ON WE MARCH:

A memoir of growing up in The Salvation Army

Bette Dowdell

CONFIDENT FAITH
INSTITUTE

*On We March: A memoir of growing up in
The Salvation Army*

published by:
Confident Faith Institute LLC
PO Box 11744
Glendale AZ 85318
www.ConfidentFaith.com

First edition

Printed in the U.S.A.

ISBN: 978-0-9717728-5-4
LCCN: 2008903856

Cover and Interior designer: The Printed Page

Publisher's Cataloging-in-Publication
(Provided by Quality Books, Inc.)

Dowdell, Bette.
   On we march : a memoir of growing up in the Salvation
Army / Bette Dowdell. -- 1st ed.
   p. cm.
   Includes index.
   LCCN 2008903856
   ISBN-13: 978-0-9717728-5-4
   ISBN-10: 0-9717728-5-1

   1. Dowdell, Charles E. (Charles Edwin) 2. Dowdell,
Bette--Family. 3. Salvation Army--Biography.
4. Christian biography. 5. Christian life--United States--
Humor.   I. Title.

BX9741.D69 2008   287.9'6'0922

QBI08-600216

To
Daddy

Charles E. Dowdell

On We March

A Salvation Army Chorus

On we march with the Blood and the Fire,
To the ends of the earth we will go,
And the Savior's love will be the theme of our song,
Because we love Him so

(The Blood and Fire is the Salvation Army's flag. The blue
border stands for the purity of God, the red stands for the
blood of Christ, the yellow stands for the fire of the Holy
Spirit.)

I'll Fight!

"While women weep, as they do now, I'll fight;
While children go hungry, as they do now, I'll fight;
While men go to prison, in and out, in and out,
as they do now, I'll fight;
While there is a drunkard left,
While there is a poor lost girl upon the streets,
While there remains one dark soul without the light
of God, I'll fight;
I'll fight to the very end!"

General William Booth
Founder of The Salvation Army

ACKNOWLEDGMENTS

First, foremost and forever I have to thank Charles E. Dowdell, a.k.a. Daddy, for loving me enough to give me confidence, encouraging me enough to dare, and living his life in a way that motivated me to give my life away to Jesus Christ, the best decision I ever made.

I also owe a large vote of thanks to Josephine Gowen Dowdell, a.k.a. Mother. While Daddy was the resourceful genius, Mother's creativity and insistence on fighting on, whatever the odds, added a large, positive dimension to my life.

Then I must give a tip of the hat to my siblings. They—brothers Joe, Charles and Barney and sister, Flo—put up with my calls and e-mails asking for verification or additional information, offering answers when they knew them and equanimity when they didn't. They're a loud, energetic group, full of great, good humor, and I'm proud to be one of them.

And, finally, thanks to Janet Wellington for her editing efforts and to the Yuneks, Bill and Benita, for offering their comments and encouragement.

THE BEST TRUTH I KNOW

People tell me I'm too honest—whatever that means. Knowing that, know also that I made this memoir as honest as I know how. Others, seeing things from a different viewpoint, may quibble, but they won't have much to work with. Anything "iffy" ended up on the cutting room floor, not in these pages.

Some names and details, but not many, drifted away in the mists of memory, and I took the liberty to exclude a few names, such as the DC, in deference to living namesakes.

Over the years, friends and family members, especially Mother, described the events I didn't personally witness—such as those occurring before my birth. Then, as I wrote, my brothers and sister added their recollections to mine to create a more complete rendition of our story.

The fact my family tells and retells our stories every time we get together helped, too—perhaps most of all.

CONTENTS

INTRODUCTION

I did not grow up in a vanilla family. Vanilla is comfortable, fairly predictable and somewhat bland. That doesn't describe us.

Some people believe the opposite of vanilla has to be dysfunctional, where anger, rage and lack of connection rule the roost. That doesn't describe us, either. We had love to spare, with parents who gave us dreams to dream and a big leg-up on the future.

My lack of vanilla predictability came from growing up in The Salvation Army, with constant moving, difficult circumstances and almost no money. But, here's the key: None of us realized we had it hard; we each thought we were living a life of privilege.

At the hub of all this optimism was Daddy, a once-in-a-lifetime man, ably assisted by Mother, always ready to take whatever hill appeared on the horizon. This is their story.

To give you an idea, people who knew Daddy routinely refer to him as either "Sir Charles" or "Saint Charles." That's the kind of effect he had. To know him was to understand the meaning of "awe," especially since, despite his manifold gifts, he had a firmly grounded ego.

And Mother wasn't exactly chopped liver. Between them they raised five children once described by a sister-in-law as "intimidating as" (I'm paraphrasing here) all get out.

I hope as you read these pages, you'll discern several things:

First, what amazing parents God blessed me with. Words strain and struggle to describe such extraordinary people.

Second, the attitude and scope of all the great work The Salvation Army does. When you write a check to the Army, make it as large as you can stretch, in memory of Charles E. Dowdell, known in these pages as Daddy.

Third, what real Christianity looks like with skin and shoes on. That is, how it gets lived out, both individually and corporately, as in a church. You'll read about several such churches in this book, especially First United Methodist Church of Huntington Beach in California, home of The Dowdell Chapel.

Last, how you can apply the lessons and the attitudes in this book to enhance your own go at life. Daddy and Mother always wanted their lives to witness, not only to God, but also to hope, to love and to optimism.

If I did it right, you'll laugh a lot—and perhaps cry some, too. I hope you enjoy reading *On We March* as much as I enjoyed living and writing it.

Bette Dowdell
Glendale Arizona

Pre-Me

Daddy was large. Not so much in height, although he stood six feet tall, but barrel-chested, with shoulders to spare. Add his enormous natural dignity and presence, and you have one awesome man, especially when he wore his midnight-blue, high-collared Salvation Army uniform.

His noticeable easy-going comfort in being who he was multiplied the effect of his imposing self. And when appearance and aura failed to strike the fear of God into the populace, Daddy's booming bass voice finished the job and brought in the stragglers.

Goggle-eyed tykes regularly asked if he were God.

But even more impressive than Daddy's awesome physical presence was his outsized heart. He appreciated and encouraged everybody fortunate enough to venture into his life, making him a "memory man." Everybody who met him remembered him—and had stories to tell.

What a blessing, then, to be his children and receive his exceptional beneficence as a birthright. Joe, named after Daddy's father, came first, then Charles, named after Daddy, then Flo, named after Daddy's sister, then me and, finally, Barney, named after Mother's brother Bern. Joe and Charles were "the boys." Flo and I were "the girls." Barney stood alone, with no need for a group name.

Fourth is, perhaps, poor placement for a high-energy, high-decibel child. Especially a usually scruffy tomboy who marched to an unpredictably syncopated drummer unheard by others. I made Mother weak in the knees.

But Daddy enjoyed my creative antics. I made him laugh, and he cheered me on. He said I lived life on tiptoes. Mother, who didn't tend toward relaxed attitudes, couldn't fully support that charming point of view, so I stuck with Daddy. We formed a mutual admiration society of two.

Daddy, Charles Edwin Dowdell, started life in Buffalo, New York, the first child of Salvation Army officers who rose high in the Salvation Army ranks. Good people, upright people, but hard. Daddy's big heart didn't reflect the rocky soil that gave him birth.

Daddy grew up all over the eastern United States, from Buffalo to Savannah and from New York City to Toledo, Ohio, where he played football and music at Scott High School. He graduated with top grades, a reputation as an outstanding musician and his name engraved on athletic trophies.

The Cincinnati Conservatory offered Daddy a full college scholarship: Tuition, fees, room and board, the works. The offer meant a college education at no cost to his parents. He planned to study music, then become a Salvation Army officer (minister). But his mother declared that only sinners went to college—on their way straight to hell. He didn't fit any part of her picture, but his pleas didn't move her.

Defying his parents meant losing them. At sixteen, with no circle of support because of the constant moving, his dream and himself belittled and his mother's dire predictions of a ruined life, he probably couldn't imagine freedom might be within his reach.

Instead of his Conservatory dream, Daddy worked a few years before going to Training College, the Army's tough, practical version of seminary. At that time, Training College consisted of one year at the college, with classes from morning until night, followed by five years of intensive home study lessons, done as you served in your given appointments. These lessons were graded at Headquarters, and all the young probationary Lieutenants needed passing grades to remain an officer.

At his Training College graduation, the brass assigned Daddy to the editorial department at headquarters in New York. He would spend his time writing and speaking. Even better, he'd play in the New York Territorial Staff Band. He could all but hear angels singing "Hallelujah!" But his father, neither a writer nor a musician, saw the appointment as sissy stuff and told the powers-that-be to "give him the hardest thing you have."

When Grandpa, an important officer in the Eastern Territory, spoke, people knew they'd better listen. Daddy ended up in Watertown, New York, struggling to revive a dying Corps (church) that couldn't afford to pay him. Single, handsome and twenty-one, he knew God had a plan, if his parents didn't manage to block it.

Mother, Josephine Marian Gowen, began life in Downend, near Bristol, England, the eighth of nine rambunctious brothers and sisters, plus two older half-brothers from her widowed father's first marriage. When she was eleven, an accident killed her father, Elias. A bicyclist ran into him, and his head smashed into a brick building as he fell.

After his death, Mother's mother, Mary, eked out a living for the family with a small farm, a country store and an occasional job hand-sewing trousers for the King of England. Her struggles added determination to her desire to gain money and, somehow, social status.

In her teens, after working a year or two as a nurse's aide, Mother decided she wanted more opportunity than England's class-oriented society offered. Not one to dawdle, she celebrated her nineteenth birthday as she sailed for New York City to join her brother, Bern, and his wife, Annie. Hired as a secretary in Manhattan, she dreamed of fame and fortune—especially fortune—certain they lay just around the corner.

Out for a walk one Sunday evening, she happened by a Salvation Army Open Air (street service) complete with brass instruments and a big, bass drum. Raised in the Church of England, she found the people's earnestness and the idea of worshiping on a street corner amusing.

Mother made a fateful decision to follow the ardent Salvationists back to their church and get some funny stories about these odd people. Her tales would gain center stage at the office and entertain her coworkers, raising her status as a sophisticated woman about town.

Instead, she most unexpectedly found herself sobbing at a mercy seat (prayer rail), asking God to forgive her sins and make her his child. She quickly became a Salvation Army soldier (member). In a short time, sensing God's call to become an officer, she willingly discarded her plans for wealth and fame to enroll in Training College.

Mother stayed, by invitation, at the Training College for an extra year as a graduate assistant, then the Army assigned her to the Bowery Corps—right in the middle of New York City's skid row. Single, pretty, twenty-three and working on the Bowery, she trusted God's plan for her future.

To offer skid-row inhabitants a way to escape their alcoholic prison, the Bowery Corps held nightly meetings (worship services). One night, just as the meeting was ending, a man, drunk almost to a stupor, disheveled and caked with grime, reeled his way down the aisle and fell across the mercy seat.

Mother, exhausted from a long day, thought about skipping the usual practice of kneeling with the man to talk and pray until he "broke through." He was probably too drunk to understand what she said, let alone make any spiritual progress. But she couldn't ignore the hope of possibility and went to his side.

Kneeling in a cloud of alcohol mixed with filth, she prayed while he babbled. She put some religious tracts in his pockets to remind him—if he ever sobered up—of where he had been. The man staggered back out to the streets, and Mother closed up and dragged herself to bed.

She didn't recognize him—in fact, could hardly believe it was the same man—when he returned the next day: Clean, shaved, hair combed and stone-cold sober, he told his story of being the editor for a New York paper before booze took over his life. Now free, he planned to stay sober and make the climb back.

They kept in touch for several years, and, true to his commitment, he never touched another drop of liquor. Mother never forgot him, the miracle she almost let get away.

Daddy and Mother met at Star Lake, the Salvation Army music camp in Butler, New Jersey. Music, especially brass bands, played a big part in Army life. Every Corps had at least a few musicians. Large Corps had sizable, excellent bands. The Army's leading young musicians gathered at Star Lake each summer, by coveted invitation only, to study under world-famous composers and conductors.

Besides the wall-to-wall music at Star Lake, Daddy loved the all-out style of baseball played there. Adding to the excitement of the game, the Stars and Stripes waved proudly from a substantial flagpole installed in deep center field. Center fielders played with their usual abandon, inhibited only slightly by thoughts of a sudden, unfortunate collision with the flagpole. These regrettable meetings happened from time to time, an inconvenience, as the game had to be halted so the wounded unfortunate could be carted off the field.

But the flagpole served as a goal as well as a menace. Every batter approached the plate with dreams of glory, determined to blast the ball over the flagpole. They didn't bother pointing a la Babe Ruth; everybody knew their goal. Many tried; Daddy succeeded. Grandma bragged about it for years.

Once a year the New York Staff Band presented a concert at Star Lake. Every Salvationist in the area tried to go. Most likely, Daddy and Mother met at such a concert. Daddy, stationed too far away to play in the band that year, came to hear the bands and lead some music clinics while Mother came for the entertainment and a chance to be with friends.

Through the years, Daddy occasionally told us, eyes twinkling, how Mother lured him into the woods at Star Lake. Mother always rose to the bait, proclaiming—without the slightest hint of a smile or twinkle anywhere—she most certainly had done no such thing, making Daddy's smile a little broader.

All we know for sure is Daddy and Mother met at Star Lake.

William Booth, founder of The Salvation Army, believed husbands and wives should be as one: one goal, one desire, and one plan of action to properly serve God. To achieve this, he set the rule that officers could only marry other officers. An officer who married a non-officer, no matter how devout, had to resign his or her commission and "leave the work."

This arrangement worked well enough for the majority who met their intended before or during Training College, but pickings slimmed out considerably after college, particularly for women, who outnumbered the men.

After two years "in the field," I believe Mother took one look at the bleak horizon and made the Star Lake meeting happen. Had it been Daddy's idea, she would have told us the whole story, leaving Daddy no opportunity to loft his line about being lured into the woods. Being the chaser instead of the chased put into question the efficacy of Mother's manifold charms, which would never do.

They proved that opposites attract. Mother, raised in class-conscious England by a mother drawn to social-climbing, and Daddy, a fully American man's man interested in sports and music, were nowhere close to an obvious match.

Even their equal commitment to God led to different approaches. For instance, in her desire to help people, Mother freely volunteered her definite ideas of who should do what, how they should do it and when. She took exception to people who failed to follow her "suggestions." Although counseled about this bulldozing tendency during her graduate year at Training College, she never understood why recipients of her ministrations would choose not to follow her obviously spot-on directions.

Daddy, while equally interested in helping, and perhaps even more so in encouraging, never volunteered his thoughts in personal matters. If you wanted his views, you had to ask. And he saw it as your decision to accept or reject his counsel.

An accomplished raconteur, Daddy appreciated all types of morally upright humor, especially when it afforded him the delight of winding his way through a good story leading to a great punch line. Mother killed every joke she tried to tell. Her humor leaned toward banana peels. Daddy couldn't understand how she found humor in somebody getting hurt, and she couldn't understand how he could miss the obvious hilarity in a banana-peel pratfall.

Even music added confusion. At some of their appointments, Mother played the piano for the meetings (worship services). Rather than play an introductory lead into the hymns, Mother simply struck a chord. Daddy, thinking it to be the starting note, would take a deep breath to start the singing, at which point Mother would suddenly play a different chord. Discussions of this surprising habit led nowhere, but Daddy finally deduced her first chord signaled the key in which the hymn was written, and her second chord gave the starting note. Mother believed proper presentation of a hymn required both, unless, of course, she forgot, in which case the first chord presented the starting note, and there would be no second chord. She insisted Daddy should realize this and sing out with vigor and confidence whenever she didn't play a second chord. Daddy, however, thought it wiser to proceed with caution lest she belatedly bang out the missing chord.

Still, these two dynamic, larger-than-life people loved God, each other and us kids so, with ups and downs of perhaps greater than average amplitude, given the strength of the participants, it all worked out. A marriage of powerful equals is a blessing for the offspring, but it surely isn't for sissies.

Captain Dowdell—Daddy—and Captain Gowen—Mother— had a short courtship, much of it via the good graces of the postal service. Because they were stationed miles apart, Mother planned their wedding without input from Daddy. It showed.

Mother dreamily envisioned two hearts dedicated to God becoming one, gathering strength to do battle with Satan. She saw her marriage as a road leading to triumphant victory for God and his church. Fully captivated by her vision, she missed a crucial detail.

The Brooklyn Salvation Army Corps lacked the center aisle so beloved by brides. Instead, two aisles flanked the center section of seats. Mother decided she and Daddy, wearing their uniforms in keeping with Army tradition, would simultaneously proceed down the two aisles and meet at the altar. To add to the loveliness of the occasion, she arranged to have Girl Guards (the Army's Christian equivalent of Girl Scouts) and Sunbeams (similar to Brownies), holding little Salvation Army flags, line each aisle.

To communicate her vision of two hearts fighting as one for God, she chose "Onward Christian Soldiers" as the processional by which she and Daddy advanced down the aisles. Unfortunately, she overlooked the second line of that venerable hymn, "Marching as to war," the relevance of which became unhappily obvious when the music began.

What with the Girl Guards, Sunbeams and their flags, the aisle had no room for Daddy to proceed, as the plans demanded, to the altar. Slim and trim at 225 or so, he weighed about 100 pounds more than Mother. Overlooking this hundred-pound detail meant each aisle had the same narrow processional channel, fine for her, but far too narrow for him. Had Mother worn the more traditional long, billowing wedding gown instead of her uniform, a simple, straight-line street dress with military insignia, she would have allowed for more space. But no.

The surprising need to thread a too-narrow needle created a dilemma for Daddy. He could not possibly get down the aisle with any style or grace, but he had no interest in dealing with the consequences of not trying. He made a manful attempt, twisting and turning his way toward the altar while the little girls, under strict orders from bride Captain Gowen to stand straight and tall, adamantly held their positions, refusing to volunteer even an inch of ground. Rather than Mother's romanticized vision of how he would come to her, Daddy resembled a pressured quarterback desperately scrambling to gain some badly needed yardage.

He struggled valiantly to stay within his allotted space, but it was the irresistible force meeting the immovable object. With the Girl Guards and Sunbeams determined to follow their orders at all costs and Daddy equally determined to reach the altar, some bumping and staggering added to the festivities as Daddy all but dragged the little girls down the aisle with him.

Mother saw the quasi-mayhem as a plot to ruin her beautiful plans. Daddy saw it as the better of two choices, the other, if indeed you can call it a choice, being not to come down the aisle at all.

And thus they met before the altar: Daddy embarrassed by his less than graceful entrance, Mother fuming at the "fact" he purposely bumped into her Girl Guards and Sunbeams. Then somebody sang their wedding song, "Because," which subtly posed the thought that God believed they deserved each other. If either noticed it, neither believed it, at least not at the moment.

And so the ceremony proceeded, the deed was done and married life began.

Daddy and Mother honeymooned briefly at Niagara Falls, then went to their temporary assignment in Pittsburgh. Since they married in April, and the Army made permanent assignments in June, it would fill in until a permanent—at least as permanent as Salvation Army appointments could be—assignment became available.

The assignment, physical director for a "magnificent gym and swimming pool," included their living quarters: A dormitory room containing six tin beds and six tin lockers, romance not being an Army priority.

The Salvation Army included Social Service Centers, or Socials, residential rehabilitation centers for alcoholics. (Socials, now called Adult Rehabilitation Centers, or ARCs, are the part of the Army that picks up donations and sells them in their thrift stores.) Residents typically came to the Social from long years of addiction. If they stayed sober long enough to come and request help, they could join the program, which included a place to stay, regular meals, clothing, medical care, Christian AA meetings, counseling and a job. Their work gave them an income and also kept the Social going.

Some men came for help. Some came to scam the system, wanting "three hots and a cot" and no interference in the way they lived life. The officer-in-charge had the responsibility to keep things moving forward, helping those who sought help, and motivating those pushing for a free ride.

The rehabilitation program required Sunday church atten-dance. The officer conducted the worship service in the Social's chapel for a congregation of all the men currently in residence—street-wise, mostly middle-aged men, old and weary before their time.

Daddy and Mother's second appointment took them to New Haven, Connecticut, to serve in such a Social. The residents took one look and mistook the young couple for greenhorns. They had no idea Daddy grew up around Socials, the son of an Army officer who eventually headed all the Socials for the Eastern Territory. They also had no idea his father proudly, and frequently, told the story of successfully putting Daddy—while still in grade school—in charge of a Social when an unexpected two-day trip came up. And, finally, they failed to recognize Daddy's blue-twisted steel and tiger-meat constitution.

Believing they had the opportunity to wrest control of the institution away from the supposed greenhorns, the men hatched a plot. On Daddy and Mother's first Sunday, six resi-dents, selected by their peers, challenged their new Captain. Rather than come to church, they stayed in the dormitory on the second floor directly above the chapel. The door to the stairs linking the dormitory and the chapel opened right behind the pulpit.

Cued by the opening notes of the first hymn, the wayward six began raising a din to announce their absence and their intention to take control of the Social away from Daddy. They wanted a fight. They believed easy victory was at hand.

Everybody in the room recognized the situation and the odds. However it might turn out, Daddy had to respond to the challenge.

He signaled Mother to take over leading the hymn, turned around and started up the stairs, closing the door behind him. Mother stood in the pulpit, waving her arms and exuding bravado as she led the singing and wondered about Daddy's fate.

The truants jumped Daddy as soon as he reached the top of the stairs. Allowing Daddy to remain by the stairs proved to be the fatal flaw in their plan.

Literally fighting for his life and realizing the impossibility of fighting all of them at once, Daddy blindly grappled to get a grip on one man at a time, then hurl him down the stairs. One by one they flew. As each body crashed into the door behind her, Mother called out, "Louder, men" and increased the vigor of her arm-waving. By the time the last body thundered against the door, the men in the service were braying at the tops of their lungs about the tender love of Jesus and Mother's arms windmilled with a velocity that threatened to take her airborne.

The fight over, Daddy came down the stairs, leaned over the body pile and opened the door. One by one, the men untangled themselves and slunk into the chapel. Last, and a whole lot more than least, came Daddy, obviously ready for whatever came next. As he scanned the chapel for their next move, the stunned roomful of men silently cried "uncle." Against all odds, they had lost the battle.

Daddy resumed the worship service. From that day on, Sunday attendance never fell below 100 per cent.

After just a year, they moved from New Haven to take over the Hempstead, Long Island, Social, now as a family of three. Joe, their firstborn, had joined the world in New Haven.

The briefest time spent in Mother's presence inevitably focused one's mind on the striking similarities between her personality and a steamroller. Ever convinced of the rightness of her cause, she lacked interest in contradictory details. Once locked and loaded, she pushed full speed ahead to take whatever hill stood in her way. Compared to Mother, the Unsinkable Molly Brown wilted to a wavering wallflower.

Even slowing her down would be a full-time career, so Daddy saved his efforts for the biggies, when the mountain loomed too high or the prognosis for the outcome appeared to be, at the least, bleak. If disaster appeared inevitable, he forbade her action, but the situation had to be extreme for him to step that far out of character. Making demands didn't fit his personality. More typically, he used reason and logic, trying to get Mother to pause long enough to consider the probable outcome, all the while wondering if he might as well converse with a wall.

She typically dismissed his well-reasoned arguments, sometimes with a "Never you mind" or an impatient wave of the hand, hardly breaking stride as she pushed toward her latest objective.

Fortunately, Daddy and Mother shared the same goals so disagreements concerned only style and tactics. What constituted a desirable outcome required no discussion. How best to reach that outcome? Ah, there was the rub.

When results undeniably proved Daddy's arguments correct, Mother announced to Flo and me this proved that a good wife always let her husband make the decisions. This idea, given the reality of how she went about life, left us thunderstruck. Before we could fully wrap our minds around the concept, though, her next crusade presented itself, and it no longer applied. At least, not so you could tell.

Watching these two very strong, very different people work together was like watching Sumo wrestlers grapple to a draw. Daddy would have settled for a truce, but Mother always pushed toward whatever she considered victory.

Mother often marveled, with enormous pleasure, about the fact none of her children showed any inclination toward passivity. How could we? The huge genetic double dose of strength aside, growing up amidst Sumos required alertness, quick reflexes and strong action.

After a year in Hempstead, Charles's birthplace, the Army appointed Daddy and Mother to lead the Corps in Altoona, Pennsylvania. A year later, the Army moved them to Milton, also in Pennsylvania, to run the Corps there.

In Altoona and, later, in Milton, Daddy and Mother, fully employed and even working what would most consider over-time, received no salary for nearly two years. Month after month, season after season, no amount of work brought sufficient money to provide them with an income. In the beautiful, remote mountains of central Pennsylvania, it was a calamitous economic time in an area that knew few good times.

The Army provided "the quarters," known in other Protestant denominations as a parsonage. The Corps income paid for upkeep of Army property, utilities, the expenses of the Corps programs, caring for the needy and, lastly, the officer's salary. Salaries were set nationally and depended on rank and years of service.

Army rules required that utilities and Corps expenses be paid first. After expenses came the needs of others. Finally, if any money remained, officers could take their small allotted salary.

Faced with enormous needs everywhere they looked, Daddy and Mother helped those in need as much as they could. Trusting God to make a way, they gave what would have been their salary to others with greater needs. Consequently, they sometimes lacked even enough money to buy food. Some of the Corps' soldiers lived on farms and brought what they could, but the cupboard sat bare on many days. Having two young children, Joe and Charles, and with Flo on the way, added to their difficulties.

On the leanest days, they had no food at all. Joe remembers at least one occasion when Daddy gathered them around the table to kneel at their chairs to pray for food. After they had been praying a short while, the doorbell rang, and there stood the owner of a meat market holding a large, handsome beef roast. He explained he could not seem to sell the obviously prime cut of meat. Rather than let it go bad, he wanted to give it to the "people at the Army." The roast provided meals for several days.

Another foodless time ended when a very annoyed grocery store owner appeared with a large chicken. No amount of effort on his part could get that bird sold, irritating him no end. He grumpily told Mother he thought he heard God telling him to take his prize poultry to the Salvation Army because the people there needed it. Unhappy about not selling the chicken, and even more so about hearing voices, especially ones that kept telling him to give the prized bird away, he rather forcefully thrust it at Mother. She received it with grateful hands and the full wattage of her most dazzling smile. And so meals for another few days were taken care of.

Through it all, God proved his faithfulness. Daddy and Mother missed some meals here and there, but they never really went hungry. And while God provided during the whole time, he never seemed to sense any urgency to show up early.

Flo arrived during their two-year stay in Milton. Mother frequently told me Flo had been a wonderful infant, a really perfect baby. Quiet. Even though Milton's hospital nursery lacked heat in the cold Pennsylvania January, Flo never cried. For some reason, Mother always stressed the word "quiet" in this oft-told tale

The Salvation Army uniform has an S on each side of the collar. Taken together, they mean "saved to serve," with "saved" meaning to be dedicated to God and "serve" meaning to relieve the cares and suffering of others.

Daddy and Mother committed themselves to this dual goal, pouring out their very lives to help others. They never turned away from it, and they never wished for any other way of life.

◇ ◇ ◇

When Daddy and Mother moved from Milton to their new assignment, leading the Corps in Scranton, Pennsylvania, the Chief Burgess of Milton sent the following letter of commendation to Scranton's mayor:

"My dear Mayor,

"The bearer of this letter, Captain Dowdell and wife, of the Salvation Army, have been residents of the Borough of Milton for the past two years and in their activities as Workers of the Salvation Army have proven to be of great energy and resourcefulness. Their work in this Town has been outstanding, and it is with regret that we are informed that they are leaving to go to your City.

"In recognition of the splendid character of this man and his wife, and the work that they have performed, I am proud to recommend to you Captain Dowdell and wife, and sincerely trust that you will cooperate and assist them in all ways possible to that they may further the great work they have been assigned to."

SCRANTON, PENNSYLVANIA

A four-alarm fire raged. As it burned through the night, Daddy manned the Salvation Army canteen, serving coffee and doughnuts to the firemen. He talked and prayed with them as they requested.

Along about breakfast time, the Red Cross arrived, with a newspaper reporter and photographer in tow. As Daddy toiled away inside the canteen, they set up their large portable Red Cross sign along the back of the canteen trailer. The sign blocked the Army's name and distinctive shield logo. Then the Red Cross workers took their places next to it, and the photographer snapped away. Then they all left.

The evening paper reported, correctly, that the canteen had served as a source of aid and comfort to the firemen throughout the night. However, the picture, including the smiling Red Cross workers, seemed to indicate the Red Cross had served as the benefactor during the fire. The reporter mentioned neither Daddy nor The Salvation Army in the accompanying article, so the picture's impression won the day.

◇ ◇ ◇

One of the Corps' soldiers needed help, so late one night, Daddy drove through a violent storm along narrow roads flowing deep with the rampaging runoff, winding his way around the mountains of northeast Pennsylvania. The back roads had no streetlights, and the storm engulfed any hint of light from the moon and stars. The night was as pitch black as the coal the area produced. In this total darkness, the howling gusts of wind hurled great sheets of rain in every direction and made the trip inadvisable, except that somebody needed help.

With headlights and windshield wipers inadequate to face the downpour, Daddy slowly crept along toward his goal. Every muscle tensed in preparation for whatever lay beyond the next curve in the road.

Apprehensive, probing his way around the twists and turns, alone in the car, he suddenly felt several sharp taps on his right shoulder. With a start, he glanced at the back seat, checking for an unexpected passenger. Seeing nothing, he rationalized the tapping as no more than a spasm of his tense muscles. He continued his slow, treacherous journey.

After going only a short distance further, though, he once again felt the insistent tapping on his shoulder. This time, he slammed on the brakes, turned off the car and turned around to search every inch of the back seat. Nothing. He looked down at the floor. Still nothing. He was alone in the wild storm.

About to restart the car, he again felt the tapping on his shoulder, stronger and more insistent than before. Thoroughly spooked, he got out of the car and flung open its back door to reveal whatever lurked in there. Nothing.

With rain sluicing down the back of his collar, he leaned into the howling storm and pushed his way to the rear of the car. He opened the trunk. Still nothing. His heart racing, he continued slipping and sliding his way around to the right side of the car. He opened the right rear door and checked the interior from there. Again, nothing. He moved on to open the front passenger's door and still found no sign of life to explain the urgent tapping.

Deciding the stress of the wild tempest had gotten the best of him, he started to make his way around the front of the car, back to the driver's door, to continue his errand of mercy. Moving cautiously, bracing himself against the car to keep his footing, his heart almost stopped.

There, in what little illumination the old car's weak headlights provided, he saw the ragged end of the road. The rest of the road had washed down the mountain just a foot or so from where he stood.

Daddy sat in the driver's seat a long time pondering the mercies of God before he slowly, slowly, slowly backed the car, feeling his way to a wide spot where he could turn around and head home.

He hadn't been alone in the car after all.

Within a few short months during Daddy and Mother's one-year tenure in Scranton, three different church denominations offered Daddy another chance of a lifetime, an opportunity that surpassed even the Cincinnati Conservatory offer all those years ago. Impressed by his abilities and his work, one by one they came to offer him a cost-free seminary education leading to ordination in their respective denomination. Additionally, they each offered him a church to pastor while he attended seminary. He would have both a place for us to live and an income to live on as he earned his ordination.

Churches simply didn't work this way, which made the offers astonishing, maybe even miraculous. One such offer was extraordinary. A set of three offers boggled the mind.

Daddy, with his love of learning, wanted to leap at the chance of more education. The fact the offers included a way to support his family made them all the more fabulous. God had called him to preach, and as long as their theology matched his, doing so in a different denomination would work for him. It seemed perfect.

But a fly, as the old saw insists flies do, lurked in the ointment. One extremely large fly.

At that time, none of these denominations ordained women, although all do now. To accept any of the offers, Mother would have to give up her calling. She could still be active in the church, as most pastors' wives are, but she could not serve God as she believed he had called and equipped her to do.

Perhaps, though, God wanted to move them in a new direction. They prayed about it, but in the end, Daddy turned each of the offers down. If Mother still heard God's call to ministry, he wouldn't argue with God.

Looking back, it's hard to see how Daddy's life—and certainly Mother's—would not have been infinitely easier had he taken any of the offers. Ministry in a standard-brand church is less demanding in every way than ministry in the Army. For that reason, I can't help but wish he had responded positively and gone where he was appreciated.

But that's only a guess. We can only know the results of the road we take. The destination that results from choosing a different path remains forever a mystery.

Part of me is glad they stayed in the Army. Again, it's only a guess, but I believe my life would have ended up far more pastel and less vibrant. I certainly would have missed most of the experiences of this book and ended up a much different person.

Still, a large part of me wishes Daddy and Mother had lived an easier life, one of recognized achievement and fewer financial struggles. And who knows? I might love being that different person.

After just one year in Scranton, the Army moved Daddy and Mother to the Tyrone, Pennsylvania, Corps.

TYRONE, PENNSYLVANIA

Five-year-old Charles started his entrepreneurial career in Tyrone. Our family lived in a second-floor apartment "on the building," (above the church) with a grocery store on one side and an auto repair shop just past a narrow alley on the other. A creek ran along the far side of the auto repair shop and served as a repository for all the non-functioning parts the shop replaced.

Charles spotted an opportunity in the auto shop's discards. Once a week he pulled auto parts, as many as he could reach, out of the creek and stacked them in his little wagon. Then he hauled the wagon up and down the street, stopping at each business to ask if they had any scrap metal to add. His route finished, he pulled his trove to a shop that bought scrap metal by the pound and waited with anticipation as they weighed it.

A big week earned, maybe, a quarter, more than enough to swank his way home to show off his treasure. In those days, penny candy actually cost a penny, so his little income gave him satisfyingly deep pockets. Whatever his little income would amount to in today's money, it started Charles on his lifetime path.

That Christmas, a month before my first birthday, Daddy and Mother set out on the drive to Grandpa and Grandma's. He didn't want to go; she insisted. Mother apparently had decided that with grit and effort, she could make peace with an irascible mother-in-law who chose to be in peace with pretty much nobody. Maybe Mother's motivation came from living so far from her own mother. Maybe she wanted it for Daddy. For whatever reason, they packed us in the car and started out.

In those days before seat belts and child restraints, Mother held me on her lap and Joe, Charles and Flo sat in the back. Of course, they started to wrestle and bounce around, so Daddy told them to get down on the floor to play.

They did so just as a large, heavy car piloted by a drunk driver careened around a bend in the highway headed straight for us. Daddy reacted quickly, steering our little car off the road, onto the berm, but the drunk driver, in seeming pursuit, smashed head-on into us.

Daddy's chest smashed into the steering wheel, breaking his ribs. His knees bludgeoned into the dashboard, fracturing bones and mangling flesh. He bled profusely from a gash that went from one side of his neck to the other. He couldn't get out of the car.

Mother reflexively turned her body to protect me. The force of the accident propelled her into the windshield, then dragged her face down the unforgiving dashboard, leaving her perfect teeth embedded in it. She sprawled across the front seat, bleeding and unconscious.

Mother's protective gesture limited my injuries to nothing more than the upholstery scraping all the skin from my forehead.

On the back seat floor because of Daddy's instruction, Joe and Flo came out unscathed, while Charles suffered only a broken nose. Charles remembers standing outside the car afterwards, unable to figure out what happened or what he should do.

Daddy and Mother were hospitalized—Daddy unable to walk, Mother not expected to live. Surgeons removed twenty-seven pieces of bone from Mother's jaw. The surgery left a small scar in the center of her chin, her only visible sign of the crash.

Mother's brother, Bern, came as soon as he heard. He walked into her hospital room and burst into tears. He said mother's pretty face looked as if somebody had pushed it through a bread slicer. Doctors said her Salvation Army bonnet, the old straw style with the huge bow on the side, saved her life.

As soon as Daddy could hobble a little, the doctors released him from the hospital, probably—with four children to care for—at his insistence. Mother remained in the hospital fighting for her life.

Daddy called his father and asked if we could stay there while he recuperated and Mother fought on in the hospital. Grandpa and Grandma lived in a large house a benefactor had left to the Army to use as officer's quarters. "The Manor" had room for everybody, plus a big barn and huge, grassy fields for play, but Grandpa said, "No."

Echoing Grandma, he said, "Four children make too much noise and too much work."

A desperate Daddy called Bern, his only other hope. Fortunately, Bern possessed a heart as king-sized as Daddy's and came to get us immediately.

Uncle Bern and Aunt Annie owned a small apartment building on East 46th Street in Astoria, and it had a basement apartment they didn't rent out. We could stay for as long as we wanted. Even forever.

Bern and Annie had lost their only child, Betty, to whooping cough, and they welcomed us with open arms—noise, work and all. They considered the additional work a joy, and Uncle Bern led the way with the noise, singing and playing games with us. Aunt Annie took a stab at shushing us because of their tenants, but her musical laughter gave away her delight. Healing love flowed like a rushing, burgeoning, spring river.

The drunk driver walked away, uninjured, from the accident. He used his wealth and an accommodating lawyer to also walk away from any responsibility. Of course, at some time or another, he still had to face God, who thinks poorly of evil.

God has permanent dibs on vengeance. We wouldn't quibble with God's resolution of the event—whatever it turned out to be.

The accident's aftereffects became a permanent part of our daily life, but I never heard Daddy or Mother ever mention getting even. The accident didn't subtract an ounce of love from them or add an iota of bitterness. Honest accountability from the other driver would have been a blessing, but they didn't let the lack of it diminish their hearts.

Mother never fully recovered from the accident. Fatigue became her lifelong companion. She continued to work hard and long, but everything took extra effort. We could only wonder how much we all lost that terrible day when the evil stupidity of driving drunk took so much of her away from us.

And forever after, we knew never to even whisper anything less than fulsome accolades about Uncle Bern, at least not within Daddy's hearing. Nobody had permission to criticize Bern, no matter what. Only praise would do, and even that was inadequate. If asked why, Daddy simply said, "Bern took us in when nobody else would."

As for me, no one on trial for drunk driving wants me on the jury.

The New York newspaper editor of Mother's Bowery days heard about the accident and wrote a lovely letter of encouragement while she recovered in the hospital. She treasured its two equally wonderful messages: He remained sober and well, and he cared about her.

William Booth's wife—and The Salvation Army's co-founder—Catherine designed the bonnet, originally called a "Hallelujah bonnet," as part of a Salvation Army Lassie's uniform. Made of fine, midnight-blue straw and shaped in the coal-scuttle shape popular for dress hats of that day, it had a wide, sturdy ribbon that went under the chin and tied in a magnificent bow by the wearer's left ear. The smooth, lustrous straw had the imperceptible added benefit of great strength.

In the early days, Army people marched down city and village streets, singing hymns accompanied by their brass instruments, and telling people about Jesus. The procession often ended at a downtown corner or in a park where the marchers held an Open Air (an outdoor worship service).

Not everybody appreciated their message, and sometimes men took extreme exception to the fact the messengers were often female. To express their disapproval, they threw rotten eggs, tomatoes, rocks, whatever was at hand, at the "Sally Anns." While nothing could protect Salvationists from physical attacks, the bonnet protected the wearer's face from flying fruit with just a quick turn of the head.

Several court cases established the Army's right to witness in public, and as people became acquainted with the Army's people and its work, the abuse abated in most countries.

However, abuse or no abuse, the bonnet continued to be part of the uniform—although adopting a trimmer and trimmer size as time went on—for nearly a hundred years. When both the special straw and the craftsmanship required to shape the bonnets became unavailable, it was discontinued.

Catherine Booth's Hallelujah bonnet, for all its fragile appear-ance, saved Mother's life when her head crashed into the windshield that dreadful December day.

After a year in Tyrone, months of which Mother spent in the hospital, the Army appointed Daddy and Mother to the Jersey City, New Jersey, Corps. Grandpa had the power to intercede and set up a Social appointment for Daddy—or, better yet, a headquarters slot. Either would have greatly eased Mother's workload and given her more time to recover, but he chose not to do so.

Jersey City, New Jersey

I vaguely remember the clapboard house at 100 Oak Street. It sat next to the Corps on a street of similar homes, a small island surrounded by apartment buildings and stores. Its across-the-front porch had dark-green latticework extending down to the ground, hiding the vacant area underneath.

When scaring our toddler socks off seemed like a swell idea, my friends and I slipped through a small gap in the latticework into the cool, spooky darkness under the porch where who-knows-what lurked. Our imaginations almost immediately skyrocketed who-knows-what into terrifying proportions, prompting our rapid exit from the suggestive gloom. The reality probably included a few garden worms and some ants, but our boggled creativity fathomed lions, tigers and bears prowling around in there, licking their lips as they stalked their prey—which would be us. A kitten brushing against our legs would have been the end of us.

One day a pair of scissors magically happened into our possession, and we snuck into our hiding place to play barber, with me as the willing customer. Well, haircuts done by three-year-olds lean heavily toward tonsorial mayhem, but haircuts done by a three-year-old in the dark reach butchering levels rarely achievable with a simple pair of scissors. The job completed, I brightly presented myself, scalp all but bald on the right side, to Mother so she could share the adventure. Fortunately, she decided to let me live.

Mother's friend arrived at the nearby train station and headed for Oak Street. Fairly confident she could find our house, she became certain of it the moment she heard a child singing a Sunday School song, "Brighten the corner where you are." She knew that must be our house.

She homed in on my voice as I energetically belted out the little chorus while playing with dolls on the front porch. I may not have understood the words, "Someone far from harbor you may guide across the bar," but whatever it meant, I whooped it out with gusto.

She delighted Mother with her story that my song guided her directly to our door without hesitation or question. Mother repeated the story many times over the years, pleased by the fact her friend instinctively knew her home would be the one with a child on the front porch singing about God.

The possibility her friend's insight might have sprung, at least in part, from the fact the child sang at the top of her considerable lungs never came up for discussion.

I don't remember Daddy with a full head of hair. Youthful pictures show him sporting a significant shock, but by the time I came along, it had mostly disappeared. Only a circle of hair around the sides remained, oddly dense considering the total lack of hair on top. Other than the fringe, he had only a single, small curl growing front and center of what would have been his hairline if he had one.

As a little girl, I loved to sit on his lap, look into his eyes and play with that curl. He would engulf me, putting his big arms around me as I all but disappeared. We smiled at each other as I fussed with the curl. His smile made me invincible. How could anything hurt me in my safe haven? For that matter, how could anybody even see me in my secret hiding place?

Love must be the most powerful force in the universe. Daddy's love gave me the confidence to add bold, adventurous hues to my life. Without him, I might never have dared. He gave me a glimpse of an encouraging God of possibility.

Curls—even sparse, stand-alone curls—can beget amazing results.

Joe and Charles attended PS 14, two of just a handful of white kids there, Joe, a proud third-grader, Charles starting out in the first grade. Most school days involved a fight. Joe's gift of gab usually deflected the impending fisticuffs and saved the day, but sometimes his mouth propelled him directly into the line of fire. Charles, better built for battle, would wade in and take care of business for Joe.

Charles had his own fights. He won them all, which only escalated their frequency. Finally, a classmate, George Washington, claimed him as a friend and told the other kids to stop. School life blossomed.

The following year, rheumatic fever sent Joe to a special "heart school" and Charles to PS 12 for second grade. Being the new kid again brought new fights, continuing until another friend, George Lincoln, spread the word they should stop.

Charles has never forgotten his two bulwarks.

The fights, it must be said, had nothing to do with race or prejudice. In fact, none of us remembers experiencing racial disharmony in our younger years. The tussles were about being the new kid and about pecking order, not anger or hate.

Daddy joined a ministerial volleyball team, a band of God's men who played with great skill, high-spirited humor and no cussing—and as if their opponents were Satan himself, come to play ball at the YMCA. Each had a facility for ragging on their teammates. Anybody who blew an assignment won a permanent nickname to commemorate the miscue.

Daddy's particular talent was spiking the ball. His size, accompanied by the ability to leap high enough to get on top of the ball, the better to hammer it home, rattled the skull of anyone foolish enough to attempt keeping the ball in play. When he rotated to the front line, then, it became a game of setting him up to spike. Whether from harsh experience or awed observation, everybody in the league knew this.

A few intrepid souls, new to the league and oblivious to the concept of ministers, of all people, cheerfully playing for blood, took Daddy's appearance in the front line with careless indifference. Unwise. Very unwise. A dizzying, ears-ringing lesson corrected their misapprehension in short order—and also served as an informal league welcome.

Mother watched them play exactly once. She told Daddy Christians didn't play with such murderous intensity, and he should play nicely. Daddy stared at her in disbelief. So he played on, hammering the ball home as often as opportunity presented itself, and she didn't watch.

After three years, the longest time we lived in one place, the Army moved Daddy and Mother to the Corps in Dover, New Jersey. To commemorate Daddy's departure, the other members of the volleyball team gathered for a raucous reading of the following "roast."

"OUR BACCALAUREATE

"Today we are thinking of the graduation of 250, not individuals, but pounds of powerful, sizzling, restless manhood. For two years Charles the Conqueror, the Dynamic Captain of all he surveys has been cultured in the Pastor Pep school of Alibyistic Arts. A student and practitioner of aggressive, blustering blitzkreiging action, the great Charles has been awarded the coveted letter "S" which adorns the collar of his uniform.

"That "S" has many meanings. Important among these meanings is the one offering assurance of ultimate SALVATION and the restoration to SANITY of those encountered by the Great Conqueror irrespective of any SIZZLING attacks or SQUEEZE plays which Charles the SALVATIONIST may employ in his engagements. The letter "S" signifies also that the

Great Charles SHOOTS STRAIGHT, is a STICKLER for SCORES, but SOFT when SCORED for his STICKLER STRIVINGS for SCORES. That "S" means also that the Captain is a SWELL SPIRITED SUPPORTER of SPORTS with STRESS on the SPIRITUAL.

"To all those collegians of the Pastor Pep School of Volley Ball and Alibyistic Arts, our Great Charlie has been a perspiring inspiration to us in many a battle. We have viewed his greatness from various angles. His spirit of cordiality has expanded him to great bulging proportions. He has a smoothness of head that rivals the highest polish of great personalities. The expanding curves of his massive citadel bespeak the strength and power that rumble and grumble within for action. Charles as we all are aware is a demon for Volley Ball. His service is slashing, fast and cruel. Some day he will master the control of his great power house which has every appearance of now being built on skids. When that day arrives all Volley Ballers will make for the woods and victory, sweet victory will be Charlie's thru all eternity.

"In graduating you, Charlie, we desire to express our deep regrets at your leaving us. We have greatly enjoyed your companionship. You have been a good scout and "Pal" and if we could, we would like to choke the guy who arranged your transfer.

"If your graduation from the green pastures of Jersey City means a promotion, then we are glad; if not, then we suggest that you write your superior officer and suggest that he pluck a few feathers from the wings of his imagination and stick them in the tail of his judgment and let you remain in Jersey City.

The Faculty
George Garniss, Equalizer
Edward J. Bubb, Chief heckler
John Q. Ledger, V.B.D.
Theodore Erdmann, Service Instructor &
Valedictorian
N. Randell Shilling, dribble All-Round Man
Joseph Swan
Edgar J. Filbert, Scoop
Julius B. Tusty"

I found this "roast" among Daddy's papers after his death. "Alibyistic arts," perhaps better rendered alibi-istic, probably relates to making alibis for bonehead plays. The Rev. Ledger added a nice touch by awarding himself a Doctor of Volley Ball honorific. And while the "S" on Army uniforms already had the specified meaning of "Saved to Serve," the various interpretations found in the roast offer a certain convivial appeal.

Dover, New Jersey

The Dover Corps sat on the town's main street amidst various businesses, about a half-block from the railroad tracks, near the noisy, busy train assembling yards. Our quarters, a second-floor apartment above the church—"on the building"—shook whenever a train passed.

On one side, the side away from the tracks, a skinny strip of land, just wide enough for the garbage cans, separated us from a movie theater. Salvation Army people didn't generally go to movies, so the proximity caught our excited attention. Temptation arrived when we saw the balcony door propped open. Joe and Charles realized they could see into the theater from the window in Daddy and Mother's bedroom. They shared the news, and we all trooped down to the bedroom. Daddy and Mother were doing the Lord's work downstairs.

Looking through the open fire-escape door, we could see the movie—and even hear parts of it.

The boys only needed to lean out the window a little way to take in next door's glamorous proceedings, but Flo and I had to stretch for it. A couple of times the boys took pity on my shortness and held my feet so I could hang my body out over the alley, far enough to see the movie. Perhaps an extra generous mood struck them. Or maybe the movie really stank. No matter. In fact, few details mattered. My brief moments of glory included only bits and pieces of silver-screen enchantment—with no beginning, no end and no plot, but ah! the wonder of it.

Flo and I learned the awful truth about Santa Claus in Dover. On Christmas Eve, Mother put us to bed, then she and Daddy went downstairs to conduct the Christmas Eve candlelight service, which would end at midnight.

Too excited to sleep, Flo and I talked and sang Sunday School songs. Finally, running out of songs and bored, we decided we needed something to eat. Our home never had snacks handy for the taking, so finding something ready to eat took serious investigation, as well as a certain amount of flexibility about what would do.

We checked every kitchen cabinet and came up empty. The refrigerator, though, had a big bowl of large, freshly peeled onions ready for chopping on their way into the Christmas turkey stuffing. The choice being onions or nothing, we each grabbed an onion and went back to bed to eat it.

As we chomped on our onions and talked about what the morning would bring, we heard the service end and Daddy and Mother start up the stairs. We crammed the half-eaten onions under our pillows and pretended to sleep. After a while, Daddy tiptoed into our bedroom, put something on the bottom of each bed then crept back out, gently closing the door behind him.

Excited about what it might be, Flo and I immediately grabbed for whatever he put on our beds. To our delight we each found a cute little stuffed animal. Then we read the dismaying gift tags: "From Santa Claus."

We never told Daddy or Mother. We didn't want to break their hearts, too.

Somebody came up with the idea that Cousin Butch, he of the black curly mop of hair, and I, called "Bright Eyes" by Grandpa, should be a cover picture for "The Young Soldier," the Army's national Sunday School paper, a signal honor indeed. "Talk about adorable!" swooned the adults.

And so we gathered for the picture-taking session, two four-year-olds, delighted mothers in tow. I don't know about Butch, but I had no clue the pictures constituted a big deal—at least in our mothers' view of it. But I knew about posing for pictures. I didn't mind. They could take pictures of me all day long.

The photographer perched Butch and me on a little end table, cheek-to-cheek, in a manner of speaking. Well, okay. I guessed we could sit close. If Butch socked me, I'd just sock him back.

Perhaps I should mention that Butch had never socked me or even shown the slightest inclination to do so. But a girl needs a plan just in case.

Gazing through the camera lens, the photographer decided the ultimate *ne plus ultra* of adorable could be attained only by having Butch put his arm around my shoulders. And thus he decreed it would be.

Not so fast here. Posing for pictures fit my established bound-aries nicely. Sitting close to Butch lay marginally within my parameters of acceptability. But that arm business didn't fit my criteria by a long shot. Butch could keep his arm to himself.

The photographer instantly leapt into his artiste, only-my-way-can-possibly-work mode. The mothers cajoled and implored. All to no avail. I remained adamant, a pint-size bundle of determination. Their pleas failed to dent my resolve. Around and around the impasse we went.

Finally, a desperate Aunt Ruth experienced an epiphany. If I would let Butch put his arm around my shoulders, she promised, I could wear her pearl necklace for the picture.

My four-year-old fortitude crumbled. The chance to wear a grown-up pearl necklace, a wondrous treasure even Mother didn't possess, would make it worth the inglorious affront of letting Butch put his arm around me.

I promised I wouldn't push him off the bench.

Aunt Ruth clasped the pearls around my neck, then told Butch he could safely put his arm around me.

And so the "Young Soldier" cover picture went forth for the world to see: Two brightly smiling moppets, the little girl's dress stylishly accessorized with pearls.

Somehow or another, Charles heard about store detectives that stopped people from stealing. He thought about the idea a long time, wondering if he should believe it. Maybe somebody just made the whole thing up. Maybe not, though.

Charles didn't like uncertainty. He needed to investigate, a thought his mind entertained with a certain regularity. Charles always checked things out.

He thought of a plan. He would walk into the hardware store, pick up a hatchet and, the purloined hatchet in full view, walk out. He had no intention of stealing. If a store detective stopped him, he'd give the hatchet to the detective. If no store detective nabbed him, he'd go back into the store and return the hatchet. Either way, his conundrum would have a resolution.

As Charles executed his plan, somebody, perhaps even a store detective, though his man's exact title never became clear, stopped him just outside the door. At that precise moment, Charles's plan sprang a leak. The man had little interest in the quickly surrendered hatchet; he wanted to see the miscreant's father, and off they marched.

Daddy, a new minister in town, sat in his office studying when Charles strolled in with a stranger and nonchalantly announced, "This man wants to talk to you."

His chipper attitude revealed a blissful ignorance of the unplanned U-turn into a predicament. Since he had no intention to steal anything, he hadn't stopped to think somebody else might not see it the same way. Meanwhile, his escort harrumphed ominous words and sounds, certain he had caught a juvenile delinquent red-handed.

Daddy asked Charles to explain why he took the hatchet, and he told the story about needing to know for sure about store detectives and the plan he created to find out. Then

Daddy explained Charles's need to know things for sure, mentioning the time Charles set the backyard on fire because he read you could start a fire with a magnifying glass and the sun, and he had to find out for sure. And the time Charles jumped off the roof waving a blanket to see if having a cape like Superman made it possible to fly.

Charles's earnest explanation and Daddy's stories about some of Charles's previous investigations won the day. Maybe the man had children of his own.

The man and the hatchet went back to the store. Charles, still unaware how close he had come to the brink, went back to pondering the world. Daddy most likely just shook his head and wondered where Charles's gift of inquisitiveness would lead him.

We left Dover after a year.

St. Albans, New York

The Army appointed Daddy to run a men's hostel in Harlem, and we lived in a nice brick house in St. Albans. The neighborhood brimmed over with children, so we kids loved it.

But our year in St. Albans may not have been the best of times for Daddy or Mother. Daddy commuted to Harlem on the train. Between the demands of the job and the fixed schedule of the trains, his hours sometimes stretched way too long—even in Salvation Army, work-til-you-drop terms. And the hostel served a short-term clientele, with no program and little time to rebuild lives. This frustrated Daddy. Day after day, he dealt with despairing men who needed all the help he could offer, but, hamstrung by the limitations of hostel turnover, he could do almost nothing for them. Finally, Daddy's schedule bothered Mother. Pregnant with Barney and not well, she insisted he should spend more time at home. No solution existed.

Fortunately, Uncle Bern, Aunt Annie and their friends, Roland and "Ted" Banner, were within subway distance, so they visited as regularly as their work schedules allowed, always happy to spend time with Mother and fill the breach a little.

Barney joined the family just after Christmas.

Our family vacationed at the Army's vacation hotel, The Kensington, a few short blocks from the Atlantic Ocean, in Belmar, New Jersey. A few miles north of Belmar, Asbury Park called to us. Filled with amusement park rides and attractions, Asbury Park motivated us to save our pennies all year so we could hit all the rides. A trip to Asbury Park highlighted our year. If our money ran out too soon, Daddy, if he had any money—a big if—would "piece us off" to keep the fun going.

We spent most days at the Belmar beach. Daddy and Mother spread towels and blankets high on the beach close to the boardwalk, above the high-tide line. We children dashed for the water as soon as Daddy said we could go. Then Daddy stood guard, scanning the water so he always knew our locations and situations.

Belmar's surf can be choppy and rough, especially for a child. Over the years, we each took our turn getting caught in the undertow—pulled underwater, eating sand, not know-ing which way pointed up, out of control, drowning. The lifeguards never seemed to notice us, but Daddy always did—and thundered down the beach to the rescue.

Fortunately, nobody ever had the misfortune to get between him and his mission. The sight of him sprinting down the beach at breakneck speed, totally focused on one spot in the water, provided warning enough to stand back. Way back. Daddy didn't have the makings of a long-distance runner, but he could lead just about any pack in a high-speed sprint.

Motivate him with his child's life, and he became an unstoppable blur racing across the sand.

Finally, my "turn" to get caught in the undertow arrived. As I scraped and bounced around the ocean's bottom, swirling underwater with the turmoil of the waves, I had no fear. I certainly didn't realize the potential consequences of my plight. I only wondered when Daddy would come. Not "if," but "when." And then his strong arms pulled me out of the water, and I returned his smile of greeting. Just as I expected.

I didn't realize I should be grateful.

Our Kensington arrangements included meals. The dining room had tables that sat four, six or eight people. Each family had an assigned table during their stay.

Barney made his premier appearance in Belmar at the ripe old age of eight months. Now a family of seven, we, of necessity, graduated to the largest table. As we ate, everybody stopped at our table to coo over the new baby, a happy, adorable towhead.

One day a lady laughingly remarked that we'd have to have another baby to fill the last remaining seat at the table. To which the curly-haired, six-year-old moppet at the table—which would be me—said, "We can't. We haven't paid for this one yet." My little *bon mot* mortified British born-and-raised Mother almost to tears.

Especially since it lacked even a shred of truth. The bills to pay for Barney's entry into the world had long since been paid. And, even if that hadn't been the case, Mother believed one simply did not announce such things to the world.

Nobody knows where I got the idea to say what I said. Perhaps I started gravitating toward the punch line at an early age.

My brief moments of indiscreet speech made Mother twitch. Since she couldn't predict either the time or the content of when I'd come out with another attempt at humor, she had no way to cut me off at the pass and save herself from embarrassment. Daddy had mixed emotions; he liked my quick thinking, but he wished I had a better sense of timing.

That first vacation after Barney came along, when all the people paraded by our table, stopping to adore the new baby, one lady broke my heart.

As everybody went gaga saying goo-goo to the new baby and remark on his perfection, she remembered her child psychology just in time. Or so she thought.

After beaming over Barney, she turned to me and said brightly, "Well, you're not the baby anymore, but you'll always be the baby girl." I staggered under the impact of her words, a blow that sent me reeling.

I was six. I was finished with all the baby stuff. I was a Big Girl. Barney's arrival had saved the day. With Barney on the scene, nobody could call me the baby anymore.

Until this lady pointed out the irrefutable, inescapable fact that I still owned the title of baby girl and probably always would.

She cheerfully, albeit unknowingly, broke my heart. Unaware she had struck such a mortal blow, she probably heaved a sigh of relief that she had caught herself in sufficient time to express a kindness.

She marched off in triumph, but left me in stunned defeat. Amazingly, I said nothing. Defeat will do that to you.

We always had dogs. For one thing, Mother loved dogs, and they loved her. She said if God had not called her into the ministry she might have become a vet, but just for dogs. Specifically, large dogs.

She seemed to speak their language. With no apparent effort, she could train a dog to do about anything. Our dogs knew all the usual tricks: Roll over, speak, sit—whatever—and they were wonderful family pets, good for wrestling or listening to our tales of childhood's woes.

But they also acted as excellent guard dogs, necessarily trained to protect us.

Sometimes, so-called kings of the highway, transients, would sneak in, or break in, and steal whatever they could carry, especially when we lived on the building. Even in those days, over half of them were ex-convicts, many with outstanding warrants for their arrest. We needed protection.

Mother favored German Shepherds. While Shepherds can be ferocious, Mother's goal was to stop intruders without doing major bodily harm. She taught our dogs to lie in silence, leap out snarling when called upon—enough to scare the most brazen intruders—then nip at aggressors' ankles to hurry them along for a block or two, away from our home and away from us.

If, without being summoned, the dogs chanced into an encounter with intruders in our home, they simply cornered them, teeth bared and snarling, and waited for somebody to arrive with further instructions. If a cornered intruder made a break for it, the dog "responsible" for that intruder reverted to his leaping, snarling, nipping ankles routine.

Thanks to Mother's training, the dogs terrified intruders routinely, but harmed nary a soul.

If transients knocked on the door to ask for help, they received it. If they did not bother with the formalities, they met our dogs. Our uninvited guests always got to make the choice.

Another Army officer asked Daddy and Mother if they would provide a home for his seasoned Old English Sheep Dog, Sammy. Faced with a dog needing a home, what answer could there be other than a yes?

So Sammy joined the family and immediately selected Daddy as his favorite. Sammy devoted himself entirely to his self-selected master, becoming his constant shadow.

When Daddy showered, Sammy bumped on the shower door to get in. If he failed in his quest after what seemed a reasonable time in shaggy dog terms, he stretched out in front of the shower door, creating a large, hairy obstacle for Daddy's egress. Especially since it could not be assumed Sammy would stay prone during said egress, and Daddy might end up in a dance to stay vertical after a large dog uprising. Loyalty can have a down side.

Each day Daddy took Sammy to the hostel—or the Social in later appointments—where the old dog spent his time shambling along after his master. The men became his second family. Everywhere Sammy went, the men eagerly gave his shaggy coat lots of petting. When Daddy worked at his desk, Sammy slept underneath, positioning himself right on top of Daddy's feet. When those feet moved, Sammy lumbered into action. His sudden appearance from under the desk—a large apparition materializing, it seemed, out of thin air—startled many a visitor.

Back home during dinner, Sammy slept in the dining room corner nearest Daddy. Sometimes, caught up in a splendiferous dream of his youthful glory days, Sammy's legs ran fast and free while his tail rhythmically whapped against the wall.

It took us a while to remember to check the activity of Sammy's tail before answering the insistent knocking at the front door. Until we got the hang of it, we opened the front door to an empty stoop a lot. We wrote off our misguided trips to the door as part of Sammy's charm.

After just five years with us, Sammy died quietly—at his post under the desk, lying on Daddy's feet.

Upon occasion we visited Grandma and Grandpa in their large Little Falls, New Jersey, home. The adults gathered in the kitchen to visit and tell stories. All the kids played in the surrounding fields. Hide-and-seek worked great because hiding only required squatting down in the tall grass. We weren't allowed to go into the big barn, but exploring the creek at the back of the property and playing in the fields provided fun enough.

The tall grass also came in handy on those evenings when we stayed out past the town's curfew. Whenever headlights appeared, we simply squatted in the grass until the coast was clear.

Sometimes, though, the weather forced us to stay in the house. Although we worked hard to be quiet, even the breathing of five kids in the house ruffled Grandma's feathers.

During our housebound visits, we could roam the entire first floor, but not go upstairs. Downstairs gave us plenty of room to roam. The huge living room had two sofas, miscellaneous overstuffed chairs and a grand piano—which, of course, we never dreamed of touching. The similarly-sized dining room abutted the living room, and a sun porch ran across the entire side of the house. We only went to the kitchen, filled as it was with adults, when we needed to speak with a parent.

We had no games to play or books to read unless we brought them with us. Even then, they didn't last long enough. Several hours of just hanging out—quietly—dragged, boring and seemingly endless.

And we faced a huge temptation. Grandma kept dishes of high quality chocolates—the likes of which we never saw except there—in decorative glass candy dishes throughout the house. These candies, Grandma decreed, were not for children, only for grown ups. To assist in enforcing her edict, each glass candy dish had a glass lid, making it impossible to silently sneak out a candy.

We, of course, found a solution to the challenge. We would station ourselves by a candy dish, keeping a careful watch for wandering adults checking on our activities. Absent any wanderers, we manned our stations and waited for somebody in the kitchen crowd to tell a joke. Then, while the adults laughed, we grabbed off the candy dish lid and sneaked out a piece of candy. If the laugh lasted long enough, we could put the lid back in one joke. Short laughs, though, meant we had to wait for the next laugh to replace the lid. We also had to keep it out of sight as we waited lest, again, a wandering adult happened upon us. Finally, lid replaced, we drifted away from the candy dish to avoid any association. It gave us a little victory over oppression.

Usually we took only one piece a day. Empty candy dishes would provide proof positive of our larceny. If Grandma noticed any candy missing, she'd brand us as thieves and lecture us loud and long—almost certainly to the end of our days.

Since we experienced no retribution, we knew she never caught on. By Grandma's lights, then, it's amazing we didn't all end up pursuing lives of crime. Even without discovering our dastardly candy-snatching, she never would have predicted all we turned out to be. Given to criticism, Grandma didn't entertain grand expectations. Our lives would have amazed her. She might've even taken to bragging on us, although she saw no cause to do so then.

Some people see a glass as half full; some see it as half empty. Grandma could never be convinced the glass wasn't bone dry. None of us knew how she got that way.

Her father, Charles Harrison, lived his life as the next best thing to a saint. Her mother, Elizabeth, was a good and Godly woman. While she could be a little sharp of tongue from time to time, that came more from spunk than spite, and her husband's quiet, "Now, Liz" calmed her in an instant.

Somewhere along the way, though, Grandma soured on life. Pity. I know for certain she had at least one son and his family who excelled at love, but she could not—or would not—join in and share the warmth.

Most Sunday afternoons, Flo and I played Sunday School with our dolls. We lined them up, and Flo led the service. After the preliminaries, she called on me, to either lead The Lord's Prayer or recite the 23rd Psalm. I never knew ahead of time which it would be. Perhaps she didn't either.

Since I got the beginnings of the two mixed up, I sometimes started the wrong one. This did not please Flo. According to her, anybody could start the right one, for crying out loud. Somehow I had to launch the one she announced, and with no restarts.

This created a problem for my five-year-old self. In her best pulpit voice, Flo would announce which I should do. I'd get in a bit of a panic and run both possibilities through my mind until I figured out for sure how to start the right one. She'd heave large sighs of impatience as she waited for me to launch.

But every week found us back at the same stand.

Each change in appointment included another adventure in Salvation Army housing, "quarters" in Army terminology. I suppose one might relate our quarters to a parsonage, but the accommodations varied far too widely for such benign wording to express the reality.

We might move from a lovely home in a privileged part of one town to an apartment in a high crime area gone to seed. Or from a large suburban house in a good school district to a business district apartment on the building and in an abysmal school district. New appointments could change everything, not just our address.

The furniture changed, too. Salvation Army quarters came furnished, right down to linens, dishes and silverware. The kitchen table in the new place might have room for all of us or it might not. Maybe each of us kids had our own bed; maybe we shared double beds. And so on. We brought with us only our "personal effects" including, since Daddy and Mother loved reading, hundreds of books.

Officers could not refuse an order to move, so we moved every year or two. Usually Daddy scouted out the location ahead of time, but we children never knew what to expect. Squeezing into the car with never less than two large dogs, we went with wonderment and trepidation, to see what lay ahead.

Sometimes Daddy pulled up to a really nasty house in a ramshackle part of town and announced, "Well, here we are!" Our hearts would sink, but then Daddy would pull away from the curb saying we had just a little further to go.

I saw it as teasing then, but I came to realize his little stunt eased those times he knew we would be disappointed if we went straight to the new quarters. We all sighed with relief when we finally arrived at a quite bad place after stopping at a disaster thinking we had to live there.

This nomadic life, with all its variations in accommodations, built some serious flexibility into us. And Daddy and Mother's positive, optimistic attitudes pulled us away from any thought that this might be a difficult way to live, moving us, instead, toward rock-solid convictions of hope and unconquerability. We became *The Power of Positive Thinking* writ large. By our lights, we lived a privileged life.

Bogota, New Jersey

I started kindergarten in Dover, right after turning five in January. When I went to St. Albans for the next school year, my swell kindergarten, plays-well-with-others résumé aside, they decreed me too young for first grade. They didn't offer half terms, so I soldiered through another year of kindergarten.

Finally, in Bogota, I made it to first grade. After just a few days of school, the teacher told me I had to stay after school. I don't know how I knew that staying after school meant trouble, but her announcement shrouded my day in dread. I didn't know what I had done wrong, but it must have been really bad.

After all the other kids went happily home, my teacher led my pallid, fearful self across the hall to the second-grade room. There, another teacher thrust a book at me and told me to read it, starting at the first page. Already in deep trouble, I read with all my heart, praying I didn't make the unknown problem worse. Trying my best to make a bad situation better, I even put in emphasis and energy as Mother had taught me.

After I read a few pages, my teacher said, "Thank you" and told me I could go home. She said she would call my mother. Call my mother? Teachers calling mothers meant disaster, maybe even the end of the world. I knew that for sure.

I dragged home with a heavy heart and concrete feet.

Mother greeted me with a big smile and said my teacher had called. I didn't understand the smile, and I didn't know what my teacher told her. I just waited to hear my punishment.

Instead Mother explained the teachers liked my reading and wanted to move me to second grade, but only if I wanted to. To tell the truth, first grade, second grade, who cared? Knowing I wasn't in trouble, now that mattered.

As relief flooded me, Mother added the wondrous, magical news that going to the second grade meant I would get to read more books. That sealed the deal for me. That's what I wanted to do. No question about it. Second grade, here I come. I started the next day.

My birth certificate recorded my name as "Betty." This worked very nicely until Bogota.

My teacher called me Elizabeth. She said "Betty" spelled with a "y" always translated to the more proper "Elizabeth," and so it would be. I didn't like it one little bit.

Not that Betty sounds like poetry. Short and stumpy, Betty doesn't fall as liltingly on the ear as the far more mellifluous Elizabeth. But that misses the point.

Daddy and Mother named me Betty. I wanted my teacher to call me by my right name.

Day after day, the teacher trilled "Elizabethhhh," raising both pitch and volume to emphasize the last syllable. I knew she meant me, but I didn't answer. She would try twice, perhaps three times, before lapsing into her lecturette about how "Betty" spelled with a "y" actually meant "Elizabeth," but I never answered to Elizabeth. My name was Betty.

Finally, I had enough of this Elizabeth business. The problem needed fixing. One day, on the way home from school, I thought of a solution.

Daddy saw me as I neared home. One look at his small, angry daughter stamping her way home told him I had a good story to tell. It brightened Daddy's day to listen to my litany after a good stomp home.

I told him about the teacher who wouldn't call me by my right name because it ended with a "y." And I said how much I didn't like teachers calling me a wrong name. Summing up, I announced from that day forward my name would be Bette. With an "e."

Daddy pronounced it a fine solution. We told Mother, and she agreed. I was seven.

From then on, the teacher called me by my right name. My latter day suspicion is Daddy or Mother helped the change along with a little behind-the-scenes activity. However it happened, "Elizabethhh!" left the building.

Changed my birth certificate, too.

I hung out with boys. We played together and walked home from school together. The boys did whatever I told them to do.

One day, homeward bound from school, I kicked my leg in the air—for reasons unremembered—and my shoe flew off, soaring like a guided missile directly into a neighbor's thorn-infested hedge. Well, I couldn't go home without my shoe, so I told my gang they had to get it out of the brambles for me. Which they eagerly did. Problem solved.

However, our neighbor, owner of the offending hedge, held quite exacting notions concerning proper deportment. Her tenets did not include boys and girls being buddies. Even more, they did not include girls behaving like hooligans, which is how she saw the shoe-in-the-hedge—among others—episode. She freely gave Mother her time and effort to sweetly explain the negative implications of each of my transgressions.

She frazzled Mother. With five children, her Army work, keeping the house, making our clothes, and on and on, Mother didn't have an hour or so to devote to discussions of, for example, my shoe in a bush.

It may be that Mother wished I didn't swing from trees or grab boys by the front of the shirt so I could lift and shake them—among my activities that gave her pause—but she and Daddy always encouraged each of us to be all God intended us to be. On a bad day, they might ponder God's sense of humor, but they persevered.

Mother maintained, perhaps for reasons of personal sanity, that, properly led, high energy, strong-willed children grew into excellent adults capable of great things while children without any vinegar ended up as passive, do-nothing adults. By Daddy and Mother's lights, parenting meant keeping us close to God, teaching us to be honest, kind and well-mannered, and convincing us we could do and be anything if we worked at it. Shoes in bushes notwithstanding.

Three-year-old Richie Helpap and his mother lived next door with Richie's grandparents on the other side of us from the hedge lady. Mr. Helpap was away serving in the military. Richie and Barney, then two, played together every day, all day, going back and forth between the two houses.

When the Helpaps went out for an evening, Charles "baby sat" for them. That is, he slept in their house with the instruction to quickly get Daddy and Mother if anything happened.

One late spring day, Richie and Barney played together as usual, and their mothers worked around the house, also as usual, keeping an eye on the two towheads as they followed their routine of periodically adjourning from one house to play with the toys in the other. At lunch time, just as Mother was about to call Barney to come to eat, Mrs. Helpap called over for Richie, and they realized they hadn't seen the boys for fifteen minutes or so. Each mother had assumed they were playing in the other house.

Well, the boys had never wandered off before, so it would be a simple matter of going to a few close-by homes to find them. When that didn't work, Mother called Daddy to come home. She and Mrs. Helpap solicited neighborhood volunteers to expand the search. When Daddy arrived home to frantic mothers and still no boys, he called the police.

The police searched. The volunteers searched. More volunteers joined the hunt, and they searched. After school, Boy Scout troops organized, and they searched. Still no Richie or Barney. Worry grew to fear as long hours crawled by.

About seven that evening, a police car, siren and red lights going full tilt, pulled up in front of the house carrying a backseat cargo of two dirty, hungry little boys. The police had found them wandering around a traveling carnival in Teaneck, a little more than two miles away.

As Mother rushed to hug Barney, he held out a fistful of nearly dead wild flowers, unfortunately on the brink of extinction. No matter. Untutored, he already grasped the age-old wisdom of the male of the species: When you're late, show up with flowers.

One day a boy who lived down the hill, one of my gang, said he was going to kiss me. His threat scared me. Our teacher had taught us about germs, and I knew for a fact that kissing would give me some dread disease. I might die. I would not live to see another birthday. Or, worse yet, another birthday party.

I hurried home to ask Mother about the danger. She didn't see the situation in quite the same perilous terms as I. In fact, she remained calm, and smiled a mysterious little smile, which didn't help at all. Strange smiles don't really answer important questions.

So, unsure of the consequences this threat posed, I decided not to take any chances. I told my would-be swain I'd beat him up if he even tried to kiss me. After that, he kept his distance. We still played together, but he never mentioned that kissing business again.

The Bogota house had a steeply terraced front lawn All right-thinking kids instinctively know if it looks like a hill, you have to play king-of-the-hill on it.

One kid runs up to the top of the lawn and screams that he (or, less often, she) is the king of the hill. This declaration signals the other players to race up the hill at top speed and top volume to rout the self-proclaimed king, shove him down the hill and return him to serfdom. And while charging the hill to depose the king, players had to be quick and alert enough to repel competitive usurpers equally intent on becoming king.

No king gave up easily; they gave maximum effort to bulldoze the attacking hordes back down the hill. No usurper gave up easily either. They grabbed for the king's shirt tail while using the rest of their bodies to repel everybody else.

So what you have, basically, is a happy free-for-all, with all the neighborhood kids shoving and pushing for the right to claim kingly status—if only for a minute or two, the usual tenure. The nonstop action ended only when players became too pooped to participate or got called home for dinner.

Our front lawn hosted many king-of-the-hill games, with Joe, Charles, Flo and me going full tilt up and down the terraces. Too small to ever muscle my way to kingship, I played with enthusiasm if not noticeable results—unless you count survival.

We kids spent wonderful hours playing in a vacant lot about a block from our Bogota home. Sometimes the Harveys, another family of five Army officer's kids, joined us, making it even more fun. Ten of us played tag, climbed trees and generally whooped it up getting dirty.

Across the street from our wonderful playground sat the beautiful St. Joseph Roman Catholic church, in which a lot of equally beautiful weddings took place. Flo and I, along with the Harvey girls, loved to attend the weddings. We would see the bustling and the fancy dress that announced a wedding, and as soon as the doors closed behind all the people and the coast was clear, over we'd go.

Not sure of our welcome, we tried to do everything just right and not get in trouble. We knew we should cover our heads in a Catholic church, so we did our best, plopping a dirty hanky, a used tissue, whatever we had, atop our wind-and play-blown hair. We crept to the back pew and sat as quietly as proverbial church mice. Had we known about genuflecting, we might have given that a try, too.

We probably didn't have to try so hard. Since wedding guests always fit comfortably in the front section of the large sanctuary while we stayed in the darkened back, our scruffy little group—and our painfully untutored attention to detail—almost certainly went unnoticed. If the priest did happen to notice us, we probably gave him a chuckle.

All eyes gazed upon the bride and groom as we craned our necks to take everything in, goggle-eyed at the glory of it all. Flowers and candles filled the whole front of the ornate church. Instead of Salvation Army uniforms, the brides wore beautiful, long, silky dresses with lots of lace; they had their hair all fancy and they wore veils. We loved every part of the weddings. Then, with the "I dos" all done—before the bride and groom reached our pew and saw us—we sneaked out as invisibly as we could and raced back to the field—dirty, sweaty, enraptured.

Every once in a while, Freddy Harvey quit playing and went over to the church, but we never knew why. He didn't wait for special events like weddings; he just went over to an empty church and disappeared inside the big doors. After a minute or two, he'd reappear and run back across the street to resume play. One day the priest called Freddy's father requesting that he please tell his son to stop drinking the Holy Water.

An astonished Freddy told us about how sometimes water got to be holy and his father said that made it special. Well, this astounding news required a lengthy, wide-eyed discussion. We had no idea water could be holy. We wondered how it got that way and how you could tell holy water from unholy water. We decided it must have something to do with being Catholic because we knew Salvation Army water was okay to drink.

After that, though, Freddy had to play thirsty.

The Salvation Army owned all the cars we drove. While red cars, especially red sports cars, caught Daddy's eye, Army regulations demanded sedans, with the color selection limited to navy blue, black or, in exceptional cases, dark gray. So he drove navy, black or dark gray sedans of varying vintage.

The Bogota car was an ancient, unreliable, black Chevy. On the many mornings it refused to start, we kids all piled out of the house and pushed the car to the corner where Daddy headed it downhill, hoping that a quick pop of the clutch as the car gained momentum would persuade the engine to turn over.

As kids, it was a grand time. Joe and Charles provided the bulk of the necessary effort—Joe being a somewhat scrawny eighth-grader and Charles a more solidly built sixth-grader. Flo and I joined in the fun, pushing as hard as we could.

While Daddy joined in the general merriment, I can't imagine he saw these events as fun. Perhaps seeing his children so willing to help—and having a great time doing it—eased his chagrin over the clunker's regular refusal to move.

Attitude is an extraordinary thing. Along with its wonderful ability to smooth bumps, it comes with the fabulous added attraction of costing nothing.

Daddy sat in the driver's seat of the old Chevy, ready to start on a Staff Band trip. We kids jumped round the car, seeing him off. He asked if everyone had their fingers safely away from the car, and we all loudly chorused "yes," so he banged the old car's rusty, recalcitrant door shut.

And a loud wail went up. In my excitement, I yelled "yes" with the others, but neglected to check the location of my digits. The door crushed my right index finger and now blood dripped everywhere.

The doctor who lived in the house behind ours stitched me up and told Mother to keep me absolutely still for a week.

Might as well tell the wind to stand still.

Mother, resourceful as usual, coped. She sent a note to school, so the "Elizabeth" teacher had responsibility for me during the school day. Then she assigned Joe and Charles to take turns telling me stories during the time after school and before dinner. Although probably not thrilled about babysitting a little sister, they tackled the assignment with gusto.

Full of the glories of World War II, they made up stories about the battles I won, throwing away every shred of reality for the goal of keeping me enthralled—and still. They would talk about the tanks rumbling across the desert, the planes battling in the sky, the Germans advancing from the west, the Japanese threatening from the east. Our armies trapped. Just as certain defeat loomed, I strode onto the scene and single-handedly snatched victory away from America's enemies. Day after day, I kept America free. I earned medal after medal.

One day, just as Charles reached the best part—the part where I arrived in the nick of time to pulverize every enemy in sight—Mother called him to set the table for dinner. That day ended my need to stay still. Now I could run and play, freeing Joe and Charles of their storytelling duties. And I never found out how I won my final victory for truth, justice and the American way.

The owner sold our rented Bogota house, and we had to move in June when school let out. Daddy and Mother found a house in Englewood, and the Army authorized its purchase. Now all we had to do was get from here to there.

Given Army austerity, we moved ourselves. Daddy brought boxes home from the grocery stores, the Social, anywhere he could find some, and we all set to packing. Since we'd learned how to properly pack a box of books by kindergarten, we veteran packers pronounced ourselves ready to take on the books, a job that kept us busy for a while.

Finally, moving day arrived. Daddy drove a truck home from the Social, and we all pitched in to fill it. Mother directed traffic and kept an eye on Barney. Daddy and the boys moved the furniture. Flo and I carried whatever boxes we could lift. With Daddy and Mother's encouragement, we kids got the idea that the move offered a special opportunity to have a great time, and, being so convinced, we did.

The refrigerator went on the truck last. Heavy and unwieldy, it couldn't be hoisted and carried by a man on one end and two boys, however willing, on the other. Even the attempt could end in injury. Daddy was on his own.

He backed up to the refrigerator and had the boys put a heavy leather strap around the refrigerator and him. Sending the boys to safety on the other side of the room, Daddy buckled the strap, raised his massive arms inside it and grasped it firmly. He took his stance and started pushing against the strap as he slowly leaned forward, pulling the refrigerator onto his back. He carried it out of the house, down the many front stairs, over to the truck and up the ramp into the truck's interior.

Joe and Charles had sense enough to be awestruck. Flo and I thought carrying refrigerators was just something Daddies did.

ENGLEWOOD, NEW JERSEY

Englewood, New Jersey, turned out to be paradise. Acres and acres of playgrounds and ball fields of a large school campus sat directly across the street from our new home. Grass carpeted the ground as far as the eye could see. The fields and playground equipment called us to play.

Daddy's brother, Joe, came to help with the move, bringing Butch along. The six of us kids helped unload the truck, sort of, then Daddy turned us loose. We raced across the street.

By dinnertime we had scattered across the acreage, none of us within sight of the house. How, beyond sending out a posse, does one round up six kids, spread over many acres, before the food gets cold? Quite easily, as it turned out. Daddy walked out on the front porch, raised an alto horn to his lips and blew a full-volume mess call.

Well, that was new. We hadn't ever been summoned home by a mess call before. I'm not sure any of us had even heard mess call prior to Daddy's vigorous rendition. But, no matter. After just a few notes, we knew he was playing our song

71

and raced home at top speed. We streamed in from every direction.

Daddy's performance—and our instant homing pigeon reaction to it—uniquely introduced us to the neighbors. I heard they laughed about it for years.

But we only lived in Englewood for ten days.

Most Army moves to new assignments happened in June. This particular June had seen a veritable tsunami of moves. During the Fourth of July weekend, right after this big upheaval, the commanding officer of the Mount Vernon, New York, Men's Social, unexpectedly died of a heart attack while out in a boat, fishing.

Grandpa, responsible for all the Men's Socials in the Eastern Territory, had a problem. While reluctant to move all his officers again, he needed to fill the job at the Mount Vernon Social, one of the largest in the Territory. He realized he had only one good solution.

Daddy had been appointed to the Hackensack Social for a three-year process of closing it down. Now at the end of the second year, he had finished most of the work. Moving the schedule up and closing it down a year early would free Daddy for the Mount Vernon appointment and eliminate the uproar—and expense—of moving everybody for a second time within a month. Given any other scenario, Grandpa would never have awarded Daddy such a plum assignment.

A few officers, though, men and women from old-line Army families, concluded Daddy got the Mt. Vernon assignment because he was the boss's son. Nepotism, pure and simple, they decided. Fat chance, that.

Grandpa despised nepotism. Either you could do a job or you couldn't; your name and your connections meant nothing. His great pride in this noble stand bruised a lot of feelings.

Some officers could trace their lineage back to the early days, not long after March 16, 1880, when Commissioner George Railton and his seven "Hallelujah lassies" came to New York City from England to officially establish The Salvation Army in the United States.

Actually, in 1872, James and Ann Jermy had asked General Booth to acknowledge their thriving mission work in Cleveland as part of the Christian Mission—later renamed The Salvation Army. The Founder replied, "So you have raised the banner of The Christian Mission in Ohio. Amen! May it never be dishonoured, but may it float over an Army of men and women whose sole aim shall be the glory of God, and the Salvation and happiness of man." This unofficially began the Army's work in America.

But the Railton date was the big date, the remembered date, the date mentioned in Army history. Some members of family dynasties dating from that era became accustomed to a certain deference in their assignments. Their attitude wasn't widespread. The vast majority of officers poured out their lives in service wherever they were sent, but feelings of entitlement did exist in some small circles.

Grandpa always jettisoned deference to favor merit. He had no concern for hurt feelings since he believed them to be inappropriate. Coming from a life of toiling deep in the Pennsylvania coal mines when he was eleven and work-ing his way up from there, he lacked patience with people seeking preference. And thus he angered a few of the oldest names in Army history. Some never forgave him, creating a bill Daddy would eventually have to pay.

Grandpa's decision launched us into chaos. In most moves, we packed only our personal belongings since the Army owned all the linens, dishes, pots and pans, curtains, etc., and these things stayed. But this move had been a different sort of move. Everything in the Bogota house had to go to Englewood, so everything—our stuff and Army stuff—got packed together. Now we had to unpack every box, take out what belonged to the Army, then repack what belonged to us for the move to Mount Vernon.

Not only that, we had to put everything in place for the new officer—furniture nicely arranged, linens stacked neatly in the linen closet, dishes arranged in the kitchen cabinets, all the beds made up with clean sheets and so on. And the house had to be left clean, which, in Mother's mind, meant immaculate. She had a week.

And Daddy had that same week to close down the Hackensack Social—the stores, the people, the accounting records, everything.

And what a week it turned out to be.

Promptly upon arriving in Englewood, Flo developed a whole colony of boils on her posterior. Soon she could not sit down or lie down, and Daddy took her to the hospital's emergency room where doctors lanced each and every boil while she yelled and ordered Daddy to beat them up for hurting her.

That night, she still couldn't sit down or lie down to sleep, so Daddy arranged himself as a human slant-board for her. He sat deep in a large, overstuffed chair in the living room, his knees pressed against the sides. Flo stood in front of the chair, between his knees for balance, and leaned her head against his chest, her arms around his neck. Daddy wrapped his big arms around her shoulders to keep her from falling, and thus they slept.

An evening or so later, I tumbled down the stairs. My head cracked into a window sill on the landing, gashing through my right eyebrow. Daddy returned to the emergency room, this time with me in tow, and the doctors sewed me up.

The doctors probably entertained dreams of a new hospital wing with us in town, but we moved a couple of days later.

Flo and I experienced a real loss in the move, a pain going well beyond our physical mishaps. Mother had bought an old vanity, fixed it up, a beautiful, multi-tiered organdy skirt as its crowning glory, and put it in our room. Easily the most gorgeous thing either of us had ever beheld, it made us giddy just to look at it.

When Flo could sit and I could refrain from falling down stairs, we took turns sitting at the little vanity, preening. Well, preening in the tomboy sense of the word. We did our best.

But the little girl in the family following us into the Englewood house had been crippled by disease, and Mother decided that giving the vanity to her would be the loving thing to do. To heal our broken hearts, she insisted God would make it up to us. And he surely has, but not always with the same magic that organdy inspires in little girls' hearts.

Fortunately for Daddy, the refrigerator stayed in Englewood.

MOUNT. VERNON, NEW YORK

Mount Vernon gave us a large, wonderful house— white clapboard, with seven bedrooms in three stories plus a basement and a sun porch graced by beautiful windows across the front. Big trees surrounded the large backyard. One smaller, specimen tree grew in a corner, offering low branches perfect for climbing.

Perhaps even better, the neighborhood was wall-to-wall kids. All our schools were close by, and a playground to end all playgrounds lay just down the hill.

But best of all, the appointment challenged Daddy's considerable mettle to see what he could make of a real opportunity. Everybody had everything they could think to ask for.

Daddy became the chaplain to both the police department and the fire department, and the newish station wagon that came with the Mt. Vernon appointment acquired a siren and a flashing light. We kids constantly urged Daddy to sound the siren, making "are we there yet?" seem like a rarely asked question. Despite all our chatter, the siren remained mute, and we gave up. For the most part.

A rusty brown dog followed Charles home from junior high school, so eager for attention Charles hardly had to coax this excellent behavior. Arriving home, the dog at his heels, Charles thought it only right to give the dog a little water, what with the effort of following the entire distance. Later, the dog still patiently in attendance, Charles broke out a small repast, quickly wolfed down by the dog. Still the dog stayed and, as night fell, Charles brought him into the sun porch for the night, that being the only kind thing to do after all.

Early the next morning, Charles proudly showed off his new dog, now named Brownie, to Daddy and Mother—who told Charles he had to find the owner. With Brownie on a leash—with a bit of a prance—Charles set out asking people around the neighborhood if they recognized the dog, hoping everybody would say "no." But, alas, somebody not only recognized Brownie, but also knew where his owner lived.

Weighed down with disappointment, Charles trudged to the appointed address. A man answered the door-bell, took one look and said the dog, which he described as half Chow and half German Shepherd, did indeed belong to him. But then fortune smiled. The man said he had two other dogs and had been looking for a home for this one. Did Charles want the dog?

Charles catapulted home, Brownie at full gallop, with his great good news. Daddy and Mother said the dog could stay if Charles took care of him. The deal struck, Brownie moved in.

Brownie gave Mother heartburn. She, who all dogs must obey in all things, did not see eye to eye with a dog who viewed obedience as optional. Charles had somewhat better luck, but Brownie, an intelligent, strong-willed dog, followed his own purposes.

Brownie chose to be a great family pet, and he chose to be an excellent guard dog. But, somehow or another, he let us know he did these things by his choice, not ours.

Brownie's attitude could be frustrating, but his dislike of other animals was a real problem. He hated cats, chickens, squirrels, sheep. If it had four feet and a fur coat, or two feet and feathers, Brownie almost surely hated it. And nothing Mother did made even a dent in this unhappy attribute.

When a squirrel ventured into our backyard, as many did, Brownie froze, waiting, as the squirrel moved farther and farther from the tree. At just the right moment, Brownie broke his pose, but rather than running toward the squirrel, he raced for the tree. Of course, as soon as Brownie broke his stance, the squirrel did what came naturally and also raced for the tree, only to be met there by Brownie, who broke the squirrel's neck with one swift bite.

This conflicted Mother. Furious with his actions, she was also awed by his cleverness. Coming down on the side of love for all of God's creatures, she settled on expressing her outrage to the beast, which momentarily replaced his proper name, and denounced his behavior.

Brownie responded by prancing and preening, proud as a peacock with his feat. Daintily picking up a dead squirrel by its lopsided head, he would carry it over to the back porch stairs and gently lay it down, a love offering for Mother. Not the slightest bit entranced by this act of thoughtfulness, Mother grew ever more frustrated. And so it played out, again and again.

Mother's love of animals, even delinquent dogs, saved Brownie. She never stopped believing she could reform him. Plus, Brownie truly excelled as a family pet and guard dog.

Lovable, loyal, independent, disobedient, Brownie was a rogue you knew you could count on when you needed him. Usually.

Our house on Egmont Avenue sat a little more than halfway up the hill from a large, multi-level recreation area. The highest level of the recreation area, the one nearest our house, contained a big playground. The next level down held an array of tennis courts. A large football field, with stadium seating on one side, filled the bottom level. The neighborhood herd of children spent a lot time whooping it up on the playground.

◇ ◇ ◇

One of the neighborhood girls, Shirley Arndt, lived further up Egmont Avenue, up where it became flat land. Flo and I envied Shirley's scab-free knees. Her long blond hair, always in perfect order, added to our envy. And we admired her talent for drawing pictures of horses, although staying in the house to draw struck us as boring.

One day a set-to at the playground ended with a small army of children, including Flo and me, marching menacingly behind Shirley, forcing her up the hill to her house. Nobody laid a glove on Shirley, but we sure scared her.

Most of the belligerents usually considered Shirley a friend, but not that day. For whatever reason. Or perhaps for no reason, as happens with kids.

Shirley, of course, told her mother about her very life being imperiled, adding what little drama a stay-in-the-house, perfect-kneed, horse-drawing girl could muster. Shirley's mother reacted loudly. She decided Flo and I were the ringleaders of the pack of ruffians who frightened her delicate daughter. She angrily called Mother, using an impressive variety of words Mother seldom heard. Promising peace, Mother arranged for Shirley to come to our house.

I knew this would not end well. Mother inevitably agreed with anybody who criticized any of us children, or even Daddy. In any disagreement, you could count on Mother to take the other person's side, usually without bothering with details—such as the topic of the disagreement. She claimed that she only wanted to be fair, but fair never included being in our corner.

Hoping to head off whatever solution Mother devised, I apologized to Shirley as soon as she hit the door. A startled Shirley accepted my apology.

And so we four—Mother, Flo, Shirley and I—sat down to chat. In short order Mother announced that Flo and I were indeed at fault. She told us each to kiss Shirley and make up. I quickly told her I had already apologized and made up. Shirley agreed, also quickly, so Mother excused me from the kissing requirement. But Flo had to pucker up and do her duty.

Well, I was delighted. First, I didn't have to kiss Shirley. Second, Flo did.

By the next day, all the neighborhood kids were friends again—even without kissing Shirley. Peace returned to the playground. Pestering Shirley lost its charm once everybody learned of the consequences.

No matter. From that day forward, Shirley chose not to inform her mother concerning playground activities. The kiss-and-make-up scenario probably killed it for her, too.

To make the Army's work known, Daddy and Mother actively participated in community organizations. One sight of them in action meant Mother's organizations asked her to be president, and businessmen in Daddy's organizations tried to hire him away from the Army. Joe remembers in Mount Vernon it was a potato chip company that tried to get Daddy to join their executive ranks.

Whenever we lived near Manhattan, Daddy played in the Salvation Army's New York Territorial Staff Band. This meant driving into the city at least twice a week, once for practice and once for Friday Night at The Temple, a worship service held at Army headquarters on 14th Street across from the old Armory. Band trips, recordings and concerts meant extra trips. He also practiced at home. Heavy time demands above and beyond his full-time assignment were beside the point; Daddy loved it.

Most weeks, we all went to Friday Night at The Temple. Army families came from all around the area, and Mother enjoyed that. We kids felt like we knew the bandsmen from Daddy's stories about them. And we really did know Daddy's friends, like Milton Kippax and Art Crater, which made it fun to watch them sing and play their instruments.

Band members called Kippax the metal man. The winner of several sports medals in his youth, he unwisely bragged about being a medal man one day on the band bus. Frank Fowler, tuba player and singer *extraordinare*, quickly agreed, saying Kippax had silver in his hair, gold in his teeth and lead in his pants. The metal-man name, of course, stuck.

Daddy gave trombone-playing Art Crater the nickname, Shaky Crater. Jazz musicians have a special slide shake that creates an effect not heard in Army bands. Upon occasion during practice, Crater threw it in, delighting the rest of the band and startling the conductor almost off his podium.

The Friday Night service starred the band. As usual in an Army service, the band accompanied the hymns. They also played at least one concert piece—a march, a somber tone poem, a bright, energetic festival piece or perhaps intricate variations on a classic hymn. For some services the band also sang as a male chorus. It was a concert with a sermon added.

Band trips and special concerts required extra practice. Whenever Daddy needed to fit practice into every spare minute, he parked his tuba under the high-legged buffet in the dining room rather than take time to constantly put it in and out of its case.

I saw the tuba as an invitation.

One day I decided to RSVP the invite. I got down on my hands and knees, huffed in several deep breaths to build capacity, jammed my lips to the mouthpiece and blew with all my might. A satisfying blat resounded through the house. Success! I decided to try it again. And again. It seemed I might even become proficient at tuba blatting.

I forgot about Mother, always a little on the jumpy side, in the next room. Each blat of the tuba occasioned her instant levitation. She unhappily accepted one unnerving blat as the normal energies of an active child. Two blats plunged her thoughts to a significantly less benign level. The third blat bolted her into action, and she raced into the dining room and forbade me, in no uncertain terms, to do that again. Ever.

Pity. With just a few more blats, I surely would have got the hang of it. When an opening came up in the trombone section soon after, Daddy switched to his preferred instrument. The move pleased him, but I forever lost my chance at proper tuba blatting.

Grandpa's sister, Aunt Pink, so-called because of her rosy complexion, planned to come for a visit. Daddy and Mother didn't seem at all enthusiastic about her pending arrival. Our questions about this never-met relative brought only lip-pursed, monosyllabic answers.

We puzzled about what this could mean until we somehow learned about Aunt Pink's distinctive claim to fame, which may or may not have caused the unrest, but it sure caught our fancy. That stump-short, softly round lady, straight out of Central Casting's idea of a perfect grandmother, owned an extraordinarily colorful and extensive vocabulary of four letter words that she kept burnished and honed by constant use. Reliable sources claimed she couldn't get from the start of a sentence to the period without larding in several choice beauties. And she belonged to us!

We didn't know Dowdells who cussed. In fact, we didn't know anybody who used bad language around Daddy and Mother—except, of course, for Shirley's mother, and only that one time when under duress and strain. Daddy and Mother sure didn't swear. I never heard a single Anglo-Saxon impropriety escape their lips ever.

And now a champion cusser was coming to our house! Well, we could hardly wait. Who knew what strange sounds would tickle our tender ears? We knew Daddy and Mother wouldn't react all that well to Aunt Pink's vivid vocabulary being bandied about. It sounded like a perfect set-up for fireworks.

She arrived. She looked like a sweet little dumpling crowned by snow-white hair, not somebody who could melt paint off walls by mere speech. And so began a very long day—at least for the adults. Aunt Pink strained to rein in her tongue. Grandpa, not usually tense, looked as though a good "boo" could put him into orbit. Daddy and Mother acted distracted, perhaps worried about the impact on us children if Aunt Pink let loose a volley. I, personally, was all ears to hear something exotic, and all eyes to see what would happen if I did.

But it turned out to be a dud of a day. Just adults discussing the weather and such. Aunt Pink and Grandpa left early, both showing signs of wear.

Just home from work, Daddy came into the living room and, with a big smile, invited Flo and me to come outside for a big surprise. We could tell that whatever he had out there would be good. We dropped everything and hurried out to see.

The station wagon sat in the driveway just outside the front door—with two brand new, red and blue bikes strapped to it, one lashed to the front, one to the back. Two wheelers. Full size two-wheelers like the rest of the big kids rode.

We had been asking for bikes, but had little hope we'd get them. Now here they were! Shiny and pretty, the stuff of birthday-candle and first-star-at-night wishes. And it wasn't even our birthday or Christmas, just a regular day.

We promptly set to helping Daddy untie those beauties from the car, chattering our delight as we worked. No sooner did we get the bikes standing on their own in the driveway, though, when Mother called us to dinner. We wheeled our precious cargo to the garage and went in to eat. Darkness fell before we finished doing the dishes. We wouldn't ride the bikes that night.

Flo knew about two-wheelers, but I had never been on one before. Daddy told me not to ride the bike until somebody had time to teach me. Day after day, nobody had time to teach me how to ride my new bike. It sat in the garage, calling my name.

Finally, I could resist temptation no longer. Lots of people rode bikes, I reasoned, and it didn't look hard at all. Besides, I could start out down the hill to get it going. So, without bothering to inform anybody of my plan, I wheeled out my new bike, got on and pointed it down the hill.

Well, one part of the plan turned out to be spot on. Heading the bike down the hill really did get it going. Faster and faster I flew. At breakneck speed, I belatedly realized I had not considered how I might go about stopping the bike.

At the same instant I recognized the stopping problem, I also realized I faced an emergency. Once I went past the fast-approaching cross street, the hill's grade became vastly more acute—just short of a sheer cliff—and at the bottom stood the sturdy, government-regulation chain-link fence of the playground.

My only real chance at survival, I decided, lay in careening around the corner onto the cross street, which happened to be a state highway, thus avoiding the sure death of picking up even more speed and crashing head-on into the fence. I almost made the turn, but somebody had inconveniently placed a telephone pole right by the corner. After an unplanned jumping of the curb, I bounced off that pole going lickety-split.

A neighborhood's worth of mothers streamed out of their houses to see if I had departed this mortal coil. Well, I was fine, and the bike hardly scratched. But the whole world knew about my crash. My parents would surely hear about the whole thing, and they would know I disobeyed the rule about not riding my bike until somebody taught me how. We're talking trouble with a capital T.

It didn't help that all the mothers agreed it had to be a miracle of God, at the least, that no cars were coming on the heavily-traveled cross street when I made my out-of-control entrance.

On the silver-lining side, the escapade made a point. Somebody needed to teach me how to ride my red-and-blue treasure before I did myself in. So, at last, I learned how to properly ride a bike, even without a hill to get started. Better yet, I learned how to get the thing stopped.

When he was about ten or eleven years old, Daddy announced, as boys that age are wont to do, that he wasn't afraid of anything. His mother immediately vaulted to the conclusion that she had a habitual liar for a son and no good could ever come of it. She set her face like flint to nip this evil habit in the bud. He may only have said it once, but she knew he cusped on the slippery slope to perdition, so she devised a cunning plan.

She gave him several chores one evening, the final one to get water from the well. The primitive, antiquated quarters, without running water, sat on one side of the small-town Corps building, with the well on the opposite side. To get water, Daddy had to walk through the empty church. Grandma knew it would be dark then.

Daddy, always eager to please his parents, industriously did his chores. Meanwhile, Grandma went into the church and lay down on the floor between two rows of seats, positioning herself to prove him a liar and give herself the opportunity to denounce the error of his ways.

Reaching his final chore, Daddy walked through the pitch dark sanctuary, metal water bucket in hand. As he passed her, Grandma reached out and grabbed his ankle. Reacting quickly, Daddy began whacking her with the bucket as hard as he could, again and again, until Grandma finally made herself known.

Grandma delighted in telling this story. From the way she told it, I think she saw it as a morality tale in which her valor and dedication rescued Daddy from a terrible fate. In my slightly different perspective, I thought she was mean. I saw Daddy's whacking her with the bucket as her just desserts.

Fortunately, the bucket part of the story came at the end of her tale, so she took my gleeful response as a reaction to her noble goal, not to the battering of her cranium.

Hanging in my home this very day is a sampler Grandma cross-stitched while a young mother. It is, I believe, the only one she ever did. The stitching shows a hearth flanked by chairs and asks "What Is Home Without Mother." Cross-stitched irony, as it were.

Delivery trucks frequented our Mount Vernon neighborhood. The boys in my gang would climb on the back bumper of a truck, squatting down so the driver couldn't see them, hang onto the rear door handles, and see how far down the hill they could ride before they were scared enough to bail out.

I was one of the guys, but I had yet to ride a truck. The longer I put it off, the louder the snide remarks about my lack of guts grew. Well, sometimes you gotta do what you gotta do. Whether you want to or not. I declared the next delivery truck mine.

My truck arrived promptly thereafter. Making sure the driver couldn't see me, I clambered onto the back bumper and grabbed the handles. The truck started down the hill. At what I deemed the appropriate moment—later, of course, than the others would have—I bailed.

My bravado marched well ahead of my information. Basic physics says I should have jumped forward to make up for losing the momentum of the truck. Perhaps such instinctive knowledge is a boy thing. It did not happen to be, at that moment, a Bette thing. I simply dropped off the truck.

And proceeded head over teakettle down the hill, the gang running after me. They apparently had some notion of getting me stopped. They failed.

When the tumbling finally ended, scrapes covered me from head to toe. But when the guys asked if I were hurt, I said, "Naw" with as much devil-may-care bluster as I could manage.

I headed home, saying I had to wash out the scrapes, which was true. Left unmentioned, I had to get home before I ran out of bravado and started to cry.

Having proved my point, I never again rode a truck. I told the gang I had nothing to prove since I already owned the longest ride. With memories of my inept exploit fresh in their minds, the gang agreed with my assessment. Some things work out.

A customer on Joe's paper route gave him a female German Shepherd of uncertain age, describing her as pure bred. A beautifully conformed dog, she looked it. We called her Beauty.

Beauty left few family memories. Quiet and passive, she had few Shepherd traits. She preferred quiet corners to the middle of the rough and tumble of playing kids. A canine Greta Garbo, she just wanted to be left alone.

Beauty did one memorable thing, however. One night, as everybody slept, she gave birth to a litter of seven pups on Joe's bed, waking him up. He took one look and yelled for Mother, awakening the rest of us and making it a family event.

Mother set Beauty and her pups up in the dog house the next morning. During the time Beauty nursed her pups, only Mother could get near her. Beauty snarled and snapped at everybody else. Her angry refusal to recognize our familial connection disappointed us, but facing a snarling German Shepherd tends to be instructive, so we kept our distance.

For the life of us, none of us can remember anything else about Beauty. Her remote personality and hermit-like nature just didn't create memories.

Mother decided to keep one pup and parcel out the rest. She said we kids could name the pup. The committee met at length to consider possibilities. We concluded our puppy's name should be Geronimo. Since his duties would include chasing after intruders, he would have to make unaccompanied journeys away from home, and we loved the idea of standing at the front door bellowing "Geronimo" at the top of our lungs to call him back. Not that a dog trained by

Mother necessarily needed to be called home, but it struck us as a swell idea.

Somehow or another, though, we never followed through on our plan. His name promptly became Jerry, and thus he would be called all his days.

Also promptly, he began working his eager, personable way into our hearts. He grew to be a good-size Shepherd-lookalike with the standard Shepherd coloring and markings. Playful with the family, fearsome to intruders and polite in mixed company, Jerry developed into an all round good dog. A great dog, as a matter of fact. My personal favorite.

<>◇<>

Whenever Daddy served at a Social, we all went there for church. First, we went to the Corps for Sunday School, then we went to the Social for church.

Church attendance was a mandatory part of the Social's program. The congregation that gathered in the chapel, then, consisted of Daddy, Mother, us kids and all the men in the rehabilitation program. Daddy led the service, and Mother assisted. Whenever the current group of residents didn't include a pianist, she played piano. She turned Barney's care over to Joe or Charles whenever something needed doing.

We sat dead center in the front row where our parents—and all the men—could keep an eye on us.

Salvation Army life was a family affair. Daddy and Mother needed and expected our support. We usually fulfilled our duties quite admirably, but from time to time, our support level sagged. One area requiring our focus and effort involved not distracting the men during the worship service, a crucial part of the rehabilitation program.

Daddy preached an excellent sermon, but we had to grow up a little to realize that. Until we did, and learned to listen, the service seemed awfully long. God didn't give any of us kids the passivity gene, and we'd get restless. A heartbeat after any restless bumping and jiggling began, a loud finger-snap emanated from the pulpit, Daddy's way of telling us to settle down. He didn't miss a beat in his preaching; he didn't change his expression; he didn't stop making eye contact around the room as he reached out to the men. But you'd have to be deaf not to hear the snap.

We sure heard it. One snap and we all jumped into our sitting-at-attention, straight-as-a-rod posture, eyes aimed directly at Daddy. No hesitation. No rebellion. The wonder is we didn't salute.

One snap per service fell in the understandable range; kids wiggle, don't you know. Two snaps elevated our trouble status to a more serious plane, guaranteeing we'd hear about it when we got home. Three snaps—the highest we ever heard—meant big trouble. Call it discipline, punishment or atonement, but whatever you called it, homecoming would not involve a party. Since not all new territory is good territory, we had no desire to check out the result of four snaps. We usually managed to be a one-snap group, but not always.

After church, we ate Sunday dinner at the Social, then spent some of the afternoon mingling with the men in the big recreation room. It gave the men pretty much their only family-like time. The gulf of their addictions separated them from their natural families, and visits from the outside were not part of the program.

On our way out of the service one Sunday, one of the younger men came up to me wearing a big smile. He said he had a daughter who would be just about my age. Losing his intended buoyancy, he started to choke up and said he didn't get to see her anymore because he made too many bad decisions in his life. Then his face crumpled. Then his whole body. Crying, he shuffled away.

I felt sad. He showed me a daddy's need for his little girl, and I couldn't imagine what it must be like to be a little girl without a daddy. I never saw him again. With as many men as there were in the program, that may not mean anything, but it would be nice to report a happy ending. I don't know if he worked the program and got back with his family or not. I hope he did.

Afternoons at the Social were light-hearted times. A few games of Rook went over the tables, but for the most part, the men seemed to enjoy the fact we were there. They asked us about school and our activities, the kind of things grown-up relatives ask kids.

We always ended our visit with a trip to the sorting room where all the donated items were separated, tagged for resale or discarded. Unsalable articles of clothing, sheets, towels—most anything fabric—were prepared for sale to the "rag man" for reprocessing. Cardboard, newspaper, etc. went to the baler in preparation for sale to a different reprocessor. Sorting took the knowledge and skill of many residents.

The sorting room was magic; we never knew what we would see. We never had a chance to go to FAO Schwarz, but I can't imagine even that magical place comparing to the wonder of the sorting room.

Daddy allowed each of us to take a book or two. Over time, Joe and Charles put together a complete set of The Hardy Boys mysteries.

The boys could also select an item or two from among the broken toys, appliances, tools and the like, that were on their way to the junk bin. The Social had nobody to fix these items to make them salable; they didn't bring enough money to make it feasible to hire somebody to do the repairs and the Social had to pay to have broken items carted away.

In terms of the Social's needs, then, small broken items were an expense, worse than useless. Daddy saw them as a teaching opportunity. He told the boys they could sell anything they fixed and keep the money as their payment for making the repair. Thus, with virtually no input from him, Daddy taught both the boys about small appliance and toy repair—and saved the Social money in the process. Charles remembers a coup of slowly gathering all the broken parts of a train set, repairing them and selling the completed set for what satisfied him as a dandy price.

Mount Vernon was a special time.

However, even in halcyon memories, there remains a bone to pick.

During our Sunday visits, the Social's residents taught Flo to shoot a pretty good game of pool. I received no such offer of instruction. It may have been my younger age, but I think it was my goofy appearance.

Flo had straight hair, so Mother let her grow up in peace. I, however, had fine hair, with a natural wave. It tangled easily. Mother solved the problem by putting my hair in long curls and planting a huge, dumb bow on my right temple. By Mount Vernon and fourth grade, I hated those curls. They embarrassed me. And the bow? Don't even ask. Which deterred Mother not a whit. With curls, she said, I looked more "up together," so curls it would be.

So, anyway, Flo showed up regular and I showed up goofy, and that's what I think made the difference. While the ability—or inability—to shoot pool made no difference in Flo's life or mine, there must be a principle in there somewhere.

Sunday evenings, we all attended services at the Corps. I wore curls.

Mount Vernon had a long tradition, enacted whenever the semi-pro football team played a home game in the stadium down the hill from our house. Neighborhood kids would sneak down to the playground, climb over the fence, skulk their way down to the stadium level, furtively make their way into the stands—then, mission accomplished, strut back home. We happily threw ourselves into this marvelous tradition.

An eight-foot chain-link fence stood as the first obstacle. Not much of a problem for, say, a junior high student like Charles, it challenged Flo and me.

First we had to climb eight vertical feet of fence with too-small toeholds. Then we had to navigate the sharp, twisted points of wire that ran along the top of the fence. One such point reached out to snag Flo on one trip over, rewarding her with a permanent three-inch scar on her thigh—a lifelong badge of some sort of courage. Lastly, we had to climb down on the other side. Taller kids might opt to stretch out and drop down, but short kids like us had to climb down.

Once over the fence, we had to get past Vito, the groundskeeper. Looking back, I think Vito enjoyed the game as much as the kids. While he sort of chased us, somehow he never managed to catch a one of us.

Even better, Vito knew us Dowdell kids and added to the general thrill of "sneaking in" by waving his arm and loudly calling out, "I go tella you pop at da Salavaish." It made us proud to be Daddy's children. Vito knew Daddy! How famous could you get?

Sometimes Vito managed to plant himself between us and our goal, patrolling back and forth, and we had to give up, climb back over the fence and go home. Sometimes, though—ah, sweet victory—we reached the promised land of the stadium stands. Then we'd leave by the front gate and swagger—as best we could—home, savoring our conquest until the next game. I don't think anybody actually stayed to watch the football game; our game ended with making it to the stands.

Spectators in the stands, veterans of the tradition, cheered us on. If Vito's efforts appeared to be verging on success, our efforts received as much attention—and cheering—as the game.

Grandpa retired at the end of Daddy's second year at the Mount Vernon Social. In immediate response, the long knives of resentment that Grandpa had created through the years came flashing out of their sheaths, pointed straight at Daddy. Thanks in large part to Grandpa, Daddy was in no position to defend himself. Especially stationed in such a plum assignment. Perhaps even more especially since he had achieved major success, any way you wanted to measure it, in Mount Vernon. Regardless, a few officers persisted in their view the assignment was nepotism. The expression, "Wake up and smell the coffee," wasn't yet well known.

We like to think church folks are above the fray of resentment and thoughts of getting even, but the fact is people are people. In any sort of group, there will be some who excel in getting even for real or perceived indignities. However noble and lofty the cause, a few people—typically a tiny percentage—will be off-message.

Most of the troops recognized Daddy's value—and situation— but a handful saw Grandpa's retirement as their chance to settle scores. And Daddy, with all his amazing talents and abilities, was not a get-even kind of person. He made a mouth-watering target for more average folk with a bone to pick.

As soon as Grandpa retired, they ousted Daddy from Mount Vernon, sending him to the small, struggling Trenton, New Jersey, Social.

Mother, in her usual fashion, saw their actions as justified. I can only guess what Daddy thought. He never complained— not about anything.

TRENTON, NEW JERSEY

We moved from Mount Vernon's large, three-floor house with a large backyard to a smallish duplex built on a postage-stamp lot. It also had three floors, but a single bedroom with sloping ceilings took up the entire top floor.

Our new neighbors, Mr. and Mrs. Alexander Graham Bell—somehow related to the telephone's famous Mr. Bell—who lived in the other half of the duplex with their middle-aged maiden daughter, probably felt the impact of the move more than we did. They radiated uncertain concern, either from a long-held view of life or their more recently acquired view of the next door multitude.

Five high-energy kids create at least a little pandemonium. Charles's decision to learn to play the trombone probably didn't help. Flo's frequent and determined attendance at the sun-porch piano may have increased our neighbor's heartburn. And perhaps Brownie and Jerry generated a touch of dyspepsia.

Adding to the numerical awe of our introduction, we started demolition on the wall between the kitchen and a minuscule breakfast area shortly after we arrived. We couldn't all fit into the breakfast nook at once, and the wall around it made the hall to the dining room a narrow, one-way, don't-plan to carry-anything squeeze. Once Daddy determined the interfering wall didn't bear the load of the house, we whaled away, reducing it to rubble. The Bells probably began compiling a long list of real estate agents to sell their place.

But the finished change improved everything. Plus, it gave us a place to eat breakfast.

As the noise died down and the shock wore off, we developed a pleasant neighborliness with our new neighbors. They found out we were polite and cheerful. What noises they heard through the wall came from exuberance and joy, not fights. They never heard bad language or crashing household goods. And the dogs barked only for defensive reasons, offering them protection, too. In fact, once they reconciled themselves to the prodigious amounts of energy of five children, which we usually managed to keep down to a low roar, it worked out just fine.

A battered rowboat came with our new quarters. Moored in the canal that ran along the Delaware River, it was tied, as I remember, to a tree. A popular place for boating, the canal gathered water to feed Trenton's water supply. The water hurried smoothly to its appointed destination, a benign appearance masking a powerful current. Eventually, the canal's water rushed and tumbled down a cement ramp into the river, right next to a huge water intake for the city's water system.

A few days after moving to Trenton, Mother agreed the older four of us could take the boat out for a test run. We planned to spend the day on our boat, our new prize.

To call the thing a boat insults any proper sort of sailing vessel. Years of neglect left only small patches of paint to cover its weathered nakedness. It leaked a bit. An old tin bucket filled with rocks served as the anchor. All in all, it looked great, and we all piled in.

Rowing didn't take much effort in the swift-moving canal, and we made rapid progress. After a while, Joe, Charles and Flo decided to jump in and swim. I couldn't swim, so I stayed in the boat. Just sitting spawned a rapid onset of boredom, and I decided to get in the water and hang onto the back of our decrepit, albeit wonderful vessel. Providentially, as it turned out, I loudly announced the plan to my siblings.

Thick, dirty grease, a gift from years of motor boats plying the canal, covered the back of the boat. Trying to find a non-gooky spot to hold on, I moved my hands—and lost contact with the boat. The current swept me away before I could grab hold again.

At that precise moment, Flo decided to dive under the boat and grab my legs, hopefully to scare me into a scream. Since legend had it the canal held many vile creatures, she thought her plan would work well. But she couldn't find my legs and surfaced to find out why.

She saw me taking in water and bobbing speedily toward the ramp leading down to the city's water intake. She yelled for the boys, and Joe came swimming after me. Fortunately, he had a powerful stroke and had saved lives before, so he knew exactly what to do.

Charles and Flo hoisted themselves into the boat to bring it down to wherever Joe and I ended up. The anchor got caught in something, so Charles untied its rope from the boat, leaving it behind as he pulled on the oars with all his might and muscle.

Meanwhile, Joe caught up with me. He swam us over to the slimy, muddy edge of the canal so he could stand while holding me and waiting for the boat. While I coughed and gasped for air, Joe, slowly sinking into the mire, bellowed about bringing the boat over before he and I disappeared into the muck. Between shouts, he terrified me with stories of snakes swirling around his legs and told me to hold on tight lest I end up amongst them. Ah, the varied duties of a big brother.

The boat arrived, and Joe and I climbed in. Stunned at what had almost happened, we all agreed not to mention anything about it to Daddy or Mother. Learning they almost lost a daughter would mean the end of the boat, so we kept mum.

But I never went out in the boat again.

That year, Flo swam breast stroke for the school's swim team. She recalls Mother showing up to loudly cheer her on—in full Army uniform, including the bonnet. Between heats, Mother glad-handed the other parents and became everybody's good friend. In Flo's eyes, Mother's popularity and the fact she came to cheer balanced off the uniform.

The Trenton school split each grade into two sections, one for the faster learners and one for those who proceeded a little more slowly. And they had a policy of putting all new students in the slower-paced class. They did not reference previous achievements, test scores or the like. One size fit all.

My slower class covered things I had long since learned. Being young and unaware of such niceties as subtlety, I failed to disguise my boredom. Instead, I offered suggestions of possible projects, proposed to do extra reading, anything. The teacher, tall, with auburn tresses on a monthly renewal schedule, decided a demon child had been sent to punish her.

She told the other students not to play with me during recess. The girls listened; the boys pretty much didn't, which worked out fine for my tomboy self.

One day, a classmate, seeing the teacher's attitude as a permission slip, whacked my hip with what he called a "German black jack," a leather sling arrangement with a ball of lead in the business end. He laughed and said even if I told the teacher, she wouldn't do anything to him.

Instead, I told Joe and Charles—both more-than-six-feet-tall high-school students—and they made a brief house call. They politely suggested to him that it wouldn't be wise to hurt me again. No threats, no muscle, just a helpful suggestion, minors to minor.

Trenton gave birth to my interest in missing as much school as I could. With a mean teacher and no learning, what could possibly be the point of regular attendance? Especially since irregular attendance still earned an A, which met the basic necessity of pleasing Mother. And even more especially since school provided daily embarrassment.

The statuesque teacher, tall, slim and well endowed, regularly set the boys to snorting and shoving—while the forlorn girls squirmed glumly—by standing in profile and "giving an example" of deep breathing. This meant throwing her chest out as far as the eye could see while turning her head to smile brightly at the class. Proper demonstrations of good breathing technique took several thrusts of her ample bosom, of course. Snort, snort. Shove, shove. It mortified us girls.

Years later and miles away, I met a woman who attended the same school a few years after I did. She howled with recognition at the mention of the deep breathing exercises, and described the teacher right down to her hair cut and color. Apparently, titillating little boys constituted part of the teacher's regular lesson plan.

But as the school year crawled on, the teacher and I reached detente. I took care of the bulletin board, graded papers, cleaned out cabinets, reminded her when the class needed new supplies and kept the blackboard clean. She decided I was a wonderful student after all.

Fortunately, considering everything else she had me doing, she never requested my help with the deep-breathing exercises.

Teachers chose to be the bane of my existence.

Our frequent moves put me into ten schools in twelve years, guaranteeing the perpetual title as "the new kid." New kids rarely make it into a teacher's hit parade. Especially new kids who get better grades than the favorites. And most especially, new kids who arrive full of energy and noise.

Many teachers demand total obeisance, but I never got the hang of that. My DNA stopped at happy cooperation, and

I lacked the skill to perform the unhappy teacher waltz. When a teacher's unhappiness with my genetic limitations expressed itself in caustic, demeaning remarks, I didn't—couldn't—respond. They had the science of putting students in their place down pat, but the practice demanded a response, and my lack of one simply raised the ante.

It always became a contest of wills, although I didn't understand it as such. I just wanted to be myself. Teachers who allowed that always loved me. They'd give me extra reports to write and busy work to do, keeping everybody happy. These teachers even said I made teaching a joy, that I reminded them why they went into teaching. Oh, but the others.

Many teachers have an unwritten rule that energetic, talkative students should get poor grades so they can be used as a horrible example of wasted potential. But, although energetic and talkative, I always got the best grades, ruining their plan, thus irritating them. It begat a death spiral. They pushed. I, not knowing what else to do, stood my ground.

By junior high, a teacher-mandated walk to the principal's office ended many classes prematurely. In high school, my geometry teacher became so regular in the practice of expelling me from class that the office workers saved errands for me to run. If anything untoward happened anywhere in the geometry classroom, the teacher, sure it was my fault, sent me packing.

And I continued to miss a lot of school days.

To my wonderment, Daddy and Mother said not a word. Mother, a natural teacher, may have wondered why the teachers chose not to see the easy, obvious solution of keeping me busy. Daddy, I think, understood my plight. Or perhaps the fact I never missed the honor roll balanced the scales. I never rocked the boat by asking what their reasoning might be, and they never volunteered.

My "problem" ended with our move to Athens,Ohio, in the middle of my junior year of high school. Stuffed to the gills with the offspring of Ohio University professors, Athens High School had demanding teachers. Better yet, the teachers actually took joy in motivating students to soar as high as they could go.

It took ten schools, but I had come home.

I even won a big, black and red, chenille "A" just like the football players, but with an "S" for "scholarship" embroidered on the crossbar.

One amusing story about the geometry teacher: It frustrated her no end that I earned the highest grade in the class. Her solution was to give a pop quiz each time I returned from a day or so away from school "resting." Of course, since I set my own days-at-school schedule, the quiz didn't surprise me, just everybody else. My grade soared even higher. She never figured out why her plan consistently failed.

We didn't eat out much. Upon occasion though—usually when traveling—we would all troop into a restaurant, Daddy in the lead, Mother bringing up the rear. Our main question, asked before the car stopped, was, "What's the limit?"

Daddy announced a dollar amount, the limit, which we could not exceed. Up to the limit, we could order anything.

The limit bought Daddy and Mother a season of absolute quiet as we pored over menus to calculate the best combination that didn't go over the limit. It took time to total up all the various options and get close to the limit without leaving any money "on the table," as it were. An exact hit constituted victory, and being the furthest away from the limit meant defeat. The limit took serious study.

Food pyramids had nothing to do with anything. If we could find a combination that maxed out the limit without threatening to make us retch and gag, we ordered it and ate it down to the bare plate.

Our ingenuity—however bizarre our choices—tickled Daddy. Mother figured these outings were too rare to damage our health. Both appreciated the math lesson involved, not to mention our time of quiet deliberation.

Other diners, not knowing of the motivating power of the limit, often complimented Daddy and Mother on our behavior. That might have happened in any case, but the limit guaranteed it.

Flo had sheet music. Where and how she garnered this treasure is lost in the mists of memory, but just the having of sheet music gave her "with it" status. She had practice books from Mount Vernon piano lessons, but that boring kid stuff couldn't hold a candle to sheet music.

This was the big time. Grownups owned sheet music. Since Flo had recently reached the exalted status of teenager, the glamour of it all fit Flo's new station in life.

Not that the song had anything to do with the Top Ten, On The Charts With A Bullet or the like. In fact, it was the very oldie, "I'm Always Chasing Rainbows," but no matter; sheet music was sheet music.

She learned the music quickly. She played it endlessly.

One fine spring day, Flo sat down at the piano on the sun porch for a lovely day of playing her sheet music. I sat across from her, reading and enjoying her pleasure and skill.

After only a few hours, though, a man's plaintive voice came through the window. "Girlie," it asked, "can't you play anything else?"

Apparently the painters working on our neighbor's house thought a hundred or so rounds of "I'm Always Chasing Rainbows" were sufficient. Perhaps they lacked the souls of *artistes*. They obviously lacked even a hint of the status of sheet music.

We decided to take a break for lunch before Flo continued her "I'm Always Chasing Rainbows" concert. The painters either learned to enjoy her playing or resigned themselves to it. In either case, we didn't hear from them again.

Should you meet Flo today, she'll be happy to play "I'm Always Chasing Rainbows" for you. The sheet music may be long gone, but she still knows each and every chord by heart. It has a real nice bouncy rhythm.

Mother started to pine for England and a chance to see her mother again. She hadn't been back for nearly twenty years. In that time, she'd married and had five children.

Grandma Gowen never came to these shores. She had raised nine children (Mother arriving next to last), much of the time as a widow. To keep body and soul together, she farmed, ran a country store, sewed for the King and, as time went on, bought low-income rental housing. Wealth finally came her way via the rental properties.

She became something of a slum lord (or would it be slum lady?). With low-income housing, rents got collected, in person, weekly. So each and every Saturday, she walked five miles getting the job done.

She didn't trust anybody to handle her rents, so the properties tied her down. She couldn't come for Mother's commissioning as a Salvation Army officer. She couldn't even come for Daddy and Mother's wedding. And she couldn't come to meet her American grandchildren.

She never left Downend, near Bristol. She had rents to collect.

And we couldn't afford to visit her. Her wealth could easily have paid for any number of trips, but Grandma Gowen attached great importance to her money and kept a tight rein on it. She knew the seven of us couldn't afford to come to see her. So be it. She never offered to help pay for us to come to Downend, so none of us ever met her.

But then, she earned her money only by great effort and perseverance, so she certainly also earned the right to spend it as she wished. The subject of not meeting Grandma Gowen never came up for discussion. It seemed normal. She just never knew what she missed.

⟨⟩⟨⟩⟨⟩

Grandma Gowen lived in a huge home. So large, in fact, the Masonic Lodge bought it as their Temple after she died. And large enough that a middle-of-the-night Luftwaffe bomb heavily damaged the far end of the house, and Grandma didn't realize anything had happened until the next day when she took her usual morning walk around the property to check for damage.

By strong choice, she lived alone with her cat. Well, most of the time. She married for the second time in her sixties, but her groom died not long thereafter. She tried marriage again in her seventies, but that husband also died within a year or two. Wedded bliss got one last chance in her eighties, but he didn't last long either. She lived to be ninety-five, but never married again.

Truth to tell, those of us on this side of the pond never knew about husbands two through four until after her death. And we never learned their names, either. Mother and Grandma wrote to each other regularly, but apparently Grandma didn't see these events as newsworthy.

Mother's older brother, Herb, pronounced Grandma's late-in-life grooms to be gold-diggers who married Grandma for her money. We later understood that chasing her money was his game. Perhaps their game as well, but definitely his.

Anyway, when we lived in Trenton, Grandma Gowen had reached her late seventies, and Mother decided she needed to visit before her mother died. Based on what little we knew of Grandma's family history, we couldn't plan on longevity. Obviously, we didn't factor in the excellent exercise she got on weekends.

Daddy understood Mother's desire to see her mother, but he also believed she needed to be with us. He applied all the logic and reason he had in him and hoped she would reconsider, putting the trip off for a few years until we were older. But Mother—locked, loaded and absolutely convinced everything would work out just fine—had made up her mind.

That May, Mother sailed—flying being far too expensive—for England. Five-year-old Barney sailed with her. The rest of us, she believed, had enough moxie to get along without her for six months.

We had good support from relatives who lived reasonably close by and from the other Army families in Trenton. It could have worked. But that summer, the Army transferred Daddy to Cleveland, away from any thread of support or encouragement.

They assigned him to the Cleveland, Ohio, Social—as an assistant. The Cleveland Social was larger than Trenton's, but still far smaller than the one Daddy ran so successfully in Mt. Vernon. He was still paying Grandpa's bill.

Joe didn't want to move to Cleveland. He had attended enough schools, and all the moving had already messed up his credits so he had to stay in school an extra year for one requirement he missed along the way. Who knew what the next school would demand? He worked it out with Daddy to stay behind to finish up his remaining credit and graduate from Trenton High School.

He got a job in the Sears warehouse. When Daddy, Charles, Flo and I moved to Cleveland, Joe moved into the YMCA and started working.

Joe discovered a wonderful side benefit in lifting and pushing large boxes around at Sears: It muscled him into significant buffness. His delight in his new physique added a euphoric bounce in his step. It rather resembled a strut, as a matter of fact, and for the next few years, you didn't want to get between Joe and a mirror.

Flo and I accepted—rather zealously, truth to tell—the duty these situations imposed upon kid sisters. We stayed ever vigilant for any need, however minor, to verbally assist Joe's humility. As an expression of love, of course. Charles didn't natter about nearly as much as Flo and I, but he lobbed in the occasional zinger as necessary

None of it fizzed on Joe. Buffness trumps lip any day of the week.

Being raised mostly on the east coast, words like "Cleveland" and "Ohio" fell strangely on our ears. In the east coast way of thinking, everything civilized and good lay east of the Hudson River. Now, living in Trenton—actually well west of the Hudson—made this thinking a little bizarre, but in the easterner's version of geography, you aren't really west of the Hudson until you're west of Philadelphia. Except, of course, for major sections of New Jersey. Well, it made sense at the time.

We kids fell back on the scuttlebutt we'd picked up from here and there. Were the streets paved? Did cowboys herd cattle through town? Inquiring, provincial minds wanted to know.

At one point in our questioning, Daddy smiled and said he'd heard there were Indians in Cleveland. The others got the joke, but I, ever literal, wondered if we would be able to see tepees from our new quarters.

The reality of Cleveland, then, came as a surprise. And we lived in the thick of it—on East 111th near Superior—not downtown, but definitely not in the suburbs.

CLEVELAND, OHIO

I hated Cleveland. Mother and Barney were in England. Joe had stayed behind in Trenton We lived in a crowded neighborhood that didn't feel safe or welcoming. School provided daily misery. Nobody my age went to the Corps. I didn't fit anywhere.

Flo didn't like Cleveland either. She went to the same miserable school, but at least she had a good friend, Mary Galloway, at the Corps. Plus, she played alto horn in the Corps band and got to enjoy the band's camaraderie. These blessings didn't balance out the ordeal of school, but they helped.

Charles hit the jackpot. He liked his school. He played in both the school and Corps bands. Unlike Army music, the school's trombone music came in bass clef, so he looked forward to proficiency in both clefs—a huge deal to a budding musician. Plus, he had a good friend at the Corps, Harold Andersen, another officer's kid.

He turned the house's old coal cellar into his music room and practiced every day, sometimes working on one short refrain for hours. Hearing the same, say, twenty notes over and over and over and over—you get the idea—turned involuntary listeners into zombies, but all that practice won the first-chair spot he aimed for.

Flo and I started alto horn lessons together at the Corps. Whether because I behaved childishly or lacked musical talent, the teacher made no bones about not wanting to waste time with me. He worked with Flo for almost the whole hour's lesson, then complained about my lack of progress. Perhaps he was right in doing so. I finally gave up.

Spending time at the Corps added to my misery anyway. The seemingly omnipresent Corps Officer's daughter sensed blood in the water in my lostness. She viewed my presence as an invitation to practice her well-honed sarcasm skills of barbed asides and mutterings. With the constant possibility of encountering her sharp tongue, I never wanted to go to the Corps.

And Flo didn't want to be around me much, either. Which is not surprising. You'd have to scour history pretty thoroughly with a stiff brush to find any thirteen-year-old girl who voluntarily spends time with an eleven-year-old sister. A vast chasm separates those two ages. But the new distance between us added to my misery—and perhaps to hers.

School was a nightmare. The huge student body had tough, worldly-wise kids, a new thing for us. Flo and I found ourselves catapulted from small, protective, suburban schools into a huge inner-city school.

Older, scarier students roamed the halls. Rumors abounded about drugs and whiskey in the lockers, as did stories about students carrying knives. Fist fights offered semi-regular diversion on the school's vast front lawn.

Leaving the school grounds meant walking a long, long sidewalk bordered by a pipe-rail fence. The older boys arranged themselves menacingly along the length of the fence and made lewd, frightening remarks—and sometimes threats— as we walked by.

The school's population split about in half between blacks and Jews. If you weren't one of those, you were on the outside looking in. If I tried to make a friend in either group, their peers would pull them away. Many of the teachers tried to ingratiate themselves by demeaning students who didn't "belong." Their verbal warfare increased animosity in the already divided campus.

Flo and I had the same home economics teacher—Flo for sewing; I for cooking—a small, wizened woman with a white, ill-fitting wig pulled back into a bun, ineffectual, but with a compensating mean streak. She couldn't control her classes. She wouldn't teach. And she radiated disdain. Worse yet, she didn't know that she didn't know how to make it work.

On the days my class "cooked," she had us bring a grapefruit from home. Cooking meant halving the grapefruit, then cutting around the inside and between each section. Of course, in the way of all cooking classes, we had to eat what we prepared.

Every day—day after day—as we worked on those wretched grapefruit, she lectured us on the evils of sugar. Sugar, she insisted, would give each and every one of us instant diabetes. Grapefruit must be consumed as is, without benefit of sweetening.

So the entire class of, maybe, forty girls had to eat hard, sour, out-of-season grapefruit, wincing and puckering as we chewed. This student body didn't come from homes that frequented upscale gourmet purveyors of freshly-flown-in produce. We didn't get good out-of-season grapefruit. We all ate the cheapest grapefruit that could be found—hard, yellow cannonballs.

As we daily winced our way through the sour fruit, the teacher ate lunch. A lunch always topped off with a large slab of the sweetest, goopiest pie the school cafeteria offered accompanied by a cup of ultra-sweetened coffee. We would drool watching her pour a torrent of sugar into her coffee. What she put in one cup of coffee could have sweetened the grapefruit of every girl in class.

I started, as educators put it, to act out.

The huge cooking classroom had heavy, oak tables with metal-covered tops, arranged back-to-back in sets of two, down each side of the room, with two girls assigned to each. A gaggle of back-to-back stoves facing the tables on each side of the room occupied a wide, front-to-back aisle and defined the center of the room.

A set of canisters, padlocked lest a student dared use the contents, graced each table. The tables had two deep drawers filled with various cooking tools. A double-door cabinet sat between the drawers and held even more cooking paraphernalia—none of which we ever used. We never baked a cake, muffin or cookie. We never concocted a casserole. We never steamed a vegetable. We cut and ate sour grapefruit, which didn't require much in the way of equipment.

The vast, wonderfully-equipped room minimized student interaction, but we managed. During our home ec period, all divisions faded away as we united against our common enemy, Miss Dragoo. In that classroom alone, students became as one.

One day, as we waited for the teacher to arrive with her sugar-laden lunch tray, I figured out how to pick the lock on the sugar canister and passed the word. After giving her little diabetes speech, the teacher applied herself to her victuals, ignoring us while we plied away at our grapefruit. One by one, the other girls drifted by my table to surreptitiously acquire a spoonful of sugar.

We succeeded in executing our sugar liberation scheme only a few times, but what a triumph! Victory, in just fifteen little calories of purloined sugar.

One day, we got together to put a row of leftover soap slivers across the floor, step one of a plan. Our soap-bar line covered the width of the classroom, halfway to the back. Shortly after class started, in step two of our plan, one of the girls seated in the distant rear of the room starting yelling and crying. As the teacher hustled back to shush the wailing student, she hit the trail of soap, levitating her into a frenzied mid-air ballet as she tried to maintain her balance—which, at length, she managed to do. She gave an excellent performance.

Yet another day she had us washing a bajillion dishes in preparation for a Board of Education dinner. She issued the strictest of orders to carry no more than three of the valuable dishes at one time as we moved them from one end of the room to the other. A girl could get old moving all those dishes three at a time, so I carried stacks—and earned the bonus of giving her the immediate vapors. Especially when the other girls began following my example. As she clucked her way around the room, nattering at the girls to carry fewer dishes, I got behind her, bellowed "Look out!" and threw down a metal tray carefully chosen for maximum noise. Her entire body jolted into a midair symphony of spasms. Upon landing, she ordered the class to cease and desist all dishwashing, return to our seats and sit with hands folded. She glared at us, daring the slightest twitch of a muscle, until the bell rang to mercifully relieve her of our presence.

I don't know who finished washing the dishes. Maybe the Board and their guests ate from dusty plates. Or maybe they weren't dirty in the first place.

Mainly, I acted out by taking pins out of door hinges.

One day the teacher planned to teach us the parts of a stove, as if we'd never seen one—or needed one to prepare our citrus cannon balls, for that matter. In preparation for the event, I took the hinges out of the oven door of the stove she had, perhaps unwisely, mentioned she intended to use in her demonstration. Lecturing irritatingly along in her shrill, nasal voice, with grand gestures to point out the stove's very standard features, she finally reached the part we all waited for: the oven. She grasped the handle of the oven door to pull it down—and sent it thundering to the floor. Even though we all resisted cheering and laughing, she abruptly canceled her helpful talk, and we never learned about the various parts of an oven—which most of us used routinely at home in any case.

Sometimes I removed pins from the hinges from cabinet doors in the tables. Unsuspecting students would open the doors to a huge bang. Crashing doors became our irregular classroom punctuation. Well, at least it made my classmates laugh even though the teacher never saw even a trace of humor in it. But then, she never found humor in anything. Nobody ever saw her smile

Meanwhile, Flo and her classmates struggled to get through sewing class each day. To give you an idea how bad it was, even the much more compliant Flo "acted out."

She led the class in a conga line from the front of the sewing room to the back where they jumped out the first-floor window one by one, then reentered the building and con-gaed their way back into the classroom—only to do it all over again. Meanwhile, the teacher darted about the room chirping unintelligible noises and fluttering her arms in a futile effort to get them stopped.

One grand day the teacher entered the room to see Flo et al, inside clothing dummies, exuberantly dancing away atop classroom cutting tables. They accompanied themselves loudly, if discordantly, straining their vocal chords to belt out appropriately celebratory music. For some reason, their creativity did not amuse her.

Fortunately, our home ec classes came to a blessed end after one semester, and nobody ever saw the teacher again. Some said she had a nervous breakdown. Others said she retired. Whatever the case, before she left, she did me the enormous disservice of sending me to the principal's office as the lone cause of her travails.

The principal came out of central casting for a reform school movie. He scowled as I entered his enormous—to my terrified eyes—office. As I sat down, he angrily asked why I acted the way I did. What was I to say? That he ran a bad school where no learning happened, where both the teachers and the kids were out of control and somebody should close the whole place down as a failure?

I said I didn't know.

He asked if I misbehaved because I wasn't very smart.

I said, "no," but I believed him.

He asked if I misbehaved because I wasn't pretty.

I said, "no," but I believed him.

He asked if I misbehaved because I didn't have nice clothes.

I said, "no," but I believed him.

He asked if I misbehaved because my parents were separated.

I didn't even argue with his interpretation of my mother's absence; I just said, "no" and hung my head even further down.

Then, having thoroughly gutted me, he said I could go.

In my shame, I told nobody.

I later learned the principal erred on every point. For one example, I owned the highest IQ score in the school, and he knew that when he told me I was dumb. A lot of water flowed under many bridges before I conquered his callously inflicted evil.

In the end, his efforts to destroy me failed because he only made me stronger.

Daddy's situation was at least as miserable as ours, but he always focused outwards, on others. While Flo and I never told him about our trials, Daddy could see us sinking and reached out from his own depleted well to help.

Down the block and around the corner on Superior sat Franklin's Ice Cream store. They sold Lollapaloozas, huge bowls of ice cream in various flavored scoops under a multiplicity of toppings and crowned with a mountain of whipped cream. You won a certificate if you could eat the whole thing. Since we rarely had ice cream and we rarely, rarely ate out—even for treats—the place and the idea dazzled us. I don't know what Daddy had to do without to afford it, but he took us to Franklin's to tackle the Lollapalooza challenge a few times. Flo always finished and won the certificate. I always ended up giving a good part of mine to Daddy. Since he never ordered anything for himself, he probably didn't mind.

A growth spurt left me without much to wear, and Daddy took me shopping for a dress. I had never gone to a regular store to try on dresses before. Most of my clothes came from Army stores. Everything else came in the form of a bargain that Mother snapped up and handed to me when she got home. Truth to tell, neither Daddy nor I knew the choreography of clothes shopping, and we bumbled around a good bit in getting the job done. After several stores, though, I found a red plaid dress I liked.

I enjoyed everything about our venture. Again, I don't know what Daddy did without to be able to afford the dress. I doubt he spent a nickel on himself during our year in Cleveland.

One day Daddy scored two free tickets to see the Indians, a rare treat for him. In an enormous statement of love, he took me along. He loved baseball and exulted in the excellent box seats, but both were wasted on me. Pausing only to gasp for air, I chattered endlessly the entire time, pretty much ignoring the game but relishing my time with him. I don't know how much he got out of being there, but he acted as if he enjoyed himself. Since he knew I would behave exactly as I did, he wins Father of the Year hands down, any year you want to name. A lesser man would have invited a baseball-loving friend or, failing that, gone alone, but he saw me sinking and threw a lifeline.

Mother and Barney were coming home from England in time for Thanksgiving. We all worked to make the house sparkle. Daddy even washed all the curtains. Telling us to keep the house immaculate, Daddy drove to New York to get them.

A few days later, we excitedly welcomed Mother and Barney home. Daddy prepared a nice dinner as Mother unpacked. Except for Joe, our family would gather again around the table.

The day we returned to school from Christmas vacation, my sour-hearted English teacher decided a good day's exercise would be to go around the room and have students list the Christmas or Chanukah gifts they received. My family had our usual lean Yule, so I had little to say. As each student rose to proudly rattle off an impressively long list of loot, my gifts appeared sparser and sparser. My heart sank lower and lower. I kept hoping the bell would ring and end the time of tribulation. No such luck. My turn arrived, and I stood to recite my gifts.

It never occurred to me to lie. A single, imaginatively ornate whopper would have saved the day. Instead, I painfully delineated my brief list. I separated gifts into their component parts to stretch things out. Since the Corps gave a small box of hard candy to Sunday School kids, I put candy in the list without bothering to elaborate that it was hard-tack candy all stuck together in a lump. My valiant, face-saving efforts aside, nothing could hide the fact Santa had scarcely slowed down as he flew past our house that year.

As I slunk back down in my seat, the teacher questioned, "Is that all?" Heavy sarcasm dripped from each stretched-for-emphasis word, completing my humiliation. I heard a few little giggles as I miserably responded, "Yes," but the situation so exceeded any level of decency, most of the class stayed silent. But no one spoke to me or even made eye-contact when we finally escaped the room. What could they say? And why would they volunteer for more of the same, or worse, by reaching out?

Day after day, she hurled her malicious digs at us outsiders. She never realized her attitude did not win friends. Indeed, it alienated the very students she sought to charm. And when their disaffection became noticeable, even to her, she clue-lessly ratcheted her efforts up a notch or so, thinking that would make it work.

By spring, English class had become a daily acid bath. About that time, Grandpa died, and we drove back to New Jersey for his funeral. Upon my return, the teacher first berated me for missing school. When I told her my grandfather had died, she ridiculed me for missing a week of school "just" for his funeral. I explained it took place in New Jersey, but she sniffed that it still shouldn't have taken that long. And marked my grade down to prove her point.

About that time I decided the small grass area in our back yard needed a swimming pool. I took up a shovel and started to dig. Day upon day, I spent every spare moment digging the pool. My dedication made the old mail carrier's line "neither rain nor snow. ." seem wimpy by comparison. I dug, and I dug and I dug. Then I raked out the dirt piles and dug some more.

Daddy let any dismay about the disappearing grass go unmentioned. If that's what it took for me to fight my struggles, that's what it took.

A few months after her return from England, Mother told us about the time she collected Grandma Gowen's rents. The signal honor of being allowed to handle the rents showed Grandma's trust in her. And Grandma didn't trust easily.

Slogging through England's seemingly perpetual rain, Mother walked the five-mile rent-collecting round, chatting with each renter and spreading her usual good will. At her final stop, responding to an invitation from inside, she let herself into a little cottage. The bedridden tenant lay on a cot in the middle of the front room, wet and cold from the steady dripping of a leaky roof directly on her bed. Water from the soggy bedding trickled to the floor below, creating a shallow lake around her bed.

Frustration, pain and cold etched her face in misery. She said nothing about the situation and asked for no remedy as she gave Mother her rent money. But the tears of defeat that coursed down her cheeks contradicted her attempt at cheerful, socially expected chitchat. Mother could no more turn away from the woman's pain than she could fly to the moon by flapping her arms.

Mother asked the tenant about her circumstances. Did she have anybody who could help?

"No," the tenant replied. She had no family, she continued, and the aide agency responsible for her care fluffed off her requests to get the leak fixed or, at the least, move her bed.

Mother immediately, as was her style, called somebody to fix the roof. She waited for him to come and make the repair, which turned out to be a small, quick job, then paid his modest bill from the rent moneys she had collected. Pleased with an opportunity to bring relief to somebody so helpless and desperate, she arrived back at Grandma's house, excited to tell the story.

Rather than give Mother a pat on the back, Grandma lit into her, spewing a long, full-throated tongue lashing. Mother had wasted money fixing the roof. Grandma knew the roof leaked. She had known for a long time. However, the bed-ridden tenant, with no family, couldn't possibly move. She would have to stay and pay her rent, leak or no leak, and Grandma would get the rent without throwing away good money on unnecessary repairs. Fixing the roof was frivolous do-gooderism. Mother showed herself to be a wastrel! How dare she!

Grandma's harangue hurt, but not as much as the realization she could be so heartless. But even recognizing the price paid in her mother's hard-won approval, Mother knew she had done the right thing. She couldn't turn away from such a need, especially one so easily remedied, and be at peace with herself. Or with God.

But she never collected the rents again. Grandma decided Mother had a heart entirely too soft to be trusted. When it came to business, Grandma didn't tolerate weakness.

Mother heard some new jokes while in England and came home eager to delight and amaze us with her new repertoire. Knowing the hilarity about to be loosed upon us, she shook with laughter before she even launched. By the middle of the first—and best, she said—of the boffo stories, tears of laughter streamed down her cheeks. Fully engulfed in the moment, she could hardly speak.

At length, gasping for air, she finished the story and stopped talking, anticipating our crescendo—no, better, our ava-lanche—of guffaws. Instead, we sat quietly waiting for her to continue and let us in on the punch line. Dismayed with our lack of wit, she repeated the last few lines of her tale and again looked at us expectantly. Still we sat, still waiting for the funny part. We didn't get it at all.

Well, she was put out with the lot of us, but perseverance being her style, she pushed on to regale us with the next joke. Again, she laughed, she cried, she gasped for air. To the same result. We smiled a little so she wouldn't feel bad, but we didn't get it. Usually a good audience for humor, we were striking out.

Nobody had told us that sometimes you throw honesty out the window and laugh just to be sociable. And even if we'd heard that, we probably wouldn't have laughed anyway lest she misunderstood and started quizzing us about our favorite part.

Deciding her absence had somehow left us more than a bit slow on the uptake, Mother launched into her third, and last, joke. Same routine; same result. Poor mother. She gave the knee-slappers her all, to no avail.

It's hard to remember a joke when you don't get it, so most of Mother's jokes are long since forgotten. One joke, however, brought stardom—at least within the family.

It took many, many years for England to recover from World War II, and Mother returned from her visit home full of stories of the difficulties and struggles the people went through. Another Salvation Army officer invited her to speak to his soldiers about England's travails, so we all trooped off to the event—and the joke.

As part of her talk, Mother emphasized the fact that, whatever befell them, the English never lost their sense of humor. And she gave this for instance:

Meat was rarely available, so everybody made do with fish day after day. But one day, a butcher put out a sign: "Beef available today!"

A long queue quickly formed around the block. After nearly two hours in line, a lady finally reached the counter.

"I'll take two beef steaks, if you please."

"I'm sorry, missus, but we sold out of beef long since. All we have left is whale steak."

"Well, then, give me two whale steaks and wrap up the head for my cat."

Mother waited expectantly for the loud eruption of laughter that would surely follow this crown jewel of humor.

Total silence.

She repeated the story.

The silence grew deeper.

In frustration, Mother formed her arms into a large circle over her head and said, "You know, whale, the big thing that swims in the ocean."

Then putting her hands close together in front her, she continued, "And a little cat."

Leaning on the pulpit, she firmly repeated the punch line, "Well, then, give me two whale steaks and wrap up the head for my cat."

No response. The audience never did get it.

But we were delighted. "You know. A whale. The big thing that swims in the ocean" entered family lore.

Because of the drunk driver who hit us when I was a baby, Mother wore false teeth. With the extent of her injuries and all the surgery on her jaw after the accident, getting teeth that fit—that is, stayed in and didn't hurt—verged on impossible.

Mother, still faithful to John Bull and a British subject, availed herself of Britain's free-to-her health plan to get new choppers during her visit. Blimey! Not only did they fit like a dream, but she saved enough money to pay for her trip. Mother became an immediate devotee of socialized medicine.

Once home, she told us about the wonders of the British plan and about her wonderful teeth. Then she told us again. And again. And again.

One day as she waxed enthusiastic about the wonders of socialized medicine, Daddy, no fan of socialized anything, said the American plan suited him better. To settle the matter, she retorted, "Well, in England, they even measured my mouth with calipers!"

And Daddy simply couldn't help himself. Sometimes when they're lobbed in fat and right across the middle, you just have to take a swing. With a smile, he asked, "What did they use in this country? A yard stick?"

Mother rose to her full regal stature, cast an imperious look that, if looks could kill would have vaporized us on the spot, and strode smartly from the room so obviously filled with Philistines.

But by the next day, she returned again to extolling the wonders of the British plan.

However, teeth or no teeth, British plan or no British plan, Mother filed for United States citizenship shortly after she arrived in Cleveland.

That spring Daddy went over to Findlay for a meeting. While Findlay itself is a lovely, lovely town, the dump of a Corps building dimmed even the limited luster of its wrong-side-of-the-tracks neighborhood.

As Daddy looked around the building, somebody asked what he would do if the Army sent him there. He laughed and said he'd light a match.

We moved to Findlay that June.

Daddy's days of punishment for being his father's son continued. My days of digging dirt—and the worst year of my life—ended.

For all its misery, Cleveland gave Daddy and Mother a wonderful gift that lasted a lifetime: The friendship of Bert and Mary Foster, soldiers in the Cleveland Corps.

Mother and Mary shared a common background of being born and raised in England. Their times together overflowed with remembrances of the old country.

The common bond between Daddy and Bert was less obvious—invisible, in fact, to the naked eye. Prematurely wizened and barely clearing the bottom rung of the bantam-weight class, Bert worked as a UAW-CIO steward at General

Motors. Nothing about the two men appeared to coincide, overlap or enjoy any measure of congruity—until you listened in on their conversation and heard their hearts. Bert had a heart large enough to match Daddy's.

Findlay, Ohio

Tall and narrow, lacking the slightest hint of charm or grace, the Findlay Corps abutted the sidewalk on North Main Street where Route 224 doglegged through town. Without an inch of lawn to soften its appearance, the brick building loomed shabbily over the shorter buildings that hemmed it in on each side. The building's ungainliness stretched back for an entire block, save for enough room to accommodate a small, unkempt back yard with a scant ration of gravel to provide a short driveway and room to park a car.

Out in front, an eye-height, store-sized picture window occupied a large part of each side of the building. Three doors crowded the middle.

The center door opened to a long staircase that rose steeply to our quarters.

The door on the north side of the set led into the sanctuary, a fancy honorific for an auditorium full of dilapidated wooden seats separated by stumpy, metal armrests and a wall behind the pulpit necessarily draped to cover the crumbling decay.

The southernmost of the three doors opened to the office, a gym and, in the back, a transient shelter. The office, another area named well above its station, sat just inside the door, immediately to the left. It occupied a small corner of the gym, separated only by two thin walls—four feet of drab, dark brown plywood topped by four feet of glass on the side nearest the door; plywood for all eight feet on the side facing the gym, which contained a somewhat less than full-size basketball court.

With the gym ceiling reaching about twice the height of the office walls, the office area in the old building stood as a stand alone cubicle. To complete proper cubicle specifications, it provided grossly inadequate space for the job at hand and a fish-bowl atmosphere. Passers-by didn't have to inquire about Major's absence or presence; they could peer in the window from the sidewalk and see for themselves.

Beyond the gym, in a cinder-block addition at the back of the building, a reclusive, sixtyish man, with rarely a word to share with anybody, ran, and lived in, a temporary shelter for transient men. He did intake, maintenance, cooking and cleaning of the small area. Typically, two or three men—three being a full house—made their way to the shelter each day to take up residence for an overnight stay, complete with dinner and breakfast.

The shelter opened to the back yard right next to the open-tread wooden stairs leading up to the screened porch spanning the back of the quarters. Transients in residence usually whiled away the evening sitting on benches in the yard and smoking. Since we usually used the more accessible back entrance, they had a front-row seat to observe our family's comings and goings.

Upstairs, fourteen large, high-ceilinged rooms—sixteen if you count the bathrooms—lined the sides of the block-long, front-to-back hall, garishly decked out in acres of wallpaper and shades-of-blue floral linoleum guaranteed never to grace the pages of a decorating magazine. Each room opened to the hallway, so the view down the empty hall revealed a long parade of doors, giving more an institutional than homey look. We lived mostly on the side of the hall above the sanctuary, using the basketball-court side for Corps functions—meetings, Sunday School classes and the like.

Four bedrooms, each with a mini-closet added in a corner as an afterthought, lined up one after the other, starting at the front of the building. The living room followed the bedrooms, then the dining room and, finally, the kitchen and a bathroom side by side at the very rear.

The stairs from the front door to the apartment ended at the door to the third room in the line-up. To reach the front two rooms required a U-turn around the end of the bannister, either to the right or left, to reach a narrow, mini-hallway taking you back to the front of the building.

Each side of the hall mirrored the other, with two exceptions. Where we had a kitchen, the other side had an unequipped room, and the rooms on the non-family side lacked the jerry-rigged enclosures we called closets.

The juxtaposition of the bathrooms in the very back of the apartment and the bedrooms, clustered up in the front, required a block-long trek to satisfy any middle-of-the-night call of nature. The next-door gas station was actually closer, but we chose not to avail ourselves of its proximity and made the necessary expedition to the home facilities.

One day, shortly after we moved in, Jerry and Brownie, lolling about in the dining room near the back of the building, suddenly jumped up and bolted into the hall, scrambled madly to get some traction on the slippery linoleum, then dashed silently, except for the clicking of their nails, toward the front steps. We went to learn the reason for this sudden burst of activity and reached the hall just as the eyes of a transient cleared the top step, at which point, what to his wondering eyes did appear but the vision of two beasts thundering down the hall at him, looking as if they intended to do great bodily harm. Instantly reversing course, he bolted down the stairs, hitting perhaps three or four in his escape.

As the dogs neared the stairs, Brownie, the older and wiser of the dogs, started cutting a turn with his front paws to access the safe haven of the little side hall and avoid sailing off into the stairwell canyon. The younger and less worldly-wise Jerry simply sat down to bring himself to a stop—only to find the linoleum greased his path to an even greater speed, hurtling him into space like a fur-covered, wide-eyed ski-jumper. He thundered into the door at the bottom of the stairs just as the transient slammed it behind him.

Brownie stuck his head between the staircase spindles to look down at the dazed Jerry, and, it appeared to the naked eye, laugh.

We congratulated the dogs and gave them a treat. Daddy admonished us to do better at remembering to keep the front door locked, and we went back to what we had been doing, another day in the life we lived—albeit one with a scary, but ultimately laughable interlude.

Since Route 224 served as the main east-west route through Findlay, it carried a lot of truck traffic. And since many fertile farms surrounded Findlay, farm goods filled many of the trucks.

Then as now, truckers drove all hours of the day and night. While it may have been our imagination, they seemed to save livestock trucks for the night runs. As the trucks rumbled down Main Street, the traffic light just past our building inevitably turned red. The squealing of the brakes got lost in the cacophony of pigs oinking their pique at being jostled by the sudden deceleration. Cows, more mellow by nature, only mooed a little, and a truck held fewer cows than pigs in any case. Pigs, though, being both more cantankerous and numerous, could wake the dead—not to mention Charles, attempting to sleep in the front bedroom immediately above the source of the tuneless barnyard symphony. After a minute or two, the sounds of the truck motor straining to get back up to speed as the driver pushed his way through the gears added even more decibels to the ruckus. But the double-clutching shimmy at least signaled the stench would soon be moving on down the highway along with the truck.

Daddy and Mother drove back to Trenton for Joe's graduation. Pleased and proud, they joined the throng of parents in the huge school auditorium. Soon the 845, as memory serves, graduates began lock-stepping their way down the center aisle to the traditional strains of *Pomp and Circumstance*. With graduates still plying the aisle after what seemed to be the thousandth iteration of the venerable tune, Daddy, with fatigue taking the edge off his delight, wondered aloud if the graduates might be exiting a back door and marching down the aisle multiple times. Mother told him to hush in the presence of such a glorious occasion.

Joe rejoined us in Findlay, a stroke of good fortune for Barney. No sooner had Barney started first grade than a larger, older boy began to bully him. As Barney walked to school, the bully rode up from behind on his bike and gave Barney a hard kick as he passed. After a few days of this, Barney complained to Joe. In the avuncular tone he used when speaking from his position as the eldest, Joe assured Barney he'd fix the problem.

The next day, Barney set out for school as usual, except that Joe walked several paces ahead of him. Bypassers would never guess they traversed the school route in tandem. The bully certainly didn't. In his now usual routine, he rode up behind Barney and gave him a ferocious kick. As planned, Barney roared the best yell he had in him. Laughing loudly, the bully sped off.

As the ne'er-do-well pedaled past, still chortling victory, Joe grabbed him by the scruff of the neck and yanked him off his bike. It happened so fast, the bully's legs still pedaled as he hung from Joe's hand. The bicycle continued on its own for a short distance, then crashed.

Joe set the bully down. Looming large over the now scared-silly kid, Joe sternly announced, his deep voice adding menace, that he never wanted to hear another word about bullying, and, if he did, he "knew who to find." It probably changed the bully's young life forever, almost certainly for the better. It certainly improved Barney's existence.

Joe began attending Bowling Green State University that fall. To save money, he lived at home and car-pooled the twenty miles to school each day he had classes. Once there, he carried a full load of classes, played freshman football, worked a university job to make ends meet and, missing the car-pool's return trip, hitchhiked home, sometimes in the wee hours. He often skipped meals to save both time and money.

After a few months of this killing schedule, he came down with hepatitis and dropped out of school. He spent the next several months slowly recuperating at home. During that time, Mother stewed gallons of beef broth, the only thing Joe could keep down.

Surprisingly, given the conditions, the Corps did fairly well, especially the Girl Guard and Sunbeam program. People came, lives got changed and the bills got paid. While not an easy assignment, Daddy and Mother experienced great satisfaction and stayed hopeful that their efforts would result in lives changed for the better.

We gathered, as usual, for dinner one evening, each sharing our day's events. Daddy and Mother had meetings most evenings, but dinner was their down time, sacrosanct family time. The dogs stretched out on the floor near Daddy, alert to eagerly approach him at the slightest hint of a friendly, morsel-laden hand moving in their direction.

As table talk gained more and more of our attention, we failed to notice Jerry and Brownie stealthily ooze their way out of the dining room into the hallway. Suddenly, the sound of growling dogs, a deep-in-the-throat growl calculated to strike terror, interrupted us. The occasional snarl punctuated the hair-raising growls.

Our dogs didn't snap and snarl just to be doing something different, but to minister a warning. Obviously somebody was in the hall, intent on who-knows-what. We went to investigate.

We found two ashen, shaking transients fruitlessly attempting to bury themselves in the wallpaper while the dogs paced a menacing arc around them, teeth bared, the hair on their backs bristling at full attention. The transients had soundlessly ascended the nearly sixteen feet of front stairs, tiptoed their way along almost the entire length of the hallway and were almost upon us before the dogs caught their scent.

As the dogs circled, Daddy made clear his unhappiness with the men's presence. He suggested they leave, telling them the dogs would do them no harm if they went quickly. They saw the wisdom of his words and left—with a dog-induced motivation adding urgency to their speedy retreat.

A large room, off to one side near the back of the gym and abutting the homeless shelter, held clothes for needy people. Responsibility for sorting and stacking the clothes by type and size fell to the man who ran the shelter, which is to say, they reposed, wall to wall, in large, haphazard piles, each accommodating all types and sizes of whatever came in as donations.

One day Daddy and Mother had to be out doing the Lord's work and called on my thirteen-year-old self to run the office in their absence. A transient arrived wearing possibly the filthiest, most threadbare clothing ever known to man. He was in the running for the malodorous medal as well.

He asked for clothes to replace what he had on, and I took him to the back room where he started digging through the piles of clothing as I watched and waited. If I left, the entire contents of the room could quickly and mysteriously disappear out the back door.

He found something he liked and, rather than take his new outfit with him—as was typically done—started disrobing in preparation for donning his new-to-him clothes. Well, I couldn't leave, and I couldn't turn my back for the same reason I couldn't leave, so I lowered my gaze to about his shoe tops.

Just then Daddy walked in. One look at the man undressing in front of me, and he let out a bellow. I left, in relief, while the man stuttered an explanation and his apologies to the "Major" (Transients call every Army officer Major, regardless of rank, although in this case the transient got it right.) as he quickly finished dressing and left.

About that time, Daddy started talking about getting a house to live in, somewhere off the building. Given the layout and condition of the building, words like "comfortable" and "homey" would always be out of reach. Plus, transients kept getting in, sneaking up the front stairs. And anybody staying overnight in the downstairs shelter would have no problem breaching our total lack of security in the back of the building. Our safety depended entirely on our two dogs.

We moved into a comfortable, white clapboard, two-story house on First Street in the middle of the school year. Flo, Barney and I had to change schools, a small sacrifice for such a wonderful change.

Returning to health, Joe got a job at Cooper Tire and Rubber in the injection-molding room where he worked on forming rubber auto parts other than tires. Charles joined him in June, as soon as he turned eighteen. The boiling cauldrons and close quarters combined to create a superheated, almost unbearable work environment. Most workers didn't stay with the hot, arduous work for very long, but Cooper paid well, so Joe and Charles stuck it out, even taking all the overtime they could get. They ended the summer at the top of the molding room's seniority list save one wizened Cooper's veteran of several years.

We all had a fixed appointment for dinner. Sometimes Daddy cooked, sometimes Mother. As we grew older, each of us took our irregular turns preparing dinner. Whoever happened to be home when time to prepare dinner rolled around became the evening's chef.

At the dinner table, everybody had an opportunity to share their day. If we had no news to contribute, Daddy improvised with geography or history quizzes. He gauged each question to the age of the questionee and delighted in a correct answer as much as we did. To properly define motivation, you'd have to see Daddy at the dinner table.

One day near the end of eighth grade, I had big news to share. Proud news. Even exceptional news. When my turn came, I grandly shared my marvelous story, imbuing it with every ounce of the considerable drama I could muster.

"Well," I emoted, "today my teacher told me while I may only be thirteen years old physically, I'm at least sixteen years old emotionally." Finishing with a flourish, I looked around the table, expecting awe enough to match my own.

Instead, I saw stunned, deer-in-the-headlights silence. Daddy struggled to respond in kind, but he lost the battle and burst out laughing. Trying to balance his laughter with words of good cheer, he only laughed harder with each attempt to speak.

My sky-high balloon completely deflated, I went back to being thirteen—without, amazingly, hurt feelings. The fizzled balloon delivered good results. My parents avoided the dread presence of a thirteen-year-old drama queen, and I escaped serious delusions of sophistication.

Eighth-grade English nearly did me in. Not the work, but the teacher, Miss T.

Each day Miss T assigned desk work. Each day I finished well before the allotted time expired. She viewed this as rebellion, a plot to undo her.

She used our desk-work time to apply make-up and flirt with herself. She laughed, batted her eyes and tossed her tight, bottle-black curls to and fro while gazing lovingly in the mirror of her cosmetics-filled case. She did not fancy the idea of students gawking at her as she made her come-hither faces and mouthed sweet nothings to the mirror, trying desperately to hold onto thirty-five while the calendar pushed her inexorably over the crest of fifty. Thus, her antipathy to my speedy facility with the assignments intended to keep us all too busy to gape.

Well, a minute or two of observing her peculiar activities sated my appetite, so I undertook busy work of my own design. At first, I filled the extra time by drawing. I liked to draw. Miss T said it made the other kids feel dumb because while I drew, they still struggled with the assignment. She decreed I would do no drawing in her classroom.

So I read books. I liked to read. After reading all the books the school library allowed eighth-graders to read, I brought books from home—which made Miss T even more unhappy than my drawing. The books belonged to my father, and men always had dirty books, said she. I informed her Daddy never had dirty books; Daddy had good books. Miss T remained unpersuaded. No reading.

One day, trying to think of something to fill the time, I absent-mindedly started to sing. Just softly. I liked to sing. Miss T quickly made it clear she did not like me to sing. No singing.

And so it went

One day I walked into the classroom a few minutes before class started. As I put my books on my desk, Miss T demanded that I leave. My inappropriate behavior would not be tolerated.

What behavior? How do you get into trouble just walking into the room? I asked what I had done wrong and she left.

Shortly, the principal appeared in the classroom door, a beckoning finger calling me to join him in the hall. I went, memories of my encounter with the Cleveland principal flooding trepidation through every cell.

The principal announced he'd have to fail me because of my behavior. Then, having my complete attention, he dropped what he perceived as the big bomb. With the usual awed view of Daddy, he ordered me to bring Daddy to school to discuss the problem.

What a relief.

Bringing Mother would have been the end of me, but Daddy would be on my side. The thing about failing scared me and I might still be in big trouble, but I wouldn't be alone.

The next day we gathered in the principal's office: Daddy, in his handsome uniform, the principal, Miss T and I. The principal asked me to tell my side of the story. I explained about all the time when I had nothing to do, and that Miss T wanted me to sit absolutely still, head down, feet together on the floor and hands folded on the desk. I told him about not being allowed to draw. I told him about not being allowed to read. I told him Miss T said Daddy had dirty books. The slightly-built principal gulped, knowing Daddy was a preacher, not to mention large and intimidating. Coming completely clean, I even mentioned the singing.

I caught the principal off guard. He expected neither a guileless, worried girl nor the story I told, so dissimilar from the one elaborated on by Miss T. He asked her about the accuracy of my account. Lips pursed, still convinced of her inerrancy, Miss T agreed I told the truth, just as she had previously described it to him.

In a few well-chosen, educationally-correct phrases, the principal told Miss T to shape up. Then Daddy added his few words. He spoke kindly, but his big, bass voice seemed to have a touch of doom in it.

The embarrassed principal asked if I were currently reading one of Daddy's books.

"Yes," I answered. He asked the title of the book.

"How To Win Friends And Influence People," I responded, too naive to notice the total disconnect between the title and the situation.

After a stunned moment of silence, Daddy and the principal started to laugh. They laughed for a long time, gathering momentum as they went. Miss T sat primly, eyes straight ahead, looking for all the world as if she had a mouthful of rancid milk.

The threatening clouds rolled away. The sun came out. My troubles evaporated. I would not fail. Daddy and the principal continued to laugh.

Some days are just good.

One early evening three boys, junior high school friends, stopped by to talk with Flo and me. After only a short time, we heard Daddy's car pulling into the driveway, causing instant alarm amongst our visitors. Panic might be a better term.

Yelling "He's here! He's here!" they darted about the living room, bumping into each other and the furniture as Flo and I looked on in amazement. Finally organizing their thoughts, they dashed for the back door, yanked it open, took the stairs in a single bound, crossed the backyard in record time and leapt over the hedge to freedom.

Daddy saw the entire escape. He could hardly get out of the car for laughing.

The boys opted to never visit in our house again. One episode of growth-stunting fright and pandemonium apparently filled their appetite for danger—even if only imagined.

But not too many nights later, they decided it would be fun to stand in front of our house and call for Jerry. In response, as they hoped, Jerry launched a barking frenzy. Since they kept calling endlessly for him, I decided it would be impolite not to honor their request for Jerry's company. I opened the door and let him out, with a little whispered "Sic 'em" to encourage him on his way.

Jerry tore down the street in full bay and, upon catching up with the now fleeing boys, started to nip at their ankles. Terrified, they initiated a group scramble up a newly planted sapling, too small to support even one of them, let alone three. In their panic, they failed to notice this limitation. As they climbed, the little tree bent over until it almost touched the ground. Of course, this lowered them, and their ankles, into Jerry's nipping range.

As their wails and curses filled the air, I decided they had probably learned all the lesson they needed to never again set Jerry to barking, and I called him back. He pranced home, his duty accomplished.

The boys avoided our house, maybe even our street, after that.

As summer ended, money lacking, we had to leave the First Street house and move back on the building. Barney still remembers Mother's distress.

Joe and Charles went to Bowling Green as freshmen that fall. Through their school years, they earned their keep through a variety of jobs. Starting out scrubbing, waxing and buffing the floors in the Student Center after it closed for the night, Joe moved onto working for the university refinishing desks and dorm furniture and doing repairs. He also emceed, sang with dance bands and did stand-up comedy—or sometimes sit-down comedy, playing the piano as part of his routine.

Charles also started with the Student Union job, then gravitated to work in his Kappa Sigma fraternity. The university paid him to be the fraternity house's janitor. He became the week-end cook, and he helped in the kitchen and served tables as a steward during the week.

Thus, Daddy and Mother's determination to raise all of us with the ability to do just about anything started to make its intended payback. While the boy's efforts lacked any specific career-orientation, they turned out to be an excellent start on "real life."

With all the farms surrounding Findlay, Brownie's big failing of enmity toward other animals became a fatal flaw. He started chasing farmers' sheep. The farmers found out who owned the rusty colored dog and came to talk to Daddy. They told him about having to chase Brownie away before he killed their sheep. Daddy expressed his regrets and promised to try to keep Brownie corralled.

Try as we might to keep him home, Brownie got out to continue his unwelcome visits to the farms. That dog could sneak out of maximum security. The farmers came to speak with Daddy a time or two more, but as much as we all tried, we could not control Brownie.

One night he didn't come home. We did all the things people can do to find a lost pet, but it seemed obvious what had happened. While the farmers had expressed great reluctance to shoot a family pet, they made it clear to Daddy they couldn't afford to sacrifice their livelihood to a wayward dog. Brownie apparently had tried to kill sheep once too often. We mourned our loss, but we understood.

The summer following their joint freshman year at BGSU, Joe got his buff self hired as a lifeguard at the city pool in Findlay's Riverside Park, a match made in heaven. In a Speedo-style bathing suit covered with lily pads—which comes up, upon occasion, for family reflection to this very day—he performed his studly strut around the pool while the teen girls clumped and clustered around him. Sometimes life is a beautiful thing.

While Joe spent his days setting his admirers' hearts aflutter, Charles went back to Coopers, working the midnight shift. His days in the hellish molding room fortunately over, he moved to the dipping room where they prepared the cords for tires. The dipping room had only the heat provided by Ohio's summer nights, and the work proved more boring than hard.

Digging in the scraggly back yard, Barney unearthed a treasure. He came running up the back stairs and into the kitchen where we sat around the table chatting just before lunch. Holding his treasure out for Daddy to see, he excitedly asked Daddy what it could possibly be. Heavy into buried treasure, as young boys are wont to be, he dreamed high-as-the-sky hopes.

It only took a glance for Daddy to identify the prize as the dirt-encrusted remains of a broken bottle from the local San-A-Pure dairy, but saying so would douse the sparkle and anticipation from Barney's eyes. Instead, he held Barney's find up to the light, slowly turning it around in his fingers and carefully examining it. At length, he announced, in serious, measured tones, "Barney, it looks like you've found a genuine piece of SanisAPuris!" and handed it back to a euphoric Barney who ran to his room to store the wondrous artifact in his treasure box.

Somewhere, somehow, Mother met a nineteen-year-old young lady, Helen, desperately in need of help. Learning disabled, abused by her parents, cross-eyed, her form one of random bumps and lumps in no particular order or pattern, Helen was a veritable symphony of genetic disarray, but with a loving heart that ached to please. She touched

Mother's heart. Upon learning that Helen's guardians, her aunt and uncle, had no plans to provide training or to help her become self-supporting, Mother invited her to come to our house each day and learn how to cook and clean. Never mind that Mother worked long, long hours; she would find time to help Helen.

The training went slowly. Even by generous standards, Helen was not an apt student. With perseverance replacing hope, Mother and Helen soldiered on. Once Mother made up her mind that something needed doing, her determination surpassed that of the Marines, Army, Air Force, Navy and Coast Guard combined. She, too, refused to consider failure an option.

One day Mother announced the time had come for Helen to start learning to cook. That very day, she would bake a cake. Helen immediately went giddy and flustered, a very bad sign, but onward and upward they went. Mother decided she could will Helen to success. As Helen made her way through the recipe, Mother oversaw the project, ducking in and out of the kitchen, working on a Sunday School lesson in the dining room while helping Helen over the rough spots, of which there were many, in the kitchen.

Finally, the finished cake came out of the oven. While it looked a little flat, Mother iced it into a work of art. At dinner's end, Helen proudly brought the cake to the table. She beamed with excitement. We all oohed and aahed, while Mother prepared to cut and serve Helen's cake.

Well, it couldn't be cut. Mother pressed harder and harder with the cake knife as the cake formed itself into a flying wedge, each side raised while the center held firm. She finally ended up with a large carving knife, all but standing on her chair for better leverage, while the cake resisted her energetic ministrations. Then Daddy had a go at it and managed, by dint of significant effort, to hack his way to success.

We still had some slight amount of hope for the cake and each took a piece only to find it also couldn't be chewed. As it entered your mouth, so it stayed. You might suck on the flavor, but masticating its shipping-carton texture into swallowable pieces couldn't be done. Helen forgot the baking powder. And who knows what else.

One day, a day forever seared in memory, Helen mentioned her aunt and uncle's exceptional success with their rhubarb crop that year. Daddy told her to congratulate them on their gardening skills. Then he fatefully mentioned that he liked rhubarb. And gave Helen a way to return the kindness she had never known before.

For the rest of the summer, Helen arrived each morning, beaming, delighted to present Mother with a giant bundle of rhubarb. A humongous bundle of rhubarb. Which, in Mother's mind, allowed only one response. Every single day for the rest of the summer, Mother included stewed rhubarb in the dinner menu. It looked like regurgitated glop, and she expected us to eat it so we didn't diminish Helen's joy in bringing her gift.

Even at that, fortune had favored us. Had Helen been able to drive, the aunt and uncle would probably have supplied rhubarb by the truckload.

At summer's end, well before Helen's training came within sight of the finish line, the Army moved us to Lima, Ohio.

I don't know if anybody continued the work Mother began or what became of Helen, too limited and sweet-natured to make it alone.

LIMA, OHIO

Army people saw the Lima, Ohio, Corps as a hard appointment, but at least the quarters weren't on the building. We lived a few miles from the Corps in a very pleasant neighborhood, in a cozy—to use real estate's tight-fit definition—two-story house with a front porch across its width and a large back yard. Cozy or not, the house's off-the-building status made it a winner.

And the Corps actually had a lot going for it. Although located downtown, Lima's relatively small population meant downtown wasn't much of a trip, which made location a minor distraction, not a real problem. The single-story, well-maintained brick building had plenty of well-arranged space—a nice sanctuary, Sunday School classrooms, meeting rooms, a gym, storage and a private office for Daddy.

The Corps owned an antiquated, bright yellow school bus to gather kids for Sunday School and other activities. Long past its time, the bus was kept alive by one of the members, an almost full-time second career. Once in a while Daddy

154

drove the bus home and parked it smack dab in front of the house, obliterating any front-porch view of the neighborhood. And vice versa. He probably had a good reason to do this—beyond humiliating his teen daughters—but we never asked what it might be.

Having a huge, glow-in-the-dark yellow bus emblazoned with "THE SALVATION ARMY" hunkered down in front of our house seemed to beg for peer abuse, but in Lima, never was heard a discouraging word. So we relaxed and even "allowed" Daddy to drive us to school in the beast. He'd pull up directly across the street from the school campus where the entire student body milled about, loathe to enter the building a nanosecond before the bell's command.

If the laboring motor of our yellow antique didn't sufficiently announce our impending arrival, the loud whoosh of opening the bifold door compensated nicely. A brass band could not have announced us more effectively.

One day, as we crossed the street to join our friends, Daddy leaned out the driver's window and boomed "Are you-uns comin' home for luuunch?".

His hillbilly accent rounded out the experience to its full ignominy, but rather than sink into the sidewalk, Flo whipped around and yelled back, "Sartainly, Paw!" They both sounded as if they'd started the trip to school somewhere deep in the back hills.

Then the bell rang, and everybody went into school laughing. Daddy and Flo occasionally repeated their performance just for kicks and chuckles; it never failed to entertain the troops.

Daddy and Barney drove to the local animal shelter to get Barney's tenth birthday present, a dog of his own. After careful scrutiny of the current inhabitants, checking them for energy and personality, Barney chose the winner, a Boston Bull Terrier he promptly named Stubby in honor of his cropped, perpetual-motion tail.

When Mother heard them arrive with their prize, she—with Jerry hard on her heels as usual—came to inspect the new member of the family. With one quick glance at Stubby, Mother announced him too small and too ugly to be a keeper. As she announced her hasty verdict, Jerry remembered his alpha-dog status and lunged for the interloping twerp.

Hopelessly outmatched by a Shepherd many times his size, Stubby didn't back down. But he instinctively increased his odds of survival by bolting into a safe harbor, the space between Daddy's legs. Thus protected, he took his stand for God and country—or whatever dogs take stands for.

The little dog's spunk changed Mother's opinion. Tsk, tsking Jerry, she told him to stop his nonsense and welcomed Stubby into the family.

None of us realized we lacked a significant piece of information about Boston Bull Terriers. We could see Stubby's face looked like the "After" picture of a high-speed crash into a wall, and his coat had the typical, undistinguished rusty brown and black speckles. We shortly learned the rest of the story.

Boston Bull Terriers have one claim to fame, if you can call it that since no other breed would condescend to claim it. When excited, they produce prodigious amounts of gas sufficiently odorous so as to peel paint within a five-foot radius and to cause eyes within an even greater distance to well with burning tears.

And they excite easily, always as a result of human contact. Anything out of the ordinary in the household routine served nicely as an opportunity for Stubby to silently introduce this most singular of talents. It might be during a loud game of Monopoly. Or perhaps as the family gathered to tell our stories and laugh. While fully involved in our merriment, watering eyes and a sudden gasping for air announced Stubby's distinctive presence.

Loving Stubby took more than a little understanding, but his personality made up for his unfortunate, unchangeable allegiance to his breed's characteristics. Stubby made us laugh.

Stubby trotted through life with enthusiasm and a certain elan. Life, to him, was immutably good. If we unhappily called his name in reprimand for fouling the air, he'd stand tall, tail whirling, expectantly waiting for somebody to pet him. He had no shame. He had no guilt. He had only joy.

When Barney put together a few nickels, he bought toys for Stubby, who received all gifts with enthusiasm. Chewing happily on a cigar-shaped chew toy, he crunched a multitude of holes along its length. Not a problem. Holes or no holes, he continued to vigorously enjoy his mutilated cigar. As the holes became more numerous, they'd catch on his teeth, making the toy a semipermanent attachment. He wandered around for hours with his cigar dangling at odd angles, looking for all the world like a drunk canine Winston Churchill with a motor in his tail.

Unlike all our other dogs, Stubby did not grasp any part of the guard dog function. His invisible gastrointestinal armament didn't frighten or deter anybody. He was entertainment only.

Our memories of Stubby are, alas, of those times his talent—his destiny—appeared in full bloom. But as long as anybody who knew him still lives, Stubby rules.

Stubby's unfortunate talent added a unique, all but indescribable dimension to social situations. He loved to meet and greet in his own unfortunate way. He was a social butterfly who wanted nothing more than the pleasure of everybody's company.

Welcoming guests presented an etiquette problem Emily Post never thought to address. Failing to mention Stubby's gift resulted in cruel and unusual punishment of guests as they strained to carry on as if breathing had not unexpectedly become a problem. However, explaining it in polite company challenged the talents of even the most euphemistically facile. Whatever we said could be off-putting to guests who arrived without the expectation of discussing the digestive combustibility of our pets.

The problem embarrassed Mother no end and seemed to have no solution. If banished to the basement or Barney's room, incessant yipping and barking made polite conversation impossible. To Mother, lover of all things canine, it seemed to punish him for his genetics, however regrettable. He only did what came as naturally, at least to him, as breathing.

Mother weighed two possibilities. If Stubby joined us in welcoming guests, his malodorous adventures would end after, say, twenty minutes. While the unfortunate twenty minutes could seem endless, the other option of loud and never-ending complaints from an unhappy dog actually was endless. So Stubby stayed.

As often is the case in trying circumstances, the twenty-minute rule had a caveat. Actual contact with a guest completed Stubby's bliss. If, after the visitors were seated, he managed to park himself on or against a guest's feet, ecstasy lifted him to new heights—in a manner of speaking—and he would contentedly emit a never-ending stream of nasal pollution. We had to keep Stubby close by us to spare our guests, but as the conversation engaged us, we sometimes lost track of him. Only signs of a guest's olfactory distress reminded us of our duty.

One day, some fellow Army officers came to visit. Mother wanted to not only welcome them, but also, having never completely overcome the social-climbing training of her childhood, to impress them. Upon their arrival, we all gathered to welcome our guests, Stubby joining in the greeting in his own inimitable style. Caught up in her goal of making a good impression, Mother felt she had to find a graceful, inoffensive explanation for the problem rather than something like a frank "With Boston Bull Terriers, it's Gas R Us."

However, when Mother experienced intense emotion, such as in prayer, anger or embarrassment, her long-lost English accent came roaring back. In her attempt to save the day, Mother, with a gracious nod and smile—sounding for all the world like the Queen of England—said, "He IS a bit gaahssy."

Time stopped. Everybody needed a moment to digest this unexpected—both in content and execution—remark. Then the stunned moment passed and laughter commenced, with Mother joining in just a little off the beat.

Poor Mother. With the demands of the Army life, she didn't have any kind of social life, even by loosest definition. She just wanted it to be nice. She knocked herself—and us girls—out getting the house to sparkle. She worried together an enjoyable meal. All for naught. Her efforts were totally upstaged by a twelve-pound beast with no sense of propriety or shame.

But she certainly broke the ice. And the day turned out to be a lovely time with friends after all.

As usual, Daddy and Mother gave their all to make the Corps a going, growing enterprise. Attendance grew. Lives changed. New programs started.

For example, reviving a disbanded Girl Guards brigade brought sixteen immediate enrollments, amazing for a Corps previously purported to be dying. A Sunbeam troop, reactivated at the same time, instantly attracted fifteen little girls. Even *"The Young Soldier"* took notice and published pictures of the two groups, with Daddy and Mother smiling in the back row, for the whole country to see.

Mother met Easter Strayker, Lima's immensely popular radio show hostess, at one of Lima's civic organization meetings. Easter—as everybody called her—began to take an interest in Army activities. She visited the Corps to see the activities for herself, and she talked about the Army on her program. A very giving lady, she had no reluctance about telling the Army's story to her listeners, giving the Corps a tremendous boost in its social service work and fund raising.

◇ ◇ ◇

Christmas always brought the year's heaviest workload—an avalanche of requests from struggling families for Christmas baskets of food and gifts. We needed the money to provide them. Daddy—with Easter Strayker's generous help—worked on raising money. Mother worked on selecting the recipients.

Of course, these demands came on top of their usual backbreaking workload. Their hours soared from heavy to crushing starting mid-November as they put in fourteen to sixteen hour days, six days a week. Other than running the morning and evening worship services and visiting the sick, they usually took Sunday off.

Money determined how many recipients we could help. Mother would willingly give out every cent they had, even if it meant receiving no salary, but spending more than they raised could sink the Army—and everything it tried to do—for months.

Her work included sorting the true from the scam. A good story didn't necessarily reflect a real need. Some people went back and forth between churches, businesses and agencies to see how much they could get. Their greed rarely sprang from urgent need, but they invariably had dandy stories to tell—often illustrated with a well-timed tear.

The truly needy, on the other hand, were often embarrassed by their plight. Their pride, battered and torn as it was, led them to rationalize the direness of their need.

But some of the loud and pushy were indeed needy, while some of the quiet and desperate had a scam going. With years of experience, Mother excelled at telling true from false.

And everywhere we moved, she developed a grapevine for finding people too ashamed to come for help. This group usually consisted of people who had known far better times and could not bring themselves to risk the further humiliation of friends and neighbors learning how far they had fallen.

One time Mother heard that a lady in a wealthy neighborhood was in desperate straits. While hardly believing it could be true, she didn't want to risk failing a need. She went to visit. Rather than her usual Army uniform, she wore "civvies" to save any possible embarrassment.

When she knocked, the door opened just a crack. At first, the lady resisted her overtures, but Mother had a way of "worming her way in," as she described it. Working her charm, Mother found herself in a lovely, unheated house with an empty refrigerator and a frightened, forlorn, somewhat past middle-age woman. Mother assured her no one in her "circle" had turned her in. Then she offered assistance, pledging to deliver it secretly, at night—if the downcast lady could accept it.

The lady wilted into tears that anybody would care enough to help her without shredding her fragile facade. She sobbed anew when Daddy showed up, under cover of darkness as prearranged, with boxes brimming over with food, enough to last for weeks. And she wept again, with relief, when he showed up after Christmas to help her begin to reconstruct her life.

One mother raising a large family on little money couldn't accept the idea Christmas help came without strings. Around Thanksgiving each year she would arrive at a Sunday morning meeting prepared to get gloriously saved from her sins. As soon as the altar call came, she bolted for the front to do the deed. She applied for help the following week. Shortly after Christmas, mission accomplished, she backslid from her religious experience. Daddy tried to explain this exercise wasn't necessary, but she wouldn't risk it.

The professionally poor were another matter. They arrived early in the season, while everybody still had money to give, insisting they had far greater need than any other living being and certainly greater than Mother had ever known. Convinced of their well-honed persuasiveness, they took umbrage when Mother exposed their scam and turned them down. They would leave in a huff, raging at the hardheartedness of The Salvation Army.

Then they'd go to grocery stores and cry to the managers; that always worked. Next they hit the governmental and charitable agencies. Unlike Mother, these folks usually bought the story.

Finally, they hit the mother lode, the churches. For reasons that escape logic, church people never entertained the slightest thought these people might lie. The members of the church might slip into a little white lie upon rare occasion. Perhaps the minister, upon even rarer occasion, might fib. But people showing up for a handout? Poor people? Never.

Back in the day, Daddy and Mother had experienced great cooperation with other churches, sharing programs and pulpits. Whether it was a change in the times or the area, though, they enjoyed precious little interaction with Lima's churches.

What galled my parents, besides desperate people having to do without while the greedy raked in windfalls, was the fact that while these folks always included, with great dramatized distress, the fact the Salvation Army had turned them down, nobody bothered to wonder why. Jumping to the desired conclusion the Army had no heart, they piled the goodies higher. Year after year, nobody thought to give the Army—my parents—the benefit of any doubt because they were too taken in to have doubts.

Sometimes ministers called to chastise Daddy about it. Clueless to the fact the Army was a church and they were speaking with a peer, they dripped condescension and judgment. Daddy saw those calls as teachable moments and explained the situation, sometimes even reading Mother's very complete report to the caller. He usually offered her expertise for a cooperative effort. An astute few ended up apologizing—then educating their congregations. Most, though, knew what they knew and didn't hear anything Daddy said.

One such, thinking to soften his pontification of a true and righteous judgment, added his concept of a bit of brotherly love by ending the conversation, "Well, I have to hand it to you, Charlie. You're certainly doing a work the churches can't do."

The doltish remark at first stunned Daddy, then annoyed him and finally amused him. It became a family byword to describe a thankless task.

One of us, observing a parent or sibling stuck with a large and unrewarding job—cleaning out a piled-high garage, say, or perhaps trying to help people who refused to help themselves—would cheerfully opine they certainly did a work the churches couldn't do. It always brought a smile, however rueful.

The good Reverend never realized he had unintentionally told a joke. He might not have gotten it anyway.

Daddy decided the Lima Corps should enter a team in the church softball league. With Joe and Charles home from college for the summer, he already had the strong backbone for a good team. Joe played a flashy first base while Charles roamed left field or pitched. Both had a nice way with a bat. And so the word went forth.

Some of Flo's friends, good Italian Catholic boys all—not to mention excellent ball players—came to join up. Daddy had to tell them as much as he'd like to have them on the team, league rules required that team members attend services at their church sponsor at least twice a month. The would-be players said they didn't have a problem with that; they'd be there. Daddy signed them up on the spot.

The team roster complete, Daddy and Charles set out to buy uniforms. Since, as usual, money impacted the decision-making process, the uniform would consist of a shirt. The Baptists would probably have complete, personalized outfits; we would have shirts.

In a stroke of good fortune, financially speaking, the local sporting goods store was unloading out-of-season merchandise and had a terrific price on some long-sleeved football jerseys. Checking other prices brought the choice down to the football shirts or nothing. Close enough. Daddy and Charles scooped up enough football shirts to outfit the whole team.

Playing all-out softball in the heat and humidity of an Ohio summer produced a heavy sweat that made even the most cold-blooded of bodies glisten and drip. Doing it in a football jersey skyrocketed the perspiration output to a virtual Niagara. Fortunately, the Army team had manly men, men willing to suffer for the glory of the game.

And the football jerseys had one great advantage. The long, heavyweight sleeves allowed base runners to slide with abandon. Cocooned in heavyweight protection, elbows always survived scrape-free, no matter how long and rough the slide. They could play "sacrifice your body" ball with nary a concern about paying a price in blood and missing skin.

True to their word, the team's Catholic members showed up at the Corps for services on the requisite semimonthly schedule. They came as a group, all slicked up in suits and ties, and sat together across the back row. Always on time and always politely involved in the service. They even appeared to pay close attention. They liked Daddy and Mother, an affection fully returned, and Daddy preached a good sermon, so perhaps reality matched appearances.

As good Catholics, they mentioned their Salvation Army attendance in confession. The beauty of that came when the priest offered accolades instead of requiring penance. We guessed their priest, like most people, didn't realize the Army was a church and thought they had embarked on a mission of doing good works.

And the good Father thought rightly. His boys did very good work. They helped the team win the league championship.

By the time we hit high school, Flo and I bought our own clothes, which necessitated, of course, earning money. I started babysitting at eleven, my eye on the clothes prize. While babysitting never generated an ocean of money in even the best of times, our constant moving really interfered with financial progress. Every move took its toll on the billfold. Mothers had to carefully check me out as they considered the advisability of entrusting their precious ankle-biters to my care. And my income all but disappeared when we moved into a business neighborhood with no resident kids for blocks. People in the Corps always seemed to have enormous extended families, making my babysitting services unnecessary.

The money flowed—well, trickled somewhat freely—in Lima. The family across the street knew the Army, trusted its people and needed regular babysitting. Not frequent, but regular. Better yet, they had great kids.

Shopping time arrived after just a few months of stashing my babysitting cash, but with a complication. Lima stores didn't rush to put things on sale; sales came only at the end of the season or the end of the style. Columbus stores, however, really knew how to do business. I wanted to shop in Columbus.

Daddy didn't have a day to spend in Columbus in my preferred time frame, which bristled with immediacy. I called around to friends known to head for Columbus, but the only offer I could dig up came from somebody who would be driving through and offered to drop me off. I'd have to find another way home.

Flo suggested I take the ride. I didn't have to worry about getting home, she said, because I'd surely meet somebody I knew, and there would be my ride. The size of the city aside, I thought the odds of bumping into an acquaintance, let alone a friend, were long, especially since I'd just talked to about everybody I could think of and all said they didn't plan to be there.

She still insisted I should take the ride—and hitchhike home. It would be a cinch to get a ride, said she.

To which I replied, "Yeah, I'll get a ride, and if I'm really, really lucky, it'll be a ride home." Flo decided I worried too much, I disagreed and we debated the hitchhiking scenario a bit more.

We didn't know Daddy overheard his teen-age daughters discussing the merits of hitchhiking. We grabbed his full, dismayed attention.

He came into the room, a very somber look on his face. He intoned (it being too serious a situation to just say something), "Girls, wherever you are, whatever time it is, if you need me, call and I'll come." And we knew for absolute certain he meant it.

I managed to get to Columbus a month or so later, which turned out perfectly. I entered the best store in town just as a mini-riot started around a table heaped with dresses. I raced over to check out the goodies. Every dress on the table, all expensive in my eyes, had been marked down to five dollars, which explained the pushing and shoving. Well, my elbows work as well as anybody's, so I got in there and pulled out a dress, a wonderful Sunday-go-to-meeting dress, with an original price many times the five dollars.

I wore that magnificent dress for years and felt like a princess every time I put it on.

I bought some other things that day, all forgotten now. What could be as memorable as a five-dollar magic dress?

In the years that followed, if I managed to snag a ride from college to anywhere near home, I never worried what unearthly hour we'd pull in. I knew Daddy would be there to meet me. I never asked if he ever rued his statement about coming to get me whenever and wherever.

Mother grilled any young man who wanted to date Flo or me, and she went at it with her usual vigor. It was her duty. Comfortably seating herself across from them in the living room, she'd start in.

"Where does your father work?"

"How many brothers and sisters do you have?" Then, names and ages if appropriate.

"Do you get good grades?"

"Do you plan to go to college?"

"What kind of work do you plan to do after finishing school?"

"Do you go to church?"

"What church?"

"How often do you go?"

And so on, for quite a while. The poor guys tried valiantly to stick to honesty—which Mother mentioned as a requirement early on in the inquisition—come up with an acceptable answer and still sound sincere, always important when dealing with mothers. And, as if the trial by questions didn't generate sufficient anxiety, she usually failed to notice Stubby blissfully ensconced atop their feet, taking the shine off their shoes as only he could. They were under the gun any way you want to look at it.

Flo, being the first to get involved in the dating scene, bore the brunt of Mother's third-degree tactics. Although the extreme scrutiny discouraged nary a swain, Flo begged the boys to intercede on her behalf. Which they did, to everybody's relief.

Trial by third degree or not, the guys we dated loved my parents. Neither Daddy or Mother ever gave an inch to appear hip or cool, but they made everybody feel welcome and accepted. It was—awkwardly at times—not unusual to come home and find a former boyfriend sitting in the kitchen, deep in conversation with Mother and eating a piece of her more-than-excellent apple pie.

Flo fit the dating world far better than I. I didn't have the right attitude.

For instance, a very good-looking young man in my tenth grade class played second-string quarterback well enough to regularly get the coach's nod to leave the bench and get in the game. And he starred on the swimming team. These top-of-the-heap credentials, as teen-age hierarchies rate things, made him a very big man on campus.

Flo wouldn't believe me when I told her he had asked me for a date. As my older sister, she knew he was too good for me.

We went out a couple times, but he scored zero in the funny-bone department and only plodded along, consistently losing yardage, in conversation. My enthusiasm swiftly waned. When, as a final straw, he didn't know the meaning of "pathetic," the starring word in my vocabulary at the time, I dumped him.

I thought Flo would understand that being a sluggard in such crucial matters as humor and vocabulary made him inferior dating material, but she didn't. She said I was a dope. She knew about these things.

A stocky missionary with severely styled grey hair and decked out in an Army uniform topped by a wool sort of semi-sari to denote her service in India, came to do a week of special services. She stayed with us in our already cozy house.

Upon her arrival, she failed to recognize Mother's miraculous ability to make a house look like a home on almost no money and decided to "fix" things. She started with the few artfully arranged artificial flower arrangements, cramming everything deep in the vase to look "less disorderly." She grouped throw pillows by color and lined them up like little square soldiers. She wrestled the kitchen into shipshape order. And so it went. Mother kept on smiling.

While the takeover of the house startled us, we hadn't seen anything yet. The real highlight of the week came at church. In the middle of the service, she started some music on her recorder, but instead of the expected vocal, she took the forefinger and middle finger of both hands, crossed them into an X, stuffed them up to the knuckle into her mouth and started loudly whistling. Very loudly whistling.

She whistled many verses of a song reputed to be a favorite in India. This insistence on doing all the verses struck me as passing strange. Without words, aren't all verses the same? Anyway, she whistled us into submission, then started preaching. There should have been a break between the two events; still stunned by the musical extravaganza, I didn't really hear her sermon.

She whistled, then preached each evening. I can't comment on the sermons, what with my boggled condition, but the number of Indian hymns sporting a plethora of verses impressed me.

I tried her whistling trick, but however many times I gave it a go, I couldn't get beyond the gagging and retching caused by having that many fingers crammed deep in my mouth. I never got out so much as a peep.

Shortly after her departure, we kids started to talk and laugh about her visit during dinner. Although equally astonished by her whistling performance and understanding of our amusement, Daddy smiled, but reminded us to honor her commitment.

Daddy disliked make-up. He didn't issue any edicts about it, but he preferred that Flo and I remain Ivory Soap clean. Well, now, there's a problem.

Make-up is a rite of passage. It starts whispering its seductive, insistent call to girls the moment their age reaches double digits. From there it builds an increasing crescendo, and from the rising of the sun to the setting of the same, it entreats, "Come, try my wares. Sophistication and glamour are but a potion away." Most of our friends had already succumbed to its powerful message. Flo and I felt impelled to also heed the tantalizing call, at least to the point of wearing lipstick.

As with any girl's first experimentations with make-up, we veered sharply toward the vivid. After all, what could be more worldly-wise to the untutored eye than a generous coating of, say, brilliant magenta—or, even better, dark purple—lipstick? Absolutely nothing. To semi-honor Daddy's feelings, we rubbed the lipstick off on the way home from school, arriving with traces of something-or-the-other—whatever could it be?—in dazzling violet smeared from cheek to cheek and nose to chin. Subtle.

One of Flo's friends went well past lipstick, strikingly glamorizing her entire face with an extensive array of enhancing cosmetics. Her appearance could fairly be described as stunning.

One day, as she sat in our living room talking to Flo—and illuminating the room with her unchecked application of various coatings—Daddy, on his way upstairs, paused and asked to which tribe she belonged. Knowing he teased us about our "war paint," she smiled brightly and said, "Comanche. We attack tonight."

Daddy chuckled "Ah!" and continued on his way.

He could have given an impromptu tutorial on war paint colors and their application by various tribes—not to mention a complete history of the Comanches—but chose not to. No sense stepping on a good line.

The Corps offered two services for the entire family each Sunday. The Sunday morning Holiness meeting helped Christians grow into Christian maturity. The Sunday evening Salvation meeting invited people to begin their walk with Christ.

Young People's League—or YPL as everybody called it—came in the hour just before the evening service. Not to break the pattern, YPL also took the form of a church service, but one by and for teenagers. Attendance tended to be sparse and the piano-playing not always ready for prime time, but it was by, for and about teens.

Daddy needed somebody to lead YPL. I volunteered my fifteen-year-old services.

Leading YPL meant responsibility for everything that happened—selecting the Scripture, choosing songs to go with the topic, making announcements and, of course, giving the sermon. My training consisted of a pat on the back and Daddy's reassurance I would do well. Given at least my share of the family's genetic imperative toward optimism, it didn't occur to me that a pat on the back might be insufficient. No doubts dragged me down. I just marched forward to make it happen.

I dug into books. I studied my Bible. I talked to the other kids about possible topics. All agreed that whatever I wanted to do suited them. I didn't have sense enough to let that daunt me.

My debut service arrived. As I strode to the front of the sanctuary exuding confidence, I wondered with each step what had ever possessed me to think leading YPL would be a good idea. But opening night is far too late for second thoughts, so I plunged ahead.

I announced a hymn, the pianist started it up and everybody sang. Cool. Whatever I said, they did. We sang hymns and choruses. We took up an offering. Everybody went along with my plans. Power welled in me, mixed with relief that my little congregation followed along so nicely instead of starting an insurrection.

The true test came when I launched into the sermonette—the only possible name for my five-minute effort. I launched with bravado, and, amazingly, everybody listened. How cool could this get! Less than a minute into my talk, I fell in love. With the front of the room. Let others tremble and quake at the very thought of speaking in public. It felt like home to me.

Now I knew why Daddy loved it so—not to mention Mother, Joe, Charles and Barney. Except for Flo, once any of us got an opportunity to speak, it bordered on lunacy to get between us and a platform. Flo, plotting her own course, wanted nothing to do with public speaking.

Rather than advertise the modest proportions of the YPL attendance and the fact most of the seats sat empty, we only turned the lights on in the front of the sanctuary. The back of the windowless room remained dark. But as I began my maiden sermonette, a glow radiated from the shadows. Daddy had come to listen and sat in the back row. Beaming with pride, he lighted the entire area around him. Artificial illumination would have been redundant.

Truth to tell, I wasn't good. The glow didn't come about to honor any level of excellence. Perhaps his pride came from my following in his footsteps or my effort to be well-prepared. Or maybe just because he loved me.

But as I spoke and made eye-contact around the room, I couldn't help noticing the glow from the back row. I remember thinking, "Daddy, even God isn't **that** good."

But Daddy's glow pleased me enormously. I decided to try to get good enough to earn it.

One day I decided my YPL services needed props. Specifically, I thought I'd try a "chalk talk" and dazzle the audience by illustrating my sermonette as it went along. I told Daddy of the need for a chalk board and set about preparing.

On the day of the big event, Daddy wheeled the large chalk board in its heavy wooden frame into place. He played it straight and didn't roll his eyes, but he must have entertained several pounds of doubt.

I titled my talk, "The Sweet P's of Psalm 23." Before YPL started, I drew what I purported to be a green sweet-pea vine all over the chalk board. Then I talked about God's wonderful promises that we could find in Psalm 23. For my purposes, these promises all happened to start with the letter "P." As

I remember, I offered five promises. Five sweet promises. Sweet P's. Clever, eh?

As I mentioned each promise, I drew—in bright pink chalk to make it unbelievably exciting—a sweet pea on the green vine. I helpfully explained my pink blobs so the audience didn't have to wonder, which, given my artistic skills, they certainly would have done.

It was stupendously goofy.

But Daddy still glowed from the back of the room. Perhaps more importantly, he managed to keep from laughing or falling on the floor.

However, in the many years that followed, whenever a lull came in a conversation, Daddy sometimes smiled his little smile and said, "Give us some of the sweet peas, Bette," and we'd chuckle. What else could I do? We're talking about a major bomb. Historic, even.

Fortunately, our family conversations had few lulls.

Mother's health continued downhill. The fatigue that had dragged her down ever since the drunk driver hit us years before, sometimes overwhelmed her. She said she believed she was born tired. She never faltered, though, in her commitment to her calling. The price she paid for her efforts could sometimes take the form of an emotional eruption.

On one particularly crushing day, I sassed her and slammed a door in her face. At least, that's how it appeared to her. She immediately launched into orbit, going about Mach 3.

Eyes blazing, she darted at me, obviously intending to punish my transgression by doing significant harm to my body. I needed a plan. Quickly.

As she ran toward me, I loped off around the dining room table, thinking to give her time to realize the wonders of my charms. She followed in hot pursuit. A couple laps around the table later, I realized my charms had zero value at that moment. She had no intention of giving up.

Fortunately, a plan sprang to my febrile mind. I knew all three verses of "Because," her wedding song. Strumming on her heart strings might resolve this current threat to my well-being. If I sang that beloved song, her heart would melt. So, as we circled the table, I started singing—bellowing might be a more appropriate characterization—"Because." I gave my all in this bull-horn presentation, but her heart remained stubbornly intransigent. It's difficult to add romantic nuance when you're running for your life.

The tender words didn't even fizz on her. She just kept coming.

Around the table we went; me bellowing a love song, her breathing fire.

And around.

And around.

Finally, as I flung the last few lines of verse three over my shoulder, Mother saw the humor of the situation and sat down to laugh.

She might have been more winded than amused, but in either case, it proves yet one more time: Always learn all the verses. You just never know.

Daddy hated school plays. We all knew that to be true, and it didn't slow us down even half a step. We jumped at every opportunity to be in school plays, revues, operettas, whatever—no matter how small the role or how dumb the play.

We also knew Daddy would always show up to watch us emote and posture our way across any stage, and he never let us down. He said when one of us added our innate luster to a cast, it changed everything and made the performance a must-see.

I joined the cast of every play willing to have me. Daddy and Mother always came to the final performance when, Daddy averred, I would play my role to perfection.

After the play, Mother would offer chapter and verse about the many ways in which I could improve my performance. The fact I had just taken my last shot at it mattered not at all.

Daddy always declared I had been the best one in it. Since Mother had earned a certain acclaim as a director of plays, accuracy almost certainly sided with Mother, but Daddy's conclusion struck me as more insightful. I went with his excellent appraisal.

For one high school revue, I wrote a solo skit in which I played a hooker and sang "Take Back Your Mink." Daddy proclaimed me the best performer in that one, too. I even made the town newspaper, picture and all. Daddy joined me in celebrating the wonder of it all. It never occurred to me that it might be a poor idea for a preacher's kid to appear as a hooker, and he did not mention it.

I never parsed Daddy's evaluation enough to realize he didn't actually describe me as good, just the best. And it doesn't matter.

The Yellow Pages listing came up for renewal. Daddy changed the listing from "organizations" to "churches." It seemed like a minor, logical decision.

But the head of the local Red Cross didn't see it that way. The new listing angered him, although he never said why. He expressed his outrage to the United Way folks. Together they decided, speaking of making a mountain out of a mole hill, to demand the listing be changed back. Further, they decided to go above Daddy's head to put a little muscle into their demand.

The United Way leader called Daddy's boss, the Divisional Commander (always referred to as simply the DC), in Cincinnati.

He portrayed Daddy as angry and difficult, recklessly endangering the future of the United Way in Lima. He further characterized him as destructive to community relations. From what we heard, the listing in the Yellow Pages never came up during the call. We know it never came up as things played out. But the call hit a bull's-eye. It provided an enabling mechanism to the DC.

The DC, a large, pasty man—part of the small group lined up to "teach Dowdell a lesson"—embodied the Peter Principle writ large. He seemed to resent both Daddy's talents and his successes. The Lima appointment had never been intended to get Mother and Daddy's picture in "The Young Soldier," or increase attendance or get accolades from the most-listened-to radio personality in town. The river of positive news flowing out of the Lima Corps only sharpened the DC's animus.

The United Way's call came as a relieving oasis in the DC's particular desert of frustration. He questioned nothing the caller said, but promptly called Daddy to say he would be in Lima the following Sunday to announce—from the pulpit—Daddy's removal. The DC allowed no conversation or explanation.

The news hit the congregation like a tornado. During the Sunday School hour preceding the service—when the DC planned to drop his bomb—the members hastily started a petition to keep Daddy and Mother in Lima. As the petition's pages went from room to room, everybody signed, using any handy writing instrument. One teacher in a class of young children signed with the crayon she happened to have in her hand.

The petitions completed, members asked the DC to meet briefly with them before the service. He refused, but condescended—there can be no other word for his attitude—to meet with them afterwards. Then the service started and he proceeded with his plan, slowed down not a whit by a sanctuary filled with stunned and sobbing people, probably made worse by the classy way Mother and Daddy handled themselves throughout the morning's ordeal.

At the promised meeting that followed the service, the DC peevishly snapped he had nothing more to say and saw no reason for a meeting. Although the power resided with the DC, the Corps Sergeant Major, as the Army identifies the elected leader of the congregation—a diminutive man several inches shorter than the DC—stood firm and as tall as a

Redwood. This godly man expressed his concern about what had happened and the manner in which it happened, then handed the petition's several pages to the seething DC.

Too incensed to exhibit civility toward even polite opposition, the DC denigrated the Sergeant Major and his efforts, then embarked on a stinging ridicule of the petition. First, he criticized the wording as insufficiently legal in its phrasing. Then he attacked the people who had signed it, asserting that educated people would refuse to sign such an inadequate, imprecise petition. And when they signed a proper petition, he continued, sophisticated people knew enough to sign in ink, not in pencil and certainly not—pointing with a sneer to the Sunday School teacher's signature—in crayon.

Nothing anybody said or did could stop the DC as he spewed his venom for over half an hour. Then he stalked out. Through it all, the people displayed magnificent forbearance. Daddy and Mother worked hard to heal wounds and to rebuild the optimism and sense of mission the fulminating DC had decimated. The people's faith remained brawny, but I doubt if anybody ever forgot that excruciatingly thorough thrashing.

Evil happens, sometimes even in church, even to good people. Signifying nothing. However long it takes, in the end, evil loses. Always.

We moved to Athens, Ohio, almost immediately, in the January of Flo's senior year of high school. Already in her tenth school, she opted to stay behind in Lima, living with a family from the Corps, until her graduation.

ATHENS, OHIO

To put it bluntly, the Athens Corps anchored heavily at the bottom of the Army's appointment barrel. It had nothing going for it. The worse-for-wear building abutted the sidewalk on Union Street without so much as a blade of grass, let alone a shrub or a tree, to soften its austere three-stories of age-darkened brick.

The building sat down the hill from The Athens Messenger building, across the street from a large wholesaler and about a long block north of a popular watering hole frequented by students from the nearby Ohio University.

In the front, a nondescript door, on the southern, downhill end of the building, led from the sidewalk to the bottom level, holding Daddy's corner cubbyhole of an office, a large multipurpose room, a huge walk-in closet filled with clothing for the needy and Sunday school classrooms. A second entrance, a wide, steep cement staircase leading to the double doors of the sanctuary on the second level, sat a little up the hill to the north,. We lived on the third floor. To reach our apartment quarters, we climbed the stairs to the sanctuary, took a quick turn and walked to the back of the building.

The walk was dark and invisible to onlookers. Coming home at night created concern since homeless people of variable repute knew where the walk led.

The small, concrete backyard ended with a two-foot-high retaining wall that held back a wooded hill rising steeply to the street behind us. The hill, taller than our building, blocked any light that attempted to bring cheer. Other buildings jammed in on either side of the Corps. Since that left only the curb for parking, it didn't take many cars to create parking problems. People don't like to walk long blocks in a run-down neighborhood to attend church.

Besides the depressing facilities, we fought severe demographics. Athens is a college town, home to more Ohio University students than townspeople during the school year. College professors tend not to go to church at The Salvation Army. Students surely don't.

For the most part, the Army comes to the minds of college students only as a point of ridicule when singing drinking songs, although I must say such songs did not occur in my presence once I became an OU student. Everybody who knew me decided they'd rather forego the songs than hear my purposely calm, cheerful and gentle little speech of how my parents were pouring out their lives for drunken bums like them—what with drunken bums being the theme of their little ditties. Nobody took offense, but nobody sang the songs. Newbies quickly quieted their squalling once others explained my sensitivities—and my little speech—to them.

In any case, trying to recruit college professors or students as church members had a virtually zero chance of success. The building didn't work as a compelling sales tool when townspeople people drove by either. And with a Yellow Pages listing as a church emphatically disallowed by the DC, nobody knew who we were to seek us out. Finally, a lack of money for church outreach efforts made membership growth an impossible dream—even with Daddy and Mother's employing their formidable talents night and day, every day.

Especially since the community's social needs drained every cent we could raise. We seemed to be the only game in town when it came to feeding and clothing the needy. Raising money became a nearly full-time occupation. Even so, our meager salary could slip away on any given week as the needs of others piled up.

Every transient passing through southeast Ohio knew how to find Daddy's office. They made it a part of their regular route. Each would, of course, claim they hadn't eaten in days, maybe even a week. They just needed a little help to get home—always in another state—where good fortune awaited them with open arms.

Daddy's rule of not helping a transient more than twice a year, though, offended them no end. You'd think they'd change their going-home story the fifth or sixth time they showed up in as many months, but they never did. What right did Daddy have to remember them or, even worse, keep records?

Trying to focus our excruciatingly limited, hard-come-by charity dollars on those really in need, Daddy instituted another rule. After each man completed his story, Daddy asked if they'd be willing to sweep what little sidewalk we had in return for a meal voucher they could cash at a restaurant uptown. All happily agreed to sweep and took the proffered broom. After a few minutes, Daddy would go out, usually to collect the broom left propped against the building.

Most of the transients just walked away. At least they left the broom behind. If Daddy found the transient sweeping away, he thanked him, gave him his meal voucher and sent him up the hill to the restaurant. It never was about sweeping the sidewalk.

Impoverished families came often, too. They'd show up in the middle of winter with coatless and shoeless children. Mother outfitted them from the closet's store, and Daddy gave them a voucher to use at the little grocery store down the street. The voucher covered almost anything they wanted to buy. It did not, however, pay for alcohol or tobacco.After hearing this limitation, close to half of the recipients stomped off empty-handed. The store's owner tried to persuade them to at least get some food for the children, but they wouldn't. Kids or no kids, they never intended to use the voucher to buy food.

Many weeks the money couldn't be stretched far enough to handle all the needs. That also meant, of course, it didn't stretch far enough for Daddy and Mother's salary. And at one point or another during our Athens years, Joe, Charles, Flo and I were all in college—obviously on the do-it-ourselves plan.

Not wanting to cut back on helping others and not able to do without a salary,Daddy and Mother pushed harder to raise money. They wouldn't ask for money without giving something in return. They offered what they had: Religious literature and themselves.

Whatever it took, it took—a part of their commitment to God and the Army. I never, ever heard a word of self-pity. Mother sometimes regretted she didn't have more energy but never uttered even a single word lamenting the demands.

On the outskirts of Athens, a huge mental hospital sat on large, manicured rolling grounds. Daddy and Mother began Sunday afternoon worship services there. They had no idea how much the patients understood, but they believed everybody, even the institutionalized, deserved to hear messages of hope and encouragement. They also wanted to give the staff an opportunity to worship.

That's where they met Glenna, an elderly patient, short and frail. During her teen years, her parents committed her to the hospital, the only way her impoverished parents could get medical care for her back pain. It was to be temporary, like a visit to any hospital, but they died shortly after Glenna's committal. Without a parent or guardian to sign release papers—and nobody to plead her cause—Glenna grew old in the hospital.

Long years of institutional living made Glenna odd as a bug, but odd or not, Mother determined to fix this deplorable situation. With the hospital's concurrence, she asked Glenna for permission to become her guardian, teach her how to clean houses and help her get jobs so she could finish out her life independent and free. Glenna giggled and gave Mother an ecstatic hug.

So Mother signed Glenna out of the hospital, and she came to live with us, bringing her institutional tics along.

"Original" doesn't fully describe Glenna's approach to mixing, matching and perhaps duplicating various articles of apparel to create wildly kaleidoscopic outfits. She vivified her frail appearance with a precise, bright red circle of rouge on each cheek. Equally bright red lipstick wandered erratically in the general vicinity of her lips. Her wispy white hair evaded all Glenna's bands, scarves and bobby pin attempts at corralling it, but she gave it all she had. Each day, her ablutions finished, she gazed in the mirror, smiling with pleasure at the lovely wonder of it all.

Glenna talked to herself incessantly. She always referred to Daddy as Major—since Daddy and Mother served as Salvation Army Majors, at least that made sense, but she called everybody in a uniform Major. She spent her days making up conversations with the Major. "So I said to Major. . Then Major said to me. . ." Her high, chirpy voice provided background noise letting us know she was awake.

One disconcerting habit was dusting with whatever her hand landed on, usually something like a sweater left draped on the back of a chair. I might find her dusting with my newest, best sweater. But she always cheerfully relinquished whatever she had in trade for a dust cloth, and we learned to be better about putting things away.

And Glenna provided mealtime entertainment. At every meal, she announced she was too full to really eat anything but she'd eat a bite or two for politeness' sake. Upon taking her seat, she promptly ate everything in sight. Everything. Glenna didn't stop until every serving dish had yielded its all. Wispy little Glenna could eat the proverbial horse.

Dinner meant knock-knock jokes. Glenna loved knock-knock jokes. She would sing out, "Knock, knock," and off we'd go.

"Who's there?"

"Mashed."

"Mashed who?"

At which point she triumphantly sang out her punch line, "Mashed potatoes" and squealed with delight at her wonderful joke. And we all laughed along with her.

One day Daddy heard loud ragtime piano music coming from the sanctuary and went to investigate. There sat a delighted Glenna enthusiastically pounding out ragtime with all she had—and doing a great job of it. Daddy appreciated her skill but not ragtime in the sanctuary, so he showed her a piano in the general purpose room. From then on, when she believed she could spare a few minutes from her work, the conscientious Glenna entertained us with boisterous ragtime concerts. Concert times were unpredictable, starting variously through the day and into the night.

Although once a redhead herself, Glenna took exception to red hair. For a while I dated a young man with hair of fire, and Glenna threw tennis balls at him whenever he came over. At first she nailed him, but he quickly learned to keep an eye out for flying tennis balls and caught them—only to hand them back to Glenna. After a little while, when she thought it would surprise him, she heaved the ball at him again. It became their game.

There came a time when Mother completed her work. Glenna had jobs all lined up and wanted a place of her own. Mother helped her find a little apartment, and we lost our beloved live-in entertainer. She visited often, but it was never really the same.

With the steep, almost unclimbable, hill behind us and buildings crowded in on each side, nobody could see the back of the building. We had no neighbors, and passers-by, walking along at street level, couldn't see the door to the apartment. Anybody could approach the door—even break it down—without worrying about being seen.

One evening Flo, an Ohio University freshman, and I, an Athens High School senior, were home alone, doing the dinner dishes, when we heard a man's voice.

We turned and saw the door into the apartment filled by a huge, filthy, roaring drunk man. He announced he planned to stay the night.

"This is a private residence," we tried to explain. Hd responded by bellowing it was The Salvation Army, and he intended to stay. With that, he lurched toward us.

Flo whispered "Sic em," and Jerry exploded, snarling, from the corner.

The intruder wheeled around, fled down the stairs in two or three bounds, scrambled out the window and staggered up the street as fast as he could, cursing The Salvation Army with every step. Jerry flew through the window after him and encouraged him up the hill for about a block, then returned home for a round of praise and petting.

We later discovered the intruder broke the window at the bottom of the stairs, unlocked it and let himself in.

Two or three evenings after that episode, Flo, this time home alone, heard the downstairs door rattling. Hard. Somebody was trying to break the lock by brute force.

Calling Jerry and grabbing Daddy's .22 rifle to look threatening, Flo went to investigate. Looking down the stairs, she saw a leg coming through the window. Failing to break the door lock, the transient had gone around the building corner and found the broken window. We had not had the money to fix it, and now another transient got in.

Snarling and barking, Jerry again flew down the stairs and through the window in hot pursuit of the hastily departing intruder. And another transient went up the hill cursing The Salvation Army with every step, his speed accelerated by Jerry's assistance.

The window got fixed that day. Or maybe nailed shut. Whatever the details, nobody came climbing through the window again.

Flo excelled with the .22, a good talent to have in Athens. The wholesaler across the street dealt in, among other things, large quantities of various grains and attracted veritable armies of rats. Exterminators came regularly, but as thorough as they tried to be, not all the rats died. Many moved into our back yard: Large, well-fed, disease-carrying rodents.

Our budget didn't cover exterminators, so Flo leaned out the window of my back bedroom, picking off those wretched creatures with Daddy's .22. If a garbage can rattled, Flo shot the garbage can and usually nailed the rat. The garbage cans developed a rather eclectic arrangements of holes, but the rats found no hiding place, and they never got in to share our abode.

Sometimes you have to do what you have to do.

In eons to come, archeologists may ponder the meaning of a hillside riddled with spent bullets. They almost surely won't happen upon the reality of killing rats.

The Salvation Army publishes a monthly magazine, "The War Cry," filled with stories about God and news about the Army. Mother handed it out each week as she went about raising money in businesses and bars.

Each Easter and Christmas, The Salvation Army published larger, special editions of "The War Cry," and we used these issues in our big push to raise money. We would go to a carefully selected neighborhood and leave copies of The War Cry at each house, inside the screen door. The following evening when, we hoped to find people at home, we returned and ask the "War Cry" recipients if they would like to make a donation for the magazine. We'd do one neighborhood, then move onto the next. Our minimum hope was to cover the cost of "The War Crys." We worked mightily to blast as far past that minimum as we could.

My redheaded swain thought we could continue dating regularly throughout the Christmas season, so I had to explain War Crys came first. If he wanted to spend time with me, it would be by going door-to-door doing War Crys. He had no connection with the Army but happily agreed to help.

The first evening went well. All we did was pass out War Crys at the houses. He worked one side of the street while I worked the other, and it went quickly. He decided I had made it sound more difficult than it turned out to be and got a bit of a superior attitude. That changed the following evening when we went back to ask for donations.

Again, we worked opposite sides of the street, this time meeting in the middle of the street every few houses to make sure things were coming along okay.

About half a block into our adventure, he walked haltingly to our mid-street meeting, ashen and shaking. His knock on one door was met by a homeowner with a shotgun aimed right at the redhead, demanding to know what the %@#*! he wanted. Red told me he had to make a quick decision: To run for it and take it in his back, or stand there and take it like a man. Being an Athens native, he knew Appalachia's people never hesitated to show a gun, but usually didn't use it unless you looked to be up to no good. Realizing that running might suggest nefarious deeds were indeed afoot, he decided to stand there and take it. Meanwhile he asked for a donation and hoped the gun-toting resident didn't view his request as a negative.

While the homeowner declined to contribute, he did lower the gun, washing relief over the redhead quaking on the doorstep. A gun no longer pointed at his mid-section impressed Red as good news indeed. So good, in fact, he started breathing again as he stiffly walked away from the house, hoping the guy wouldn't change his mind before he got out of range.

We talked about it for a while. When his color returned, I asked if he was ready to continue. We still had blocks to go. Startled at the thought, he stared wide-eyed at me for a long moment, then slowly agreed we might as well finish. We agreed not to worry my parents by telling them about the shotgun.

Red did "War Crys" every night that Christmas until we had handed out—and collected for—the very last one. And he kept dating me, too. I must have been a whole lot cuter than I realized.

The summer after her high school graduation, Flo worked as a counselor at a Salvation Army camp for underprivileged children near Cleveland. Ed came from Windsor, Ontario, to work at the same camp. They met and fell in love.

At summer's end, Flo returned to Athens, and Ed went back to Windsor. Both forlorn. As often as he could, Ed hitchhiked the 300-some miles from Windsor to Athens to see Flo. One weekend he brought along a friend, Bob, this time traveling in luxury by Greyhound.

Ed and Bob arrived just before dinner. His first sight of the building probably started Bob to wondering what he'd gotten himself into. Then I answered the door wearing a cumbersome brace of black leather and steel, borrowed from a friend for effect, around my wrist and thumb. Holding my heavily braced hand in an I-am-injured pose, I allowed as how my weekend schedule would not include athletics and led them upstairs.

To chaos. Even for us.

The door to our apartment opened into the dining room. The living room lay just beyond, overlooking the street. From the door, visitors had full view of both rooms.

That semester, Flo, a phys ed major, took tap dancing to pile up phys ed credits of any stripe. On a scale of one to ten, Flo viewed tap dancing as significantly south of one. Then it turned out the final exam, on which rested her entire grade, consisted of her performance of an original tap dance routine. Flo didn't want to mess with choreographing a tap dance, but she didn't want to deal with the ignominy of failing a tap dance class, of all things. Just thinking about it brought her to tears.

Mother said she would help, which sounded to all of us as a kind of non-offer. As a somewhat matronly preacher, what could she possibly know about tap dancing? She whip-lashed our view in a trice when she pushed back the area rug between the dining and living rooms, hiked up her skirt and started tapping up a storm. The woman could go! Who knew?

So the first thing Ed and Bob saw when they reached the door was Mother, skirt hoisted and feet flying, and a teary, sniffling Flo shuffling, slapping and counting away to the dreadful music that is a tap dance specialty.

Adding to the scene, Charles, a music major at Bowling Green, sat cross-legged on the floor next to dancers, drumming to the emphatic beat of the music. Home for the weekend, my 42 Long brother decided to take advantage of the opportunity to practice his drumming. Wailing away on the hardwood with his sticks, he provided extra accompaniment for the dancers.

Beyond them, Barney sat next to a living room window overlooking the street, his cast-encased leg propped up on a chair. Playing Tarzan by swinging from a large tree by a rope, he let go when the rope started to burn his hands and landed—in a gold-medal display of marksmanship—on the lone brick buried in the play area sand. The brick smashed his knee. After surgery and a stay in the local hospital, boredom set in. Now, armed with water balloons, he leaned out of the window targeting pedestrians, mostly college student going to or from the bar down the block. His loud cheer with every hit punctuated the rhythm of the tap dance music.

Around and through all of this skittered Glenna, dressed in her usual attention-getting style, chirping about conversations with "the Major" and dusting furniture with somebody's sweater. She circled near Bob to get a good look at the new guy.

Stubby joined in the welcome with his usual greeting.

We were a five-ring circus, but Bob took it all in stride. He could never have guessed what awaited him.

Ed and Bob arrived in Athens on the very day scheduled for going house-to-house asking for donations for the Easter War Crys we had left the night before. We invited Bob to join us.

I should probably tell you Bob, raised as a proper Canadian Presbyterian, knew nothing about the Army. And he had never in his life gone door-to-door asking for donations. But he agreed to help. Perhaps the alternative of staying home with Glenna, Barney and the dogs influenced his decision. Hard to say.

Ed, Bob, Flo and I worked as a four-person team, with one person going to each house. That way, we could solicit four houses at once. Again, we met in the middle of the street every so often to check our progress.

Halfway through the evening's chores, Bob heard a man's voice thunder, "Who's there?" in response to his knock on the door.

Looking up in the direction of the voice, he spotted a shotgun sticking out of a second-floor window, aimed directly at him.

In a strained, newly-discovered soprano voice, Bob quavered back "The Salvation Army?" The man grunted for Bob to wait, unnecessary instructions since Bob stood frozen in place.

Shortly, the front door, where Bob stood fearing what would happen next, opened revealing that the man had thoughtfully left his gun behind. Reaching for his wallet, he pulled out some bills and put them in Bob's shaking hand.

The other three of us howled when Bob related—step by scary step—his near-death experience. We savored our terrific new, can-you-top-this War Cry story while he stared at us in disbelief. To assuage his concerns, we explained the local firearm customs and insisted the only real danger came from the possibility of dying of fright. It seemed the better part of wisdom not to bring up Red's episode from the previous Christmas. Even with that tactful omission, I don't think he bought our pacifying tales. After his quaking subsided, he agreed we needed to finish up, probably realizing any talk of immediately going home was a waste of breath.

He left on Sunday and never came back.

Salvation Army uniforms came custom-made by Army-hired tailors. As you might guess, they were expensive, especially on an Army officer's salary, and bought infrequently. But Daddy's uniform showed its age, and another cleaning might result in total disintegration of it. A new uniform could be put off no longer.

Mother took Daddy's measurements and sent them in. His new uniform soon arrived. He looked better than ever—if possible—in my eyes. He beamed with pleasure. That afternoon, for reasons forgotten, he had to go up the hill to town and decided to walk. I went along.

No sooner had we turned onto Court Street, though, when Daddy saw a student lying in the gutter, drunk and covered with his own vomit, and went to help. He started to kneel, to position himself to lift the young man out of the gutter.

Seeing he would end up kneeling in vomit, I could only cry out, "Daddy! Your new uniform!"

He looked at me and said quietly, "No father's dreams for his children include seeing them lying in a gutter." He picked the boy up, vomit or no vomit.

Here he was, big enough and tough enough to be the worst bully in town, intelligent and talented enough to run rings around most people in most things, yet loving and humble enough to kneel in a gutter to help a young stranger who obviously didn't love himself. Daddy was, simply, a living, breathing example of Amazing Grace—with a great sense of humor.

Daddy loved to read. He had a series of books, *A History of Nations*, with each major nation represented by a fairly chunky book, about thirty volumes as I remember. He would head off to bed and, a natural speed reader, finish a volume before sleeping. Finishing in an hour what would take me several, he seemed to inhale information.

Since he never forgot what he read, he made a wonderful resource for school reports. Ask about, say, Norway, and he'd rattle off names, places, dates, population, major industries, form of government, etc., etc., etc. My reports—and probably those of my siblings—always sourced a volume of *A History of Nations*. Teachers never learned of our information Vesuvius at home.

Each Saturday afternoon, Mother worked her business route, going from business to business, talking to the owners, giving them religious literature, answering their questions about faith—and raising money. I joined her on most Saturdays.

Donning my Army uniform in preparation for the afternoon's work always occasioned mixed emotions. While proud of the Army and equally pleased to be helping out, I still felt compelled to barrage Heaven with fervent pleas to protect me from running into friends, which would require me to explain the outfit, my lack of lipstick and the activity, all so alien to everything they understood. Week in and week out, God honored my prayers.

The route included two neighborhood bars, simple, dimly-lighted, down-home places where friends, mostly farmers, gathered to wile away a few hours over a beer. They all beamed when Mother arrived. She'd go from table to table, greeting and counseling—and, of course, exchanging religious literature for a donation. As she counseled her way around one side of the bar, I went around the other. Since the counsel of a sixteen-year-old never has much of a market, I stuck to chitchatting and raising money.

Everybody, including Mother and me, was a regular. If one of the men failed to show up, the others would check to make sure nothing bad had happened. If Mother didn't feel well enough to go, I'd do the route alone, and the men at the bar would ask about "the lady," solicitous and genuinely caring about her well-being. And on any Saturday I didn't go, they always asked about "the girl." Neither of us ever had a name beyond "the lady" and "the girl," but they didn't seem to need a name to care.

Spending Saturdays asking strangers for money may not be the stuff of most teenagers' dreams, but you can't pay for training like that. Until you've gone into a bar using religious literature to raise money, you haven't really learned to work a room.

One Saturday when I worked the route alone, I went into a hotel to speak with the manager. I introduced myself and offered her some literature, asking for a donation. We chatted a bit. She seemed quite pleased I had come and gave me a nice contribution.

At home later, Mother didn't know quite how to hold her face as I related, a bit crowingly it must be said, my success. She had stopped going to the hotel after that same manager had turned her down too many times. And now, here I'd made the sale, as it were.

Mother had to sort it out. She delighted in thoughts of my following in her money-raising prowess footsteps. My display of initiative, a trait she highly valued, pleased her, too. But a bit of a miffed feeling muscled its way in as well; nobody before had ever succeeded in raising money where she had failed. After the briefest of considerations, her pleasure won the day.

And in the Saturdays that followed, she made a point of following the trail I blazed at the hotel, always with the same excellent results. I gladly ceded back to her the metaphorical Queen of Money-Raising sash and tiara.

Saturday nights found Mother in the bars favored by the OU students. Students never gave much money, but although the Corps needed money desperately, money never took first place. She meant her love and her literature to touch hearts more than to raise money, and Saturdays nights topped the needy hearts list. Watching college students at play can be bracing for a caring heart, but she always tried for an opportunity to make a difference.

As the students got to recognize her, they greeted her with a warm welcome. They often had questions to ask. Some started looking forward to a chance to speak with her, to continue a running conversation from week to week. The conversation and their questions showed they had been thinking about things she had said, provoking a flicker of encouragement in her always hopeful heart.

She didn't expect immediate change or noticeable signs of religious interest. It takes enormous strength to be different on a college campus. She had to trust that her words would stay with them for future reference.

As she gained popularity, her bar-hopping stints extended late into the night. The long hours and the energy she expended caring about the students took more of a toll than she could really afford to pay, but she counted it worth the cost.

The Army had national salary levels, based on a formula. Married couples, with two people working for the salary, received more than single officers. They added an allowance for each child, up to a maximum of three children, until the child reached 18—known in many circles as college age. Twenty-five years of service earned a weekly increase of a dollar; if both husband and wife had twenty-five years of service, that meant they could live it up on an additional two dollars a week. Any monies received for performing weddings, funerals and the like, became income to the Army, not the officer.

Salaries never added up to a big pile of money. Not even a little pile for that matter. More a pebble-sized bump at best—and available only if no unpaid bills remained. In Athens, getting paid took everything we had in us. Combining the old sayings about getting blood from a turnip and water from a stone only hints at our financial struggles.

Money or no money, though, we needed a car. Too many things didn't happen because we couldn't get to where we had to be to make them happen. Daddy made the case for a car to the headquarters people in charge of decisions, and they approved the purchase.

While headquarters wielded the power to say yea or nay to auto acquisitions, the Corps officers—Daddy and Mother, in this case—had to raise the money to pay for them. Given our financial constraints, Daddy focused on finding the most car for the least money.

An extensive search led him to a new, light-green Plymouth left over from the previous model year, sitting in the far reaches of a desperate dealer's lot. While not regulation navy or black, nobody would describe the appropriately drab color as loud or attention-getting. Believing the fabulous price and the subtlety of the color, not to mention the lack of any real alternative even close in price, would work a little flexibility into the rules, as happened from time to time, Daddy signed the papers and submitted a requisition to headquarters for approval.

The headquarters people in charge of decisions, however, turned him down. Bargain or no bargain, green cars did not meet Army standards.

Daddy had just bought himself a car.

Now he needed a salary more than ever. Our financial situation went from devastating to double dire.

The car payments drained us dry, but Daddy's unintentional ownership of the car turned out to be an example of God filling a need before the need existed. At the time, though, the payments nearly sank us.

And what would Christmas be without the ubiquitous Salvation Army Christmas kettle? Its familiar tripod stand and shiny red iron kettle about the size of a slightly deflated basketball are part of what December has to be. While most people see them simply as part of the season, we depended on them to bring in money for the big Christmas push.

Athens presented a major challenge. The Corps faced huge needs, but we had scant few potential bell ringers, at least of the affordable volunteer variety. Spending Saturdays, the biggest kettle day, standing outdoors in Ohio's winter weather, ringing a bell and asking for money didn't appeal to everybody.

Daddy went to the various service clubs—Lions, Kiwanis, etc.—to speak about the need. Each club volunteered for the specified Saturday, with one club manning one kettle. Daddy told them he'd report back the total of each club's take, so it became a sort of goodwill competition—as Daddy hoped it would. Competition helps. Nobody wants their team to lose because they dropped the ball by not showing up, so Daddy could be sure they'd all be there.

Flo and I worked a kettle, too. We wanted to help in the huge challenge facing Daddy and Mother. Thus, we informally entered the kettle competition.

During our kettle-tending time, we tried various fund-raising approaches. Sometimes I accosted people, walking with them down the busy street, smilingly suggesting I could tell by the look on their face they really wanted to help the less fortunate. It worked pretty well. More often than not they accepted my premise and dropped money into the kettle.

Every once in a while somebody got grumpy about my approach, but when I offered an ultra-goofy apology of sorts, they always left smiling, sometimes laughing. I didn't amuse them enough to change their minds about contributing, but at least they didn't leave mad at the Army.

I also earned success, of a limited nature, by smiling and waving my eyebrows at little kids. Entranced by my dancing eyebrows—first one up and the other down, then reverse, then both going the same direction—and my singsong incantation about the joys of putting money in the pot, they all wanted to put something into the red kettle. They'd ask their parents for money, but invariably received only small change to donate, the reason for the limited success. We appreciated every nickel we received and thanked the kids profusely, but those Christmas boxes cost a whole lot more than small change.

Some of my best results came from a pair of play glasses with bloodshot eyes painted on cardboard glued to the end of springs, and enhanced by a bulbous nose and mustache hanging below the frames. With eyes bouncing maniacally at the slightest move of my head, I waved my eyebrows and did my best—but truly atrocious— Groucho Marx imitation, duck walk and all. But it made people laugh and they gave.

If things slowed down, I whipped out a small, plastic toy flute and offered to play an original tune for anybody putting ten dollars (as I halfway remember the amount) in the kettle. Now, as a matter of fact, I had no idea how to play any sort of a flute, so when somebody kicked in the requisite amount, I had to vault into overdrive. Wearing the glasses, eyes wildly flopping in every direction, I shuffled around in a sort of dance, my exaggerated finger motions randomly closing holes in the flute. Predictably, I produced one foul note after another, as loud and proud as I could blow them.

The flute routine always attracted a crowd. Sometimes it generated enough laughter to motivate additional donations large enough to require an encore or two. I would shake my head, creating an avalanche of bouncing-eye activity, stagger as if I couldn't go on, then relaunch. Given the ad-lib nature of the flute playing, I could solemnly assure every contributor they had earned a debut performance of an original composition.

Meanwhile, Flo played a great straight man, smiling and chatting with onlookers. For all I know, she may have been agreeing with them that I might be certifiable, but our routine worked. I brought many in with my looniness; she brought in the rest with her charm and big smile.

How I got to be the buffoon and Flo the straight man remains a puzzlement. No matter. It's always a wonderful day when a ham gets to chew the scenery and do good at the same time.

The Kiwanians et al did their duty on that cold December day. Flo and I had fun. Our results, of course, beat the tar out of theirs. The Bible says God loves a cheerful giver; human nature says people in a good mood become more cheerful—and better—givers.

But we figured the profound stuff out later. At the time we just knew Daddy and Mother needed our help, and we gave it our eye-ball-bouncing best.

The Army sent Joe Bosco, a Lieutenant new to the ranks, to Pomeroy, a town twenty miles southeast of Athens on the Ohio River. Pomeroy had, if possible, even less potential than Athens. And to Joe, a New York City boy who had quite possibly never ventured west of the Hudson River before, it might as well have been Uzbekistan. While the language sounded fairly similar, attitudes and the pace of daily life were totally foreign. However, being a native New Yorker, he felt confident he could shape the locals up in short order, never for a moment considering they might think the shaping up should go in the opposite direction.

But Joe had a big heart and a lot of vinegar, so Daddy and Mother set out to help him. They even smiled when he showed up, day after day, right at dinnertime with urgent questions to ask Daddy—his timing coincidental, of course. After a few well-chosen words about not wanting to barge in, he always saw his way clear to accept Mother's invitation to join us. We all liked Joe, even Glenna, who was particular with her affections.

Flo and I volunteered to work a day on Pomeroy's Christmas kettles. Joe needed help, so off we went. Straight to disaster.

Lt. Bosco had never worked a kettle. He had never managed a kettle crew before. He didn't have a clue about kettles, and we, to whom kettles were second nature, had no idea he had no idea. We had never before met an Army person who didn't know how it went.

He set our kettle up at the edge of a warehouse-business district, directly across from the Ohio river, wished us well and went about his other business. Standing on a street-corner across from the mighty Ohio on a December's day can freeze your tuchus in short order.

This freeze-the-volunteer fact is well known to kettle people, and they make arrangements for "warming" breaks. This understanding, however, eluded Joe—which we realized about the third time he drove by waving happily. We would serve our seven hours straight—no warming breaks, no potty breaks and no lunch.

The kettle, cast iron in those days, could be removed from the stand. In a pinch, risking a hernia, you could lug the kettle to someplace warm. Our poorly-chosen location, though, didn't offer a refuge. We had no money to buy lunch, and no place to buy it in any case. We wouldn't abandon the kettle

207

and risk losing its contents, however meager. And neither of us saw the area as a place to leave the other alone. We were stuck.

We tried to wave Joe over each time he cruised by, but he misunderstood the motions of our frozen appendages as friendly gestures, not pleas for help. And he didn't hear us bellowing for him to stop. And so it went for the entire day.

Had he stopped, besides getting a chance to thaw, we could have educated him on the proper, as in profitable, placement of kettles. Joe, Flo and I would all have ended up a whole lot happier.

We had given our word and we knew the need, so all day long we rang the bell and tended the kettle. Few people went by. Fewer yet put anything in the pot. We paced about in an attempt at sufficient animation to generate internal heat, but with frozen bodies refusing to cooperate, we ended up stumping around like alien monsters from a Grade B movie. Joe kept driving by. We kept waving and hollering, to no avail. It was a very bad day.

Finally, our kettle time came to an end and Joe came to collect the tripod, the pot and us. By then neither Flo nor I felt remotely inhibited from informing him exactly what he had put us through and how we felt about it—and him. Poor guy. He hadn't given a thought to what it must be like for us, and now he felt dreadful. And he had to explain to Daddy, his lifeline, how it came to be that his daughters arrived home frozen as solid as cod.

After feeding, thawing and properly commiserating with Flo and me, Daddy had a talk with Joe. While unhappy about the freezing of his *kinder*, he knew Joe had intended no harm, and after an unsmiling teachable moment, chalked it up to youthful inexperience. Since Daddy's teachable moments tended to strike fear in the hearts of listeners—perhaps greater than their fear of God, what with Daddy being visibly present and large—my guess is Joe's kettle workers received excellent treatment ever after.

And Joe kept arriving in Athens just in time for dinner. Coincidentally, of course.

Christmas trees, we thought, constituted a necessary part of Christmas. They added a festive note to the celebration of Jesus' birth. Who doesn't decorate for a birthday party?

Flo and I, especially, fancied a tall tree for the Sanctuary and a regular-sized one for the quarters, but we had no money for trees. However, with the family credo of never giving up, we hatched a plan. A plan with a certain genius to it, I must say.

Many of Ohio University's array of buildings sported grand and wonderfully decorated Christmas trees to stylishly celebrate the season. But when the university closed for the holidays about the middle of December, all those trees ended up abandoned in the alleys behind their respective buildings, nude, save for a random strand or two of tinsel. Flo and I announced we would make dark-of-night acquisitions of two fabulous trees selected from the bounty now discarded as so much garbage.

Daddy and Mother expressed little—and even that stretches the point—enthusiasm for the plan, but it was either our plan or no tree. And so it would be. Flo and I would go up to the campus and select a wonderful tree. One of us would heft the top while the other grabbed the bottom, and thus we would lug it home for redecoration, allowing the forlorn, abandoned tree to once more shine in all its glory. And then we'd do it again.

We set out on our tree-rescue mission the evening Ohio University closed for Christmas.

We went first to the alley behind the Student Center. The Center had many large and lovely trees, giving us a nice selection. Our search revealed a ten-foot beauty just waiting for a new home.

As planned, Flo grabbed one end, I grabbed the other and we headed for Union Street and home, about a half mile away, flush with success. Allow me to explain that hefting a tree of that size required more than a fingertip grip on the trunk. We had to wade into the depths of the branches and wrap our arms around the trunk. From this necessary position, we could barely see for all the foliage sticking in our faces, and, except for our fast-moving feet, we could not be seen at all. A casual glance at our plan's execution presented the astonishing vision of a large, horizontal, seemingly self-propelled fir fleeing down the street as if pursued.

Athen's main intersection is Court and Union. The Army building was on Union Street down the hill, across Court Street from campus. Our trip necessarily included crossing the intersection.

As we approached Court Street, the light glowed red against us, and we lurked behind the store on the corner as we waited. The moment the light turned green, we exploded from our hiding place, racing through the intersection past startled drivers and pedestrians. We may have motivated a few spectators to swear off the sauce, what with the bizarre vision of a mobile tree torpedoing its horizontal way across the intersection before their very eyes. On we ran, slowing to a walk only when safely back in the shadows of nightfall, lugging our precious cargo home to serve as the Corps tree.

While Daddy and Mother put the tree in its stand and started decorating it, with Barney's help, Flo and I headed back up the hill to repeat our tree-nabbing exploit. This time we searched for a somewhat smaller tree for our living room. With so many choices, we quickly found the perfect specimen and reprised our hoist-and-dash routine a second time. Anybody who happened to see both trees flying low through the intersection that evening can be assumed to be on the wagon to this very day.

And thus we celebrated Christmas in the glow of lights strung around the two lovely trees. As usual, we did not see ourselves as deprived. In fact, Flo and I felt pretty darn smug at our successful solution; we saw the problem and conquered it with energy and enthusiasm—at least in our eyes. And the pine sap scrubbed off in a day or two.

In a single Athens summer, Joe graduated from college and went to Fort Campbell, Kentucky, to serve in the 11th Airborne Division; Flo postponed college to marry and go off to live in Windsor, Ontario, and I graduated from high school. Charles had also expected to graduate from college that summer, but ended up spending another semester at Bowling Green in one of those good news/bad news things.

He registered for a required course the first semester of his senior year, only to learn it required a new, very expensive textbook. Charles, planning, as usual, to buy a used book, couldn't afford the new book. Ever optimistic, he had some thought the text would prove to be, in the manner of many textbooks, unnecessary. But when the professor turned out to rely on the textbook rather than his lectures for exam questions, Charles had to drop the class. It didn't seem like a problem; he would take it the next semester. With the bookstore awash in used textbooks by then, it would work out just fine.

Beginning the bad news part of the story, the college didn't offer the required class the second semester. He would have to stay on for an extra semester to earn his degree, a semester for which, of course, he had no money. Since he had been entertaining celebratory thoughts on how scratching his way through college was almost at an end, it made for a very low point.

Now comes the good news part. On a choir tour at the end of the extra semester, he got to know a lovely young lady, Nancy, an alto, who would become his wife. He decided she more than compensated for the late-graduation snag.

A speeding car, not unusual for Union Street, hit Jerry one night, shattering his hip. The vet could do nothing, even to relieve the pain, so Mother had to have him put down. She cried for days. I continued for weeks to take a giant step over him at the spot between my dresser and the closet where he had for so long blocked my path each morning as I dressed, each step bringing a new wave of sadness. But then, a great dog like Jerry is worth whatever mourning it takes.

That summer of graduations and weddings, we received news that Grandma Gowen lay dying. Well into her nineties, she had been hale and hearty, walking the five miles each week to collect her rents, but suddenly her health had failed.

Even more suddenly, Uncle Herb stepped in to take care of her. Strange, since in years past he hadn't revealed an iota of concern for her well-being. For instance, she once asked him to fix a minor electrical problem in her house. He agreed and upon finishing the job, presented a bill for his services—which she paid. And now Herb had morphed into a devoted son taking care of his ailing mother's every need.

As we digested this latter-day attitude transformation, word arrived about Grandma's new will, a will leaving everything to the already wealthy Herb—wealthier by far than any of his brothers or sisters. Two doctors who employed Dolly, Herb's hospital-nurse wife, witnessed this new will, written about the time Herb pronounced Grandma too far gone to take a phone call from Mother.

Herb intended to have it all and leave his eight siblings with nothing. To insure things went his way, he kept the rest of the family away from her bedside, even by phone or letter. For some reason, the brothers and sisters looked to Mother to remedy the situation. The others feared Herb; Mother feared nobody.

She wrote a letter to Herb. Prone to a writing style that misjoined words in startling ways—what Mother thought and what she wrote were not necessarily synchronous—she always asked Daddy to check her letters. They offered unexpected adventures into strange and mysterious thought processes, and he cheerfully plunged into the exploits of Mother's writing. He especially wanted to offer his services for this letter. The stress of it all had ravaged her meager energy resources, and she needed help.

With only a quick glance, though, Daddy burst out laughing. The letter started, "Dear Herb, You dirty dog." The juxtaposition of two contradictory emotions gave birth to another Dowdellism: After this, any coupling of incongruous sentiments immediately met with "Dear Herb, You dirty dog."

And Mother laughed along with the rest of us. Even she couldn't believe the direction her pen took, seemingly without her consent or control.

Grandma died just after Christmas, but Mother couldn't afford to go to Downend for the funeral. For the moment, Herb had his way.

But it seems his actions poked God in the eye. While Herb gained Grandma's substantial bounty as his own, his life began crumbling around him. His health started a long, downward slide. Dolly died, leaving him alone. He joined swell clubs where his money made friends for itself. As uncontrolled diabetes diminished his faculties, his "friends" routinely took financial advantage of him. He couldn't understand why his sisters didn't step in to care for him in his hour of need—at no charge, of course. What else is family for?

Mother kept touch with Herb, encouraging him, preaching at him, trying to prepare him to meet his maker so he'd have some peace, but nothing could pierce his armor of self-pity.

Mother's share of Grandma's fortune would have helped in countless ways—bought the house she never had, for one thing, but the real tragedy, to me, is that everybody paid far too high a price. Herb stole enormous, needed blessings from the very people he supposedly loved and, in return, received nothing more than a bowl of gruel that destroyed him.

Mother's health finally reached the end of a difficult, punishing road in Athens. Doctors warned she would die within a year if she continued to work her incredibly long hours under so much stress. It seemed nothing in her body could function properly, and every day brought such a profound fatigue she could barely get up, let alone get moving. Doctors offered no nostrums.

Both the stress and the work came with the Athens appointment. The constant lack of money, the run-down building that attracted nobody and a Divisional Commander (DC) who refused to let Daddy advertise as a church so people could understand why we even existed, created obstacles no amount of work could overcome. If either she or Daddy stopped working their endless hours, there would be no money to pay the bills, let alone their small salary. Staying in Athens would be a death sentence.

Daddy made an appointment to meet with the DC. Daddy, Mother at his side, started the conversation by sharing the news from the doctors. He asked for a transfer to an appointment that would be easier on Mother. He probably hoped for a temporary headquarters assignment that would demand nothing of her, providing the time necessary to regain her health. He had long since given up hope for plum assignments, so anything would do.

The DC, however, insisted any such move would have to wait until the following year; June had just passed, and he could only move people in June. Apparently he had changed his approach since our September move to Lima and January move to Athens.

Daddy pointed out the doctors predicted Mother would die within the year without some sort of relief. She couldn't afford to wait for the natural ebb and flow of Army life. The DC, large and unkind, but otherwise relentlessly mediocre, simply repeated himself, unmoved.

Daddy said the unwillingness to offer any accommodation forced him into a choice between his wife's life and the Army. The DC agreed.

Well, how large must it be written in the sky? After eight years, the anti-Grandpa crowd had finally made the kill.

Daddy asked the reason for his forced resignation, and the DC launched a malicious personal attack. He said Daddy lacked intelligence, had not a shred of talent, proved himself lazy to the core and on and on. Since Daddy worked most of his waking hours, had an IQ sufficient to humble your average genius and daily exhibited an incredibly wide range of talents, the DC knew he lied. His rant simply defined and aired his jealousy and animus—and revealed his belief Daddy and Mother had plotted the chilly welcome when he arrived in Lima to announce their exile to Athens two and a half years before.

The DC finished his invective by averring the Army had carried Daddy as so much dead weight for years and would carry him no longer. And, he added, instead of the pension Mother and Daddy had earned with their combined 57 years of hard labor, he would authorize only a payment of a few hundred dollars. Take it or leave it.

Mother, of course, reflexively agreed with the DC. (She, usually so discerning, never seemed to understand the impact of this habit. Through the years, she told me—on several occasions—all that had occurred that day, always with a "what's a person to do" sort of attitude.)

Daddy knew he could win his pension with a law suit. Others had sued for withheld pensions, and they all won, but Daddy didn't have the heart for it. He believed in the Army's enormous goodness, and he didn't want to risk its more-than-well-deserved reputation over the actions of an unfortunately well-placed few. Adding to his reluctance, Mother pronounced such a law suit would be wrong. Daddy, she said, caused his own problems.

It was over.

At 49, Daddy had no job, no house, no furniture, no savings. Not even a dish to eat from—or a fork to eat with, for that matter. Nothing but his faith, a very sick wife who sided with the people bent on destroying him, a résumé listing 28 years of diligent work in a position nobody understood enough to respect and the Plymouth, a blessing with payments due.

Joe, Charles and Flo were out on their own. In college on a scholarship I could, one way or another, make it. Barney, though, had just finished fifth grade.

Somehow he had to find a future.

As always, Daddy's faith held, the only light in that profound darkness. However bleak the circumstances, he still believed God would make a way.

◇ ◇ ◇

Bert Foster, his friend and a union steward at a Fisher Body plant in Cleveland, wangled Daddy a job in human resources. Called to preach, Daddy dreaded the thought of, as he understood the job, sitting at a desk pushing papers. But as they say, "A man's gotta do what a man's gotta do." While typically applied in situations involving a lot more derring-do than accepting a desk job, the saying aptly summed up the circumstances.

Daddy pointed leaden feet toward Cleveland and started packing our few belongings.

Nobody except family and friends knew about the split with the Army. Daddy told us he didn't want anybody to blame either side. Almost certainly, although he never said so, he didn't want anybody asking Mother about it.

We thought nobody in Athens knew.

One evening, the phone rang. John Versteeg, the local Methodist pastor, wanted to speak with Daddy. During our time in Athens, they had been jointly involved in various church projects, such as Good Friday services, but didn't keep in touch. Unbeknownst to Daddy, Rev. Versteeg held him in high regard.

"Charles," he declared in his famously rapid speech, "I hear you're leaving The Salvation Army. Well, I told my district superintendent about you, and he says you can have your choice of three churches he needs to fill. You just drive around and decide which one you want. We'll work out the details later."

Daddy, always fast with a comeback, stood speechless—nonplused doesn't even come close. After a few seconds of involuntary silence, he asked how Methodist beliefs compared with those of the Army. Rev. Versteeg told Daddy to come by the parsonage and check out the Book of Discipline. As in right away.

Daddy, with small, vivid rays of hope tentatively piercing the gloom, dashed out the door.

He came home a new man, surprised by grace. Reverend Versteeg, a man he held in esteem had declared him to be exceptional. Army doctrine turned out to be a carbon copy of Methodist doctrine. When General Booth left Methodism to found the Army, he took along its theology in toto. All the pieces fit. The decision made, Rev. Versteeg gave him the names of the three available churches and told Daddy to drive around to see which he wanted.

First, though, a fairly significant detail needed to be handled. The next morning Daddy, Mother, Barney and I trooped into the Methodist parsonage where, in a matter of minutes, Rev. Versteeg made all four of us proper Methodists and welcomed us into the fold.

John Versteeg, straight-on in his faith and unorthodox in his methods, must have delighted God.

BEVERLY, OHIO

The District Superintendent wanted Daddy's decision by, oh, say, yesterday. Hated to rush matters and all, but he had to know which pulpits he still needed to fill.

Daddy and Mother chose Beverly, a lovely little town on the Muskingum River, in the rolling hills of southeast Ohio. The white, steepled church sat across the street from a park, its parsonage two short blocks up the hill, high atop a terraced lawn.

The Beverly appointment, called a three-point charge, included churches in three different towns: Beverly, Coal Run and Lowell. Daddy would conduct services in Beverly and Lowell each week. Twice a month, he'd swing by the tiny rural church in Coal Run and conduct a short service there.

He called Bert Foster with the unexpected news. Bert's jubilation matched Daddy's. If anybody belonged in a pulpit, Daddy belonged in the pulpit, Bert said. Asking all about it, Bert learned of a three-week gap between when the Army quarters had to be vacated and the Methodist parsonage became available, and offered his and Mary's home.

With arrangements all in place, Daddy, Mother, Barney and Stubby (I had departed for a summer job by then.) loaded up the Plymouth and drove off to Cleveland, bidding adieu to Athens and the Army. The Fosters welcomed them warmly, but Stubby—and his unfortunate talent—stayed in the garage. Even the best of friendships have limits.

Daddy and Mother devoured the Plain Dealer's classified ads for furniture and found wonderful bargains in beautiful, graciously used—as they say in the trade—furniture. Spending all their "retirement" money—and a bit more—they got everything they needed to furnish Beverly's three-bedroom parsonage. And they took a significant step up in the quality world.

Mother took special delight in a Duncan Phyfe-style dining room suite with its china cabinet, sideboard, marvelously expanding table and covey of chairs. It provided not only beauty, but a way for our scattered family to come home for holidays and join together for holiday meals.

Daddy and Mother arrived at the Beverly parsonage a little more than a month after their meeting with the Army DC, still a little shell-shocked with the sudden upending of their lives, but ready to go. While Daddy hit the books to figure out Methodism, Mom set about decorating a home—for the first time in her life. She hooked a large dining room rug, made drapes, sewed curtains and worked her magic. With more creativity than resources, she put together a gracious, welcoming home.

Only a small crowd of regulars worshiped at the little church in Coal Run. They loved their church and supported it generously, but it had pretty much reached the end of its days. As members died off, it would fade away. The Bishop wanted to close it down.

Shortly after Daddy arrived in Beverly, he met with the Coal Run church board, hardworking, small-time farmers. He asked about their dreams and hopes for the church. They spoke lovingly of all the church meant to them. They hoped Daddy would be willing to conduct services for them and convince the Bishop to allow them keep their beloved church home going. After the meeting, Daddy called the Bishop with his desire to serve Coal Run and won a reprieve for the little church set so peacefully amidst a clearing in the trees. Pretty bold action for a brand-new Methodist pastor, but Daddy always went to bat for what was right.

The lay leader of the Coal Run church, a man pushing eighty, from the far side, still worked his farm. Rather than a watch dog, he had a huge watch turkey. A completely naked, if that's the word, watch turkey. Not a feather anywhere in sight. Maybe that's what made him so mean.

Whenever a car drove up and stopped on the property, the turkey launched an all-out assault on the driver's door to prevent egress. The first time Daddy came to visit, the turkey trapped him in his car. Fortunately, he was expected, and the sound of the first enraged gobble brought the old farmer out to greet Daddy—and explain how to handle the turkey.

"To establish your right to exit your vehicle," he yelled over the turkey's din, "you open the door and kick the turkey." Daddy, not wanting to injure the bird, gave it a gentle nudge, which accomplished nothing.

"No, no," the farmer shouted, "you have to really show him who's boss." With that, he gave the turkey a mighty kick and sent it sprawling. At the end of a tumbling skid, the turkey righted himself and staggered away in defeat.

Daddy, ever the city kid, delighted in this bit of who-could-believe-it country living.

He explained the sequence to us when he came home: "I drive up, kick the turkey a good lick, then go visit." After a while, Daddy and the watch turkey reached a kind of rapprochement, with the ugly, naked bird needing only an occasional reminder.

Every visit ended with the lay leader giving Daddy two pounds of butter, home-churned by his wife. The first such gift heartened Daddy, but as he drove the two or three miles home, a strong, acrid aroma flooded the car. At closer inspection, he realized the butter was rancid. As was every pound of butter he received from then on.

Ever practical, Mother wanted Daddy to tell the lay leader about the butter's rancidity so we could perhaps get better butter. But Daddy would not risk hurting the old couple, so he said nothing but "Thank you" as he accepted each pungent gift. After all, they ate the same butter, so apparently they liked it that way. And who knows? Perhaps the unique attributes of the butter explained their hearty longevity.

Whenever Daddy's booming bass voice joined the congregation in singing a hymn, he couldn't stop without creating chaos. If his strong voice—Mother used to tell him "even when you sing soft, you sing loud."—stopped midstream through a hymn, the congregation took that as a signal they, too, should stop. As the organist kept on playing, now suddenly as an unexpected instrumental solo, a wave of puzzled looks swept across the sanctuary as the congregation, eyed each other in confusion and wondered if they should resume their singing along with the organ or remain in silence with Rev. Dowdell. No congregation ever got on to it. If Daddy wanted to check his notes before preaching, he had to remember not to start singing the hymn just before the sermon.

But Daddy's big voice carried its own blessing.

Daddy, ever the musician, had a thing about dragging organists. Hymns intended to be slow were one thing; up-tempo hymns played at a snail's pace irked him. He selected hymns for both meaning and tempo, but usually struggled with organists stuck in low gear. Heaping praise on the organist when things went right worked pretty well.

Sometimes, though, no amount of encouragement worked. The Lowell organist offered a particular challenge. Nothing Daddy said or did could get her to pick up her coma-inducing pace.

One Sunday, he tried new approach. He sang each hymn at its proper tempo, paying no mind to his lagging accompanist. The congregation naturally followed his booming voice, leaving the organist with no choice but to scramble to keep up. At the end of the service, she beamed with delight as Daddy praised her—at great length—for playing with such energy. Things went better after that.

Through the years, whenever Daddy and Mother came to visit in the various places I lived, they accompanied me to church. Daddy would join in singing the hymns, always noticeably since he had no other choice. And since his voice doesn't range high enough to sing lead, he sang the bass part.

By the end of the first few bars of music, you could see the organist start to twitch in the presence of a gift from above: a true bass voice, sight-reading and singing with authority. Organists in small to medium-sized churches can go their entire careers without such a voice in the choir. Daddy was music to their ears. They tried to maintain focus on the service but could hardly contain themselves through to the benediction.

While the final "Amen" still resonated in the air, the organist would bolt at full speed for Daddy, all but going over the backs of the pews, to recruit him for the choir. When they learned he was only a visitor and would be leaving in a few days, their faces sagged in a sadness that could make Superman weep.

The Salvation Army eschews most rituals and doesn't celebrate Communion. Daddy had never in his life taken Communion, but since it is a regular part of Methodist worship, Daddy had to learn about it—not least, how to do it. The Worship Committee came to him with questions about setting it up and what, if any, changes he wanted. They would offer suggestions. To respond, he had to know what the Discipline said about it. As he studied, he came to love Communion—the meaning, the serving, everything.

And he loved the story about how good Methodists founded the Welch's grape juice company to provide a source of consistently good grape juice for Communion. He celebrated the fact the company never manufactured spirits until the Welch family sold their interest in it. He saw it as a great business success story.

However, Welch's excellent grape juice created a problem for Daddy: He was allergic to it. The very smell made his nose run, a difficult thing when, in his preferred method of serving Communion, he handed each kneeling communicant a little glass of the grape juice that represented the blood of his precious Savior.

He solved the problem by placing handkerchiefs—snow-white, starched, ironed and folded—at strategic locations around the altar and Communion rail before each service. And you know what? Even though I knew about his allergy and the handkerchiefs and knew he used them every time he served Communion, try as I might, I never caught him in the act.

Flo and Ed married young, and struggled in the early years. Daddy and Mother didn't really have money to spare but helped as much as they could.

After his first Methodist wedding, when the groom gave him a check, Daddy gave it to the church treasurer, following the Army rule that all income belonged to the church. Learning, with joy, that the money belonged to him, Daddy sent it onto Flo and Ed.

At the time, Flo and Ed budgeted via the envelope system, putting money in envelopes labeled for each expense so they'd have it when needed. The system did not account for emergencies. When their new baby, Fred, fell ill, the required medicine emptied their rent envelope.

Rent day arrived with the envelope still empty. They would have to explain to a demanding landlord unsympathetic to tardiness. That day's mail included Daddy's wedding check— in the exact amount they needed.

And so it went for nearly three years until their finances eased. On each day of financial desperation, a check would arrive from Daddy, a gift to him for officiating at a wedding or a funeral.

Flo and Ed never mentioned financial needs they couldn't meet. Daddy never asked. Nobody tried to coordinate any sort of a plan. But whenever a need arose, a check came.

One day Flo mistakenly told Mother that she didn't have a dresser. She and Ed had only a little furniture, and it didn't include a dresser.

Well! Mother saw her chance to help. She had a spare dresser, somewhat dilapidated and cast off to the basement by a previous minister, but a dresser is a dresser. Large and bulky, it could hold vast quantities of anything. Two plus two had never equaled four as much as this dresser equaled Flo's need. Daddy could just strap it to the top of the car, and off they would go from southeastern Ohio on a mission of mercy to Windsor, Ontario. Flo would be so pleased.

Daddy didn't see it in quite the same way. While eager to help Flo, strapping large objects to the top of the car and proceeding hundreds of miles thus encumbered lacked any shred of appeal. He had to respond quickly to stop this particular train before it left the station. Grasping for a rationale that might let him escape this ignominious assignment, he announced the dresser too shabby to give to Flo and went back to work. Even after years of coping with Mother's steamroller tactics, he somehow thought that ended the discussion.

Not many days later Mother greeted Daddy with the wonderful news she had used a little paint to completely transform the dresser. It now looked as good as new. Possibly even better than new. Her efforts, she announced, metamorphosed the dresser to a thing of beauty, surely pretty enough to take to Flo. With Mother's forceful encouragement, Daddy reluctantly trudged down to the basement to see this remarkable transformation.

Shock and awe rendered him mute. In her haste to do this good thing, Mother used the only paint available in the house: A bright, shiny, pea-green enamel. And there the dresser sat, all but glowing in the dark. Daddy made a valiant attempt to resist the inevitable, but Mother pushed on with an invincible determination to help her eldest daughter in an hour of need.

In the end, assisted by a Niagara of Mother's helpful suggestions, Daddy wrestled the humongous, shiny, pea-green dresser onto the car roof, strapped it down and started off on the long drive to Windsor. His dismay grew with each passing mile as startled motorists reacted to his astonishing cargo.

The final blow came at the Canadian border. Instead of stopping Daddy to ask the routine questions, the customs official took one look at the dresser, burst into laughter and, wiping his eyes with one hand, waved Daddy through with the other.

By the time they reached their destination, Daddy, speech-less with humiliation, could only sit and stare, but Mother glowed in triumph.

Flo and Ed, surprised by this unexpected—in so many ways—gift, hurried the dresser into their apartment, grateful for its utility if not for its pea-greenness.

In not too many years, Daddy recovered sufficiently to join the laughter at the oft-told story.

Rev. Firestone, a retired Methodist minister, a gallant with a thick mane of snow-white hair, lived just up the hill from the parsonage. In his eighties, he had recently been widowed for the second time. He preferred marriage to living alone and soon found Bertha, a spinster, to use a culturally harsh but definitive word, a woman in her sixties with a warm and generous spirit.

Love bloomed, with but one concern. Rev. Firestone came to ask Daddy's opinion about his marrying somebody young enough to be his daughter. What would people say?

Daddy told him not to lose an opportunity at happiness with somebody you love because of a concern for the opinions of others. They were both legally and morally free to marry, and Daddy suggested they accept the authority of their hearts.

He ended the conversation with, "Of course, I'm assuming you're both of legal age." They laughed together, then the elderly minister walked up the hill toward home with a sedate new spring in his step.

Daddy married them soon after.

Grandma, who by then lived with us several months each year, decreed the marriage a disgrace, an affront to the morally upright. The nerve! The gall! A minister, of all people, robbing the cradle! From sunup to sundown she exhaled harrumphs about the impropriety of it all, but she saved her real fire for the nightly domino game with Daddy.

I can't recall Daddy ever suggesting a game of dominoes in Grandma's absence, but she loved to play and he willingly laid out the "bones" each evening. With the beginning tile in place, she'd start in on Rev. Firestone's inappropriate behavior, using phrases like "old goat" and "out to pasture." Daddy would smile and mildly ask why two people shouldn't be happy, whatever their ages. She had no answer for his question, but that didn't soften her outrage. She gave up venting only after she realized her efforts not only didn't change his attitude, but didn't even bother him. How can you get a good vent on if nobody reacts?

Surrendering her outrage about Rev. Firestone, she reverted to her time-honored practice of pronouncing Daddy a chiseler every time he won their nightly domino game. She smiled when she said it, so I think she meant it as a joke. Returning her smile with a larger one of his own, he certainly seemed to take it that way. Or maybe he meant to get her goat. You could never be sure.

Grandma had her own, fixed idea about the food pyramid. Basically, it was a flat-line consisting of a single food group: doughnuts. Not the greasy, glazed things filled with air, but the proper cake-style doughnut with heft and dunkability. Her taste buds demanded bulk.

Given Mother's shaky health, Daddy did a lot of the cooking, and he expected people to appreciate—and eat—his excellent culinary efforts. But Grandma accepted meat—and especially vegetables—grudgingly and often decided to skip them entirely. Concerned for her health, Daddy tried to jolly her into an attitude change, telling her to take some meat and vegetables, that she needed them, they'd be good for her disposition. She'd fire back her all-purpose answer, intended as the ultimate in hilarious responses, "Then you'd better take two helpings," before grumpily complying.

You could count on the byplay at least once a meal, so when it started, we'd wait for her finale before resuming our conversation. It became a sort of Muzak for the dining table.

The East Ohio Conference met in annual conference at Lakeside, Ohio, each June, starting on Father's Day. Daddy and Mother loved Lakeside and its summer resort atmosphere. A big cement pier jutting into Lake Erie offered benches to sit and watch the waves, which in a lake as shallow as Erie, could be impressive. The little shops on, as Daddy called it, "the stem," a business district about two blocks long, offered wares of interest to Methodist ministers.

Daddy enjoyed the conference atmosphere. Where Salvation Army Officers' Councils were all business and all clergy, the Methodist conference allowed ample time for socializing and church members attended—and voted—right along with the clergy. And where the Army had the military style pecking order defining who interacted with whom, Conference worked more like a democracy, with few formal lines of communication.

Daddy always remembered the first time the Bishop approached him—in his rookie year as a Methodist—and asked his thoughts on an issue before the conference. Realizing the Bishop wasn't practicing some form of ecclesiastical *noblesse oblige* but really wanted to know, astonished him.

Most of Lakeside's summer rentals lacked phones. To reach somebody at Conference, you called a central number. Emergency calls sent people scurrying all around Lakeside to find the called. Non-emergency calls got posted on a huge, outdoor chalkboard across the street from the conference hall. The Bishop got calls. District Superintendents got calls. Ministers in large churches sometimes got calls. Daddy always got at least one call. Conference, after all, started on Father's Day every year. It tickled him that I went to all the bother, and he got to assure those who asked, as he erased his name from the board after we talked, that everything was fine, his daughter just called to say, "Happy Father's Day."

By his second Annual Conference, the Bishop, Hazen G. Werner, realized Daddy had made himself an expert in the Discipline. If questions arose on the floor, Bishop Werner, turned to Daddy to confirm it or, if the Bishop wasn't sure of the answer, to summarize what the Discipline said.

Daddy fit the role perfectly. He enjoyed the give and take—and the politics—of the Conference sessions, so he always arrived on time, sat down front and paid attention. He churned the happenings around in his mind to see how they applied to him and his local church. By the time Conference ended, he had all the resolutions, changes, et al worked into the following year's goals. In the meantime, the Bishop could use his attentiveness.

Besides knowing Discipline cold, Daddy never spoke beyond its actual words to freelance his opinions. And Bishop Werner knew Daddy wouldn't be a sycophant; if the point went against the Bishop's argument, so be it. And Bishop Werner appreciated Daddy's strong faith and optimism, commenting on them frequently, both privately and publicly.

Rays of appreciation from the hierarchy had never fallen on Daddy before. Obviously, he relished the new environment. But I wouldn't know any of this if I hadn't asked a lot of questions. Good, bad or indifferent, Daddy cruised through life without volunteering personal comment.

I went to Conference sessions with Daddy several times. Judging by his enthusiasm, I expected fireworks, but the sessions turned out to be eye-glazers.

For all the Bishop's accolades, though, Daddy had no vote in conference matters. Methodist rules decreed the Salvation Army Training College education and twenty-eight years of devoted service to preaching the gospel did not equal a seminary degree. Seminary trumped Training College, and his years of service were the same as if he had, say, sold life insurance. He couldn't become a full member of a conference, only an approved supply, a secondary classification. Approved supplies could lead small churches; hatch, match and dispatch members of their congregations; pray and counsel with their people—everything, in fact, but vote and climb the hierarchal ranks.

Daddy would have loved having all doors open to him, but he so appreciated being in a pulpit, he didn't mourn his loss. He still had the opportunity to continue in God's calling to preach, so he saw his glass as more than half full. Other Methodist ministers remarked on the punishing load he carried with a three-point charge, but Daddy reveled in all the free time he had to study and prepare—and simply to live—compared to his Army days. Life was good.

Methodist theology mirrored Salvation Army doctrine, but similarities between the two pretty much ended there. Army officers served in a military-style structure, with the limited latitude that implies. Within generous guidelines, Methodist preachers pretty much ran their own show in the local church. Within the local church, though, things reversed. In the Army, Daddy and Mother decided what needed to be done and set out to do it—or, if possible, find somebody to do it. The Methodist Church took a consultative approach, with committee upon church member committee to make plans and execute decisions.

Committees present challenges, but having people ready, willing and able to serve delighted—and somewhat astonished—Daddy. Especially since the church members demanded more of themselves than of him, which took some getting used to. Even so, committees are committees. A strong-willed member with bullhead tendencies can tie them in knots, particularly since everybody's a volunteer, and they lack organization charts to bestow clout.

A member of the Beverly church, a gaunt, tallish woman of a certain age with jet-black hair and long church experience, determined to sit on as many committees as she could get elected to, then use these committees to change virtually every aspect of church life to her personal liking. Her way contradicted most of what Methodists held dear, and soon committee meetings turned into sessions in hell. With each committee determined not to go her way, and she determined to prevent their taking any other path, frustrations ran high and church planning screeched to an almost audible halt.

In his studies of Methodism, though, Daddy had come across a church-saving proviso: When the need arose, the minister could assume the chairmanship of any committee. Well, obstructionist behavior can kill a church, so the Beverly church certainly had a need. Daddy visited each committee chairperson to announce he would be taking over for the time being. With nary a question, they all willingly stepped aside, probably hoping his smile meant he had a plan to go over, under or around the roadblock.

And so he did. Exuding energy and optimism, he dedicated each meeting to God and *Robert's Rules of Order* and simply failed to recognize the hard-charging reformer during the meetings. She spluttered and fumed, squirming in her seat and waving her hand whenever his eyes seemed to be coming in her direction, but somehow he never managed to call on her to speak. Her consternation and agitation escalated with every tick of the clock. After the committee accomplished the business of the day, just as she cusped on terminal apoplexy, Daddy invited everybody to bow their heads in prayer to again ask for God's guidance and wisdom. Well, when the preacher's praying, you have to join in if you want to keep your image up amongst the folks. So everybody, including she-of-the-frayed-nerves, prayed, adjourning the meeting.

Committee meeting after committee meeting, Daddy broke the log jam. After each meeting, he arrived home exultant, fingers strumming with joy at his sides, booming out, "Democracy is wonderful!" We laughingly allowed as how it didn't sound much like democracy to us, but he would have none it. Progress blossomed and bloomed.

Nobody knew about Daddy's conversations with the recalcitrant lady that helped her understand her value to God and the church, to realize she didn't have to exert control to have significance. Her actions obviously—obvious to Daddy at least—sprang from a strong, if misguided, desire to make things better, which made her salvageable. You can't do much about someone who chooses to remain embittered, but her desire for good allowed for a wonderful outcome.

Church members deemed it a miracle as she became a real partner in church activities. It may not have happened by itself as they thought, but Daddy never saw a need to tell them otherwise.

We all gathered for holidays during the Beverly days. Later, distances increased and growing families needed to establish their own traditions, so the practice dwindled off. While it lasted, though, we almost blew the roof off the place.

A family of boisterous, energetic folks gathered to practice competitive storytelling at full throttle, we each contributed our considerable energy and decibel quotient to the joke-telling festivals. We all understood and supported the basic rule: Don't wait for a break in the action; there won't be one. Simply jump in a little louder than the others and take over the conversation. We saved the news about our daily lives for side conversations; dinner called for entertainment. Through some natural, unspoken process, we deemed reminiscing, including, of course, a round of dog stories, to be an evening, living room event. Holidays afforded us a yakking jubilee.

We started building our supply of jokes, bon mots and funny tales a month or so before the great event. With Daddy, a born raconteur, and Joe, an entertainer who put himself through college in large part with his comedic skills, leading the way, we were off and running as soon as we hit the door. If it fit the circumstances, we broke into song, with "The Preacher and The Bear" being a favorite.

And, mind you, this all happened in a Methodist parsonage where the strongest thing served was coffee—and that over objections from Mother, who preferred tea. Apparently, once people taste coffee brewed in England, they refuse to drink the beverage the world over.

One day, as the usual reunion pandemonium filled the dining room, we suddenly started to gasp for air as our eyes sprung leaks. Stubby! Stretched out under the table, making absolutely no effort to control his excitement, the blissed-out beast silently expressed his enjoyment of the day's events in the only way he knew. We all chorused his name in an accusing, indicting tone, which bothered him not at all, then adjourned to stand in the living room and continue telling our stories until the stench dissipated. When whoever had the courage to test the dining room air sounded the all-clear, we regathered around the table, never missing a beat.

On another holiday we got so involved in the noon meal's round of stories, we found ourselves still at the table when the time for the evening repast rolled around. Fortunately, Mother had been attending to a few kitchen duties while listening to her brood, so dinner was ready. We pushed the dirty dishes into the middle of the table and put clean plates around the perimeter. Mother served the new food, and we kept going until well after dark.

Still another time, a Thanksgiving, Mother pulled the supposed-to-be golden-brown turkey from the oven only to gaze down on an almost raw bird. Gathering around the stove for the usual full-family, full-throttle consultation, complete with a variety of feigned foreign accents, about the source of this development, we discovered the oven dial was off by a hundred degrees, The oven got warm enough to take the chill off, but not hot enough to actually cook anything. No matter. We ate vegetables and salads for the feast and had our turkey and stuffing that evening. It worked out well. At first flustered by the uncooked turkey, Mother ended up laughing too hard to care.

Since such gatherings were our normal fare, it didn't occur to us to consider the possibility that somebody who grew up outside our milieu might see us as a little off the charts.

The boys, in turn, brought their intended to meet the family during one of these holiday gatherings. It's a testament to the boys' charms—and to the bravery of their future wives—that they did, indeed, end up married.

After each intended bride made her debut, Mother fretted about whether she would fit well in the family, what with being so quiet—a state of being that puzzled her. It might indicate timidity, a mysterious attribute as far removed from Mother as heaven is from hell. What then?

I tried to explain the stunning effect we had on newcomers and assure her each would participate more fully in time, either by developing the fortitude and volume to leap into the conversation or deciding to simply sit back and laugh until their ribs hurt. We accepted performers and audience members equally, perhaps even preferring the latter since they buttressed an area short on family members. My hopeful comments fell on deaf ears. Mother would not be assuaged. In her mind, our family defined normality, and she couldn't divine a single reason for anybody not to join right in.

During our holiday celebrations, the women prepared while the men cleaned up. The kitchen seemed to shrink in the presence of the five men—Daddy, Joe, Charles, Ed and Barney—the shortest of whom, Daddy, stood an even six feet. Since bantering and jokes constituted a large and integral part of the cleanup efforts, they took a while.

Once during the cleaning-up festivities, Joe decided he needed a bathroom break and went down to the basement to use the facilities there. A two-story laundry chute ended right next to the basement toilet. Daddy opened the chute's door by the kitchen sink, telling the others, "Watch this."

He started pouring small amounts of water down the chute, catching Joe's attention. Thinking to be helpful by telling Daddy of what looked like a problem, Joe put his head underneath the opening and, in his best Master of Ceremonies voice, called out, "Say, Dad!" at which point Daddy dumped a pitcherful of water down the chute.

Laughter and cheers broke out when the kitchen crew heard Joe sputtering and realized Daddy had scored a bulls-eye.

Even Joe laughed. For a moment. His laughter ended abruptly when he realized the cloth he picked up to dry his face was, in fact, a wet diaper.

Hilarious or not, after that episode, the Johnstown flood could have come down that chute, and none of us would have made a peep.

Alone in the parsonage on a summer's evening, I answered the doorbell. At the door stood a man, probably in his sixties, a stranger. He asked to speak with the Reverend.

When I said he wasn't home, the man turned to leave. Something told me not to let him go. I suggested that he stay, promising my father would be home in just a few minutes.

He questioned the predictability of Daddy's arrival, but I explained my father's habit of punctuality. When he set a time, you could depend on his arriving by the promised time, maybe even earlier.

With that, the man allowed as how he'd wait for just a few minutes. I invited him in, but he preferred to stay on the porch. We each selected a chair and sat rocking as we chatted about the weather.

We hadn't rocked long when, as predicted, Daddy arrived. He parked in back, then came around the house and up the front stairs to meet the stranger on the porch. I introduced them, then went inside so they could speak privately.

The moon neared its apex by the time the man left. Daddy came in and congratulated me on my instincts in keeping the man from leaving.

The visitor told Daddy he didn't see any reason to live; his wife had died, and he couldn't figure out how to go on. He had planned to commit suicide that night but felt he should talk to a man of God first.

Daddy helped him see a path through his grief. When he reached the other side of his overwhelming pain, Daddy told him, life would be better. He would still miss his wife, but life would become worthwhile again.

The man sent a letter of thanks a year or so later. He said life had turned out just as Daddy said it would.

The only downside to Daddy's punctuality arose from our absolute reliance on it. On those rare occasions when Daddy, for whatever reason, did not arrive by his predicted time, we immediately leapt to conclusions of doom. Something dreadful had happened. Perhaps he lay dead in a ditch somewhere. Surely nothing else would delay him.

Daddy's slightest tardiness constituted a news event, a reaction he found puzzling.

I inherited Daddy's punctuality. And I agree: Having others react to a brief delay with weeping, wailing and gnashing of teeth is a little much.

Whenever I came home from college, I "rode the circuit" with Daddy. He liked to bring me along, and it pleased the Lowell and Coal Run members to see the Reverend's children.

One Sunday, a trio sang special offertory music for the Coal Run service. The lay leader's wife led the group. As she walked over to take her place next to the piano, I could see that she wore seamed stockings. In fact, several seamed stockings encased each leg. Where the first one had a run, she twisted the second to cover. Where the first and second stocking had overlapping runs, she twisted a third stocking to cover. And so on. The seams created intricate, deranged patterns spanning the backs of her legs. Coming out of frugality rather than need, the stockings provided a little object lesson that probably explained their substantial wealth.

The trio launched, boldly singing their close harmony with an Appalachian twang, one singer doubling as the piano player, straining her neck as she threw her head back in close proximity with the others, the better to harmonize. They proceeded through the hymn with vigor. Every once in a while, though, the pianist hit a clunker and immediately stopped singing, leaving the little group without their strongest singer. She'd snatch her head away from the harmony, cast it down so close to the piano keys her nose practically played its own note, fumble around to situate her hands properly, then hurl her head back into position and rejoin the other two who had gamely continued singing during her noticeable vocal absence.

Well, it tickled me. In my amusement, I did a dangerous thing: I looked at Daddy. Sitting behind the pulpit in his black robe, looking serious—almost stern—as usual, he looked back at me. Our eyes met. When something amused Daddy, his eyes twinkled, no matter what expression graced his countenance. You had to know him well to spot it, but as our eyes met, I could see his eyes all but doing the fandango. And I began to lose it.

I simply couldn't laugh at those dear ladies. They sang with a sincerity that clothed their efforts in grace. There could be no laughing.

From previous experiences of high amusement, I knew that reading would control my laughter. I grabbed a hymnal from the rack in front of me, blindly opened to a hymn, any hymn, and started to read. I read until the trio finished. They sang a lot of verses, so I read a lot of hymns.

After the service, several church members expressed their pleasure that I searched the hymnal to find the words the trio sang and said from then on they'd announce the number of the hymn so people didn't have to go to the trouble of finding it on their own. I felt like a jerk as I thanked them for their thoughtfulness.

In Lakeside for Conference, on his third anniversary as a Methodist, Daddy had a heart attack. The Lakeside doctor pinned the crushing chest pain on the unfortunate result of an encounter with a too-greasy doughnut. However, since heart disease killed his father, Daddy, while hoping for the best, knew what had happened.

A few days later he drove the several hours back to Beverly. By the time he arrived home, he'd long since dismissed the doughnut story. The local doctor confirmed that he'd had a heart attack. His total treatment plan consisted of telling Daddy to lose weight.

The tricky part in following the doctor's terse orders came from the fact that, although a big man, Daddy didn't eat all that much. For him to shed pounds, he needed to limit himself to the calorie count of a debutante striving for a quick, five-pound fix.

However difficult and daunting, though, he set out to lose weight. When I visited, it hurt to see him eat his meager fare, no more than what a sturdy five-year-old might eat, but he stuck to it. Slowly, ever so slowly, the scales settled on lower and lower numbers.

Meanwhile, he rested and took it easy. If parishioners needed to see him, they came up to the parsonage.

Mother took over the pulpits each Sunday. Few members had heard a woman preach before, but any concerns they may have had quickly faded. Mother did not consider herself a woman preacher, but a preacher who happened to be a woman. Anybody who expected girly-girl soft soap got a big surprise. With people dying and going to hell, she intended to make sure they had to get past her first.

After her first Sunday in the pulpit, Reber Bright, a leader in the Beverly church and a friend, came up to the parsonage to check on Daddy's health and bring him up to date on church happenings. As he left, he stopped just before going out the door and told Daddy not to feel any need to prematurely rush back to the pulpit. Josephine, he allowed, would do just fine until Daddy recovered fully, however long it took.

Reber's comment brightened Daddy's day. First, it meant the church members still felt cared for and happy. Second, any compliment to Mother was a compliment to him. Third, doing something substantive again made Mother feel better. If tending three churches left Daddy scratching his head about utilizing his suddenly acquired spare time, she, with no defined duties, had really felt at sea. She glowed at the recognition of her calling—and he glowed along with her.

One day I called to chat about Daddy's progress, and Mother announced she had a big surprise for him. While the doctor still wanted him to lose more weight, she decided to reward his hard work and diligence by baking him a cherry pie, his favorite.

I all but jumped through the wires that connected us, "No! No! No! Don't do it. That'll kill his diet." She insisted it wouldn't.

Mother had never been on a diet. My comments sounded absurd. As a veteran of the calorie wars, I tried to explain the psychology of dieting. Especially with a diet as severe as Daddy's. But, locked and loaded to do this good thing, she could not be stopped. I begged. I pleaded. I cajoled. I all but turned myself inside out. To no avail.

Sure enough, the pie pleased Daddy, both in its taste and the thought behind it. Unfortunately, as I had predicted, it ended the diet. Perhaps, though, more than the pie, was the message from a non-dieting partner tired of not having anything good to eat—like potatoes, gravy and desserts—a powerful motivator I hadn't thought of.

No longer active in any sort of athletics, Daddy regained his weight mostly around his waistline. He no longer had the built-like-a-wall physique that awed my childhood friends, but he was still Daddy, and he still looked awfully good to me.

He probably would have looked even better to all of us had we realized how close we came to losing him. We still thought he was indestructible.

One Sunday, on his way out of church, Reber shook Daddy's hand and said, "Charles, you wear well." Daddy always described it as the best compliment he ever received.

Daddy traversed life lightly. Walking with an amazingly light step, he took exception when we stomped instead of walked. Scuffing our heels always elicited his "pick up your feet" reminder.

As frequently necessary, he would tell us to lower ourselves into chairs rather than employ our more thoughtless aim-and-drop approach.

He would not abide open-mouthed chewing, "snickying," in his words. Dinner time in our early years included many calm "Don't snicky" rumbles from the head of the table. His second inviolable rule at the dinner table involved elbow placement. Never missing a two-for-the-price-of-one educational opportunity, he'd tell us to resist the impulse to "use your elbow as a fulcrum." To enhance our education in the use and misuse of our upper appendages, a gentle jab of his fork applied to any table-based elbow guided us to a permanent assimilation of the lesson.

He frowned on gum-chewing, saying it reminded him too much of a cow ruminating her cud. Gum-snapping lay well beyond any pale, perhaps the secular version of the unforgivable sin.

And he saw banging doors as anathema. Every door-slamming episode occasioned his observations about preferable ways to close a door.

He didn't depend on volume or yell. He remained calm, but constant. Every infraction earned its own unruffled reminder.

He impacted my psyche. I flee from stores containing gum-snapping customers. Floppy slippers don't find a place in my closet since I'd have to prance like a high-stepping majorette to keep from scuffing. If eating with a known snickier, I try to sit next to the offender so as to suffer only the sounds—and not the sight—of mastication. And even now, supposed adult that I am, letting myself drop into a chair brings an instant flashback of Daddy's disapproval—and instant repentance.

By Beverly, these lessons had been drilled in deep enough to strike oil.

It was all the more flabbergasting, then, when one day he banged the kitchen door with a loud crash and burst into the house punching the palm of one hand with the fist of the other, an almost maniacal grin on his face, an Appalachian-twanging, basso profundo loudly declaring, head jerking and bouncing, "I ain't no fancy preacher! I ain't no book-larned preacher! I just bang on the Book and brag on Jesus!" He was in rare form, enjoying himself immensely before his small, stunned and speechless audience. Who was this person who looked like Daddy?

Well, Daddy liked to listen to backwoods radio preachers as he drove. Their zeal more than made up for anything they lacked, and Daddy appreciated enthusiasm. As he neared home that day, the "bang on the Book" litany captivated him. Plus, he liked the underlying sentiment, so he immediately adopted it. Once home, without warning or announcement, he repeated the words and tone for us, embellishing it with his uncharacteristic slam-bang entry.

He used the line, from time to time, for the rest of his life. If anybody asked what he planned to preach on, he might well announce with a grin, "I'm just gonna bang on the Book and brag on Jesus." He always got the expected laugh.

But it irked Mother. She liked to add her input during his sermon preparation, and when he came out with that "Brag on Jesus" line, she knew persistence would only earn her the entire litany, reenacted with gestures and the appropriate accent. Getting to use his line always put him in high good humor, but she'd walk away peeved. Whether her reaction came from not getting to help form his thoughts, at seeing him turn into some kind of caricature or simply at the rough-hewn, don't-plan-on-having-tea-with-the-Queen nature of the phrase, I cannot say.

But I can report I got the same reaction years later when she decided to help me prepare to teach a Sunday School lesson and I spoke the fated words. I said it with a smile and meant no harm, but she was not amused.

In our younger years, maybe even through junior high, whenever Daddy saw us chewing gum, he'd put his hand, palm-side up, just under our chin. Without a word, we understood we had to relinquish our wad to his waiting hand.

One day he spotted Barney energetically chewing and initiated the gum-dropping routine. Daddy's expression never changed as Barney, wide-eyed, but doing his duty as he knew it, opened his mouth to drool a mouthful of very liquid chocolate-covered cherry into Daddy's waiting palm.

Daddy readily agreed to the bride's request that her uncle, a retired minister, assist in performing her wedding. On the evening of the rehearsal, the long-retired uncle shakily tottered up the aisle to take his place alongside Daddy, pleased as punch his niece included him in her big day. The rehearsal went well. Daddy, as usual, took the bride's side in any disputes with either of the mothers. Somehow he always managed to do it in a way that left everybody happy. It would be a beautiful wedding, all agreed.

The next evening, the church resplendent with flowers, candles and gussied guests gathered to witness the nuptials, Daddy and his vintage assistant stood behind the altar, their little books containing the historic words of the wedding ceremony in hand. The flower girl came down the aisle sprinkling petals and smiling brightly, not crying as some are wont to do. The bridesmaids glided into place, each lovelier than the next. Everything flowed beautifully. The mothers could already be seen dabbing at the corners of their eyes.

Then, just as the organ boomed out the first notes of "Here Comes The Bride," somebody doused all the lights in the church—a planned development nobody had bothered to share with the clergy. Candles cast a soft glow around the sanctuary, but up in the altar, the two men responsible for getting the job done stood in total darkness, their little books useless.

Well, it's not really possible to maintain dignity—not to mention the romantic beauty of the occasion—and call out questions about the lighting just as the bride commences lock-stepping her way down the aisle. The coal-mine ambiance of the altar would remain.

Daddy turned to the little man beside him and whispered, "We're going to have to wing it. I'll start." The passion of his clergy calling rising in him, the uncle nodded. Somehow, they'd make this work.

Daddy's solemn, rumbling voice started, "Dearly beloved, we are gathered here," and continued until he ran out of gas. Pausing, he kept his eyes on the happy couple, smiling benignly. After a few moments, his superannuated helper picked up, in a surprisingly strong voice, continuing the words of the historic ceremony. After a bit, he fell silent, and Daddy, after allowing an appropriate pause, carried on. And so it went through the ceremony. When they reached the final instruction of "Husband, you may kiss your bride," they were easily as happy as the bride and groom standing in front of them.

During the reception, guests gushed congratulations to Daddy and the uncle for the beautiful way they worked together to make the wedding so memorable. They bubbled over about how much effort such intricate coordination must have required. Daddy and the uncle just smiled.

Daddy, of course, performed the wedding ceremonies for each of us kids. When Charles and Nancy's turn at the altar arrived, Nancy didn't know what to expect from her future father-in-law. She wasn't about to say anything about "obeying," but how do you bring that up to a man you hardly know—who's partial to the guy you don't intend to obey and who will be a large part of your life ever after? What if he's old school? How could she politely decline a time-honored part of the ceremony without raising hackles? It put her in a bit of a tizzy.

As the participants gathered for the wedding rehearsal, Nancy mentally rehearsed various approaches to the subject. As she fretted, Daddy came over and asked, "You don't want to include that part about obeying, do you?"

Except for her stint in the pulpit after Daddy's heart attack, Mother had been away from her clergy calling for a very long three years. It seemed more like an eternity. So, although still battling constant fatigue, she applied for Methodist ordination. After a summer at Garrett Seminary near Chicago completing an "intensive training" course, she dragged home, sleep deprived, head spinning. Cram courses are killing for people whose vitality tank sits perpetually on empty, but she made the cut.

Bishop Werner ordained her, like Daddy, as an approved supply. As in Daddy's case, her Salvation Army training and twenty-nine years of service counted no more than if she came to the ministry as years as secretary or teacher. And again, the rules disappointed her, but, few other places offered anything to middle-aged women. Besides, being clergy again meant more to her than any details. Especially since the Bishop assigned her to her own church in Neelysville, nine miles northwest of Beverly along scenic Route 60.

A challenge accompanied the opportunity. Mother didn't have a license to drive so she could get to Neelysville. But she'd driven years before, persuading her she could again. After a few practice runs with Daddy, she went for the test.

She breezed through the written portion of the driving test and confidently expected to sail just as smoothly through the road portion as well. And so she did—until the officer ordered her to parallel park. Why would she want to do that?

She explained to the officer she needed a license only to drive to her little country church in Neelysville. Its wide, gravel driveway didn't require parallel parking; everybody just pulled off to the side. Coming back to Beverly, she continued, she'd pull into our driveway and park there. So, she earnestly—and optimistically—concluded, given the parameters of her driving, she really had no need to parallel park.

Somehow, the officer didn't see it her way and again ordered her to demonstrate her qualifications for the coveted license by parallel parking in the appointed space. She panicked, a side-effect of her health problems that came roaring to life whenever she felt pressed, and she missed the parking slot by a mile. No license.

She took the driving test two or three more times, but the first failure did her in. Panic took over just getting to the test location. She must have felt overwhelming defeat. She who had faced down anything and anybody, now lived at the mercy of her unreliable nerves.

However, "ours not to reason why; ours but to do or die" and all that. Barney, she announced, would drive her on Sundays, and he or Daddy could drive whenever she had to get to her church during the week. Daddy twitted her a little about "sheep stealing," since the Sunday driving took Barney away from the Beverly church.

The Neelysville church adventure went swimmingly, to use Mother's phrase. The people loved her; she loved the people. Lots of good things happened in the church and in the lives of its members. But this wonderful time lasted only two years.

Even by the greatest dint of will, she could not summon up the energy to continue.

She kept her ordination, preaching here and there upon rare occasion, but Mother's full-time, active service days had ended. She accepted it as God's direction.

We never knew exactly what assailed Mother's health. The problems started with the severe head trauma she suffered when the drunk driver nearly killed her. That so-called accident impacted her life for all the years that followed. Striving with grit and tenacity against the vicious undertow of fatigue, she simply could not overcome her constant exhaustion. All because some evil fool chose to get behind the wheel drunk.

We lost the irreplaceable Stubby when he got out of the house, decided to chase a car and, slowed by age, ended up under its wheels. He left an amazing legacy for a squirt of a dog. Just say "Stubby" and all of us break into smiles, the stories start and pretty soon, we're laughing. We should have bronzed his mutilated toy cigar as a memorial.

CLEVELAND
(COLLINWOOD) OHIO

After eight years in Beverly, Daddy and Mother moved to Collinwood Methodist Church in Cleveland. None of us knows why. The most likely scenario is the Bishop asked for help in a place he thought they could make a difference, and they offered to give it their best try. That sounds the most like them.

However the decision got made, Collinwood presented a dying situation too far gone for resuscitation.

The church huddled in a small corner of a city block otherwise occupied by Collinwood High School. Squeezed more and more by the school and the surrounding growth of businesses, with aging, limited facilities, Collinwood Church's older, inactive congregation dwindled weekly as people died or moved to the suburbs. Caught in an ebb tide, Collinwood slowly drifted toward the oblivion that would arrive a few years later.

On their moving-in day, I drove down from Detroit to help. I shanked up the front walk, trailing a few feet behind two moving company men who had also just arrived. They had no idea I walked behind them. When Mother came barreling out the front door, arms widespread, saying "Oh, honey, I'm so glad you're here," her wavering voice suggesting tears would follow shortly, they stopped dead in their tracks thinking she meant them. While they stood motionless, puzzling over her intentions, she blew right past them to get to me—much to their obvious, grinning relief.

Mother had moved into her first pig sty. Army rules and regs ordered the quarters be left white-glove clean for the next officer. The Methodist's more *laissez faire* approach didn't edict such things, but the people in the Beverly church, as in most, made sure the parsonage welcomed new ministers. The Collinwood parsonage, though, appeared not to have experienced even scant acquaintance with cleaning implements or materials for a very long time.

The encrudded refrigerator bothered Mother the most, so as she instructed the relieved moving men about what went where, I attacked the refrigerator. To kill the various and sundry living organisms, I started with a round of lavishly sloshed bleach, then followed with soapy water, scouring vigorously with a variety of brushes sized and shaped to reach into every crevice. The refrigerator almost seemed to shrink back from this attack of foreign substances threatening its putrid integrity. It took four muscle-straining hours to make the refrigerator safe for food.

Then came the stove. Since the previous residents had obviously approached that appliance upon only rare occasion, it hadn't yet attained the refrigerator's status of total blight. However, since the usage, though infrequent, clearly excluded the wiping up of spills and splatters, I still had to muscle away on it for an hour or two. For three days, from sun up to well past sundown, I cleaned.

My maximum effort achieved two excellent results: I relieved my parents of the work and stress of an almost uninhabitable house, and my normal sixty-hour week as a Systems Engineer at IBM started to look pretty cushy.

Collinwood school and church sat at the point where five streets met, a confluence that provided the area's Five Points name. The streets, especially the two leading directly toward the church, had small, well-patronized stores and shops crowded along them for several blocks.

During the Christmas shopping season, Daddy decided to advertise the church via the bell-tower speakers. Each day at noon, he turned them on and played a half-hour of Christmas Carols on the church's wonderful organ. Given the quality of both the organ and organist, it made for a nice midday concert for Five Point shoppers and workers—and a time for Daddy to do something he loved: Make music. He hoped it might get people to notice the church and think about attending.

One day during my Christmas visit, he came into the house with the mail—and a surprised, pleased expression. Holding out some letters, he said "They're sending requests!" As he hoped, people noticed his brief, daily concerts—and started to ask for their favorite carols.

But no new faces joined the congregation. Their jobs required Five Points employees to drive there each day, but without a paycheck to lure them, they didn't return on Sundays.

When the Bishop called, after just a year, to offer Daddy a move to the Malvern charge, they were more than ready to go. The condition of the parsonage when they arrived had proved to be a metaphor for everything else.

The Collinwood members, pleasant in a chilled, camaraderie-on-ice sort of way, expected church life to be only and ever about them. They expected to have their desires satisfied by others without any obligation for reciprocity, insisting they had given more than their fair share of time, talent and treasure in years gone by. Now "the younger people" should shoulder the load. They didn't offer any suggestions about where those young sprites might be hidden in the sea of congregational grey hair. Daddy's smiling suggestions that being alive meant God still had things for them to do fell on deaf ears.

Daddy and Mother gave their customary all-out effort in Collinwood, but with members who chose to remain aloof to both visitors—potential new members—and service on the host of committees that make up Methodist life, progress fell under the heading of wishful thinking. Even Daddy and Mother's most charming and beguiling words couldn't rouse the members into making an ounce of effort to gain the prize of becoming more than they were. Comfort zones are killers.

The "frozen chosen" congregation's self-engrossed attitude produced only death rattles. They never grasped the reality that they could change the church's destiny by simply caring about others.

Malvern, Ohio

Daddy and Mother arrived in Malvern in time to dedicate the new parsonage, a handsome one-story brick house with generous rooms and a full, finished basement. After Collinwood, Mother declared herself transported straight to parsonage heaven.

Mother's delight pleased the church members. Her talent for decorating made their buttons pop as they ogled the beauty of the sturdy home they worked so hard to build. And since Mother's idea of preparing for company included cleaning back to the walls, closets and all, members realized the house would remain forever new in her care. Everybody was delighted.

Again, the parsonage revealed the church. Members participated fully, appreciated Daddy and each other, and worked together toward all they hoped the church could be.

The Malvern Youth Group invited Daddy to join their hay ride, a singular honor for any preacher, let alone one their grandfathers' age. Along with the invitation, several of the teenagers made a point to tell him they sure hoped he'd come. How could he say no?

Perhaps he should have checked into local hay ride customs. Arriving at the appointed time and place, he saw an open buckboard with no side walls to lean against and just enough hay to give the ride its name, not nearly enough to cushion the bumps. His fellow hay-riders yelled enthusiastic greeting huzzahs, bulldozing any possibility of turning back. So everybody clambered aboard, the driver fired up the tractor and off they went, lumping and bumping their way into the brisk, starry night.

In what turned out to be the accustomed style of Malvern hay rides, they traversed unpaved country roads for hour upon hour. No brief, perfunctory jaunt this. Nosirreebob! They hit every unpaved road in the county—or so it seemed.

Daddy joined in the banter and singing, trying to ignore the fact his body shrieked its unhappiness with every bump. a travail that grew louder and screechier with each mile. But paying attention to his body's lament and missing the fun, struck him as a waste of a wonderful opportunity. How often does a grandfather get to hang with the teens?

At the hay ride's end, with great force of will, he dropped gracefully off the buckboard and walked casually—with no sign of unhappy, aging joints—to his car. But by the next morning, force of will had nothing to do with anything; his body pretty much matched the buckboard—stiff and unyielding. Just rolling out of bed turned into several minutes of torture. As he hobbled down the hall for breakfast, Daddy decided he had a pressing obligation to spend the day studying and preparing his sermon, activities requiring, by coincidence, no more physical effort than sitting at his desk.

But he always smiled in retelling his adventure. He said if it weren't for the honor of the thing, he would have said "no," but we knew, if asked, he'd do it again. Without hesitation.

Some of the kids milled around the church after Vacation Bible School ended for the day, so Daddy suggested a game of baseball in the large field separating the church and the parsonage. The kids pointed out, half in sorrow and half in the hope Daddy could whomp up some kind of miracle, the lack of enough players to fill two rosters. Besides that, a stray mutt (Well, actually, he belonged to some people a couple of blocks away, but he acted like a stray.), a semipermanent fixture around the church, always got in the middle of things, darting around, barking and generally making it hard to play. Not a problem, announced Daddy; they'd solve both problems by letting the dog play the outfield. For both teams.

While Daddy's solution to the problem was not quite up there with the healing of lepers, the kids instantly saw the genius of his plan. The stray turned from problem to asset. Daddy split the kids into teams and called, "Play ball!"

Purists might recoil from describing the frivolity that ensued as the hallowed game of baseball, but the participants had a wonderful time cheering each other on and encouraging the dog with loud descriptions of the finer points of fielding— which only incited him into ever greater frenzies of barking. The dog's whirling paroxysms encouraged the kids to call out more instructions, which further incited the dog, and round, and round—a rising spiral of cacophony urging everybody forward.

The idea of using the same outfielder for both teams worked well since nobody could convince the dog to leave the field and running anywhere near him could leave you with a cast on one limb or another for the rest of the summer.

Whenever the four-legged outfielder "caught" the ball, Daddy had to go out and coax him, with much scratching behind the ears, to surrender it. Upon rare occasion, the dog would voluntarily return the ball to a player, generating exuberant cheers from his human team mates. This, like the fielding instructions, launched the dog into whirling, barking spasms of delight.

Everybody had a grand time—perhaps especially the dog, what with all the unaccustomed attention, cheering and petting he received. The daily ball game became an integral part of VBS that year. No matter how many kids showed up to play, though, the dog covered the outfield. How does one explain the concept of being benched to a dog?

Daddy and Mother went to London where Daddy served as a delegate to The World Methodist Conference. They added time for a vacation, going from place to place so Daddy could, at last, meet Mother's family and friends.

Before their trip, Daddy asked if I wanted him to bring something back for me. I said I'd love to own a pewter tea service. I set a price range but left the details to his good taste.

Once in England, Mother declared the tea service an immediate priority lest they not find anything nice later in the trip. They soon found pewter perfection. Turning down the store's shipping service, she wanted the store to deliver the set to their hotel. She didn't want to trust their overseas service, and she wanted to avoid the necessity of returning to pick up their purchase later. Carting a few pieces of pewter around wouldn't be a problem, she declared, so they'd take it with them on their travels.

The store promptly sent two men along to the hotel with the tea service, solidly packed, heavily taped for shipping and clearly labeled for customs. The plan seemed to be working, but when they prepared to head out for their next destination, lifting the box buckled Daddy's knees. His sudden weakness perplexed Mother, but after momentary consideration, she announced it simply proved he wasn't as young as he used to be. That encouraging thought, of course, pleased Daddy no end.

Every time they traveled to a new place, Daddy groaned inwardly at the thought of hoisting that box. He didn't bother to complain out loud, lest Mother launch into her getting old speech. He simply grappled the box into his grip and started a bowlegged march to whatever public transportation would take them to their next stop.

Near the end of their month's vacation—and its many opportunities to wrestle with the dreaded box—the store located them after a frantic search. With profuse apologies they announced there had been a mix-up. The box Daddy had hauled over half of England contained a complete set of Wedgwood china, with service for twelve, the weighty equivalent of a crate of cinder blocks. So much for getting old and weak.

Poor Daddy.

After four years in Malvern, Daddy and Mother accepted a move to Hayesville, Ohio. I drove down to do the packing, by now our customary practice.

Mother's health had continued its slide. One evening as we cleaned up after dinner, she fell against me, mumbling she felt faint. Using the considerable lung power I inherited from Daddy, I started bellowing for help as I wrestled to get her down the hall and into bed. She struggled against my efforts, saying I shouldn't strain myself in my late stage of pregnancy. It would have made a physical comedy classic, with me loudly caterwauling for help as the two of us staggered and bumped our way, at cross-purposes, down the long hall.

HAYESVILLE, OHIO

Hayesville memories come only as a brief blur. Daddy and Mother lived there for a single, uneventful year.

With the move to Hayesville, Grandma Dowdell shifted from visiting for several months each year to being a full-time member of the family. She brought along her bedroom furniture and a few favored chairs. Since only the largest bedroom in the Hayesville parsonage afforded adequate space for it all, Daddy and Mother squeezed into the next largest bedroom—although "large," in this instance, suggests a quite misleading and fulsome description. Almost wall-to-wall with furniture, one traversed their bedroom via narrow slits of space which might generously be called aisles had Daddy or Mother been the size of, say, the average five-year-old. Getting from bed to dresser to closet required the focus and precision of threading a needle, the penalty for failure being barked shins and stubbed toes.

And when we kids came to visit, bringing along spouses and offspring, we slept in the room Charles's wife, Nancy, dubbed "the closet." That cozy room held, in close proximity, a double bed and a dresser. No chairs. Even a wastebasket took too much floor space.

The bed, longer than the room was wide, fit only along the euphemistically described "long" walls of the room. Placed on the windowed long wall, it blocked access to the closet. When pushed to the opposite wall, several inches of mattress overlapped the door to the hall, which meant, of course, no door-closing would be going on.

Only a sliver of space separated the bed and the dresser. The dresser's bottom drawers jammed against the bed after opening just a crack, requiring the blind insertion of a hand into the drawer, followed by groping to select items by feel. The upper dresser drawers opened all the way, but you had to stand on the bed—or play PlasticMan—to use them. Mother decided the limited access to the dresser meant the closet had to be usable. The bed would overlap the door, privacy, unfortunately, be hanged. Which meant, speaking of hanging, the men of the family slept with feet stuck out for hallway display.

Grandchildren bunked downstairs on the living room floor atop beds of quilts and comforters.

The three bedrooms' diminutive dimensions might at least partially explain Daddy and Mother's short residency. "The closet" limited visits to one of us at a time, and the remote, makeshift accommodations for quite young grandchildren concerned everybody. Worse yet, Daddy and Mother's bedroom daily tested the fortitude of their shins, leaving them black and blue.

My first trip to Hayesville, to show off six-month-old Joanna, took me into an unpredicted, swirling and blowing March blizzard, virtually a whiteout. Visibility ended a few inches in front of the windshield. My headlights did nothing to pierce the dark night or the swirling tempest. Unable to see the road, let alone any road markings, on the unfamiliar freeway, I realized the intensity of the treacherous storm made it foolish to keep going. I decided to get off the freeway and find a motel. I would finish the trip in the morning.

But as I strained to see the road, I could make out each snow-covered exit only as I passed it. As time stretched on, Joanna started crying in the back seat. I couldn't reach her.

Meanwhile, local drivers, familiar with the road, zipped past me as if driving at high noon on a balmy spring day. They passed within inches of stripping off the side of my car and cut back into my lane, if indeed I was in a lane, dangerously close as they sailed along the temporarily unmarked freeway. Equating familiarity with visibility, many piled it up, making it a busy night for police and tow trucks. Sirens and revolving red and blue lights increased my tension to terror.

Joanna's screaming escalated along with her hunger. Surrounded by the local demolition derby crowd and unable to determine a possible location for the side of the road, I couldn't risk stopping. I needed to somehow find a way to get off that freeway before Joanna and I became statistics.

Meanwhile, Daddy and Mother waited for us in Hayesville, agonizing. Finally, Mother could stand it no longer and ordered Daddy to get in the car and go find me, to "lead me in." While Daddy would willingly have risked any storm for any of us at any age, he had no idea where I could be, what route I had taken or how to find me. He only knew I was somewhere out there in a record-setting blizzard, in the night, with my new baby, so they prayed.

That made three of us.

As I frantically searched for an exit, with Joanna's shrieking cries all but turning her inside out by now, a sudden lull in the storm, which some might call a coincidence, allowed me to see the next exit in time to take it—and to also read the exit sign. It was the exit to Hayesville. Thankfully, the lull continued the rest of the way.

Daddy and Mother heard me tap the horn as I turned into the driveway between the parsonage and the church. They burst out of the house before I rolled to a stop. With our safe arrival, relief flowed like a river. We prayed a fervent prayer of thanksgiving as soon as we got indoors.

Not many minutes later, rattling windows announced the return of the storm's fury. It roared through the night, abating only as the sun broke through the darkness.

Daddy took college classes just about everywhere we lived. While in Hayesville, a Methodist college, SMU if I remember correctly, put together his many credits—probably enough for multiple degrees—and awarded him his long-sought sheepskin.

East Springfield, Ohio

East Springfield, a little town with a population of maybe a thousand hardy souls—on a day when everybody stays home—lies nowhere in any sort of proximity to Springfield, Ohio, as its name might suggest, but more than 250 miles to the northeast. The tiny town included an older, but homey and comfortable, parsonage and two Methodist churches.

Christ Methodist met in an attractive, well-maintained white clapboard building in town while The Church of the Cross held services in a new, brick building out on State Route 43, just a few miles away. The Church of the Cross built their new facilities, not many years before Daddy and Mother arrived, when they had a denominational connection to Evangelical United Brethren. Shortly after the building's dedication, the EUB church merged with the Methodists to become The United Methodist Church. Thus it came to be that little East Springfield had two active, thriving Methodist churches, each with their own history and well-loved building.

The Bishop believed it made sense to consolidate the two congregations, almost within spitting distance of each other, and asked Daddy to see about making it happen. The Bishop, however, hadn't taken a close up look at the situation. Both congregations shared a common theology, actively pursued their faith and energetically lived it out. However, along with everything they had in common, each church had its own memories, methods and approaches. Neither church could be faulted, but they didn't present good merger material.

Daddy described the style and history of each church to the Bishop and said he believed forcing them to unite would end up destroying both. The Bishop accepted his analysis, and Daddy served both churches. Talks of unification have occurred a few times since, but the churches remain happily separate—and thriving—to this day, each now with its own pastor.

At the time, Mother lived a dogless life, an unhappy state of affairs for her, if not for Grandma Dowdell. One night, in the deepest dark of the night, some dastardly soul threw a bag of newborn kittens onto the parsonage lawn. Mother discovered them the next morning. As one who mourned the necessity of swatting even a mosquito, she, though not a cat person, reacted with a righteous wrath about such an inhumane act.

She cleaned and fluffed the discarded little things and began finding homes, successfully placing all but one. Her best salesmanship, usually so effective with its commingling of sweetness and steel, failed to win that final home. Sending the cat to the animal shelter amounted to a death sentence, so Mother became a cat owner.

In keeping with her customs, she started training the cat to behave well and do tricks. She ignored the fact her other pets barked while this one meowed, performing her usual tried-and-true training routine. In a short time, with little apparent effort, Mother trained that cat to be a dog.

Cats don't make very good dogs.

The housebreaking added a nice touch since it did away with the need to deal with a litter box, although the cat's sniff—apparently the cat equivalent of a bark, took a sharp auditory sense to detect. Fortunately, the cat had enough regard—some might say awe—for Mother to hold everything until somebody noticed and opened the door to let him out.

Other feats met with varying, usually lesser, degrees of success. When enjoined to sit up and beg for a treat, the cat looked like a petite, furry Tower of Pisa during an earthquake. He stayed on his haunches, bobbing and weaving until the treat came his way, but nobody ever remarked on the grace and beauty of his accomplishment.

The same with the rolling over trick. Dogs, when told to roll over, pull their legs into the tuck position and do a snappy little roll. Cats, however, don't have an instinctive appreciation of the tuck position. They wobble over with all appendages flopping haphazardly, a spectacularly ungainly, slow motion achievement of the near-impossible. As long as he got a treat, though, the cat seemed willing to do his rollover flop all day.

The heeling portion of cat's repertoire worked well, though it took some getting used to for cat people. It looked weird—the only possible word—to observe a cat, a species known for their disregard, even arrogance, concerning humans, obediently strut close to Mother's heels as she walked around the garden.

Mother even sought to impart guard dog—or guard cat in this instance—skills. It's difficult to see how a hard-sniffing cat would warn the family or scare an intruder, but guarding constituted an integral part of the skill set Mother deemed necessary. I never witnessed the guard cat in action, so I can't say how well it all went, but I'm confident Mother had the best guard cat ever—for what that's worth.

Both Mother and the cat had a fine time. Indeed, through the astonished word-of-mouth of parsonage visitors, the cat who thought himself to be a dog became something of a local celebrity. To top it all off, Grandma didn't grump about cats. Well, at least not much. When grasping for a conversational topic, she sometimes verbally landed there, but with no serious intent.

Each summer, Daddy and Mother took a vacation swing across the country visiting children. Flo's boys—and, in turn, my son—excitedly joined their Grandpa in a game of "Last Tag Finnies" during every visit. Nobody knows the origin of the game, what "finnies" means or, for that matter, exactly how it's spelled, but they all enjoyed it immensely. The game's entirety consists of touching another player, crossing your fingers so they can't tag you back and calling out, "Last tag finnies." No score is kept, and the game has no known conclusion.

Finnies started immediately upon Grandpa's arrival, continued throughout his stay and stopped only when his car rolled down the street headed out of town.

Grandchildren somehow learned about Daddy's amazing punctuality almost before they could walk. One day, expecting him at any moment, Flo's boys stood along the wall by the front door, which would hide them when opened, ready to jump out and tag Grandpa the moment he arrived. Well, that day Grandpa didn't arrive on schedule, but the boys maintained their positions, not moving a muscle or making a sound—which might, after all, be a dead giveaway of their position. After an hour of watching her sons silently standing ramrod stiff, with no idea of just when Daddy would finally arrive, Flo tried to coax them away to read, watch TV, anything. No go. TV they could watch any day, but they could hardly ever surprise Grandpa with "last tag finnies."

He finally arrived about an hour and a half late—car trouble, as I remember. The boys leapt out from behind the door chorusing, "Last tag finnies," as he reacted with great feigned surprise, and the game commenced.

Daddy introduced my son, Matt, to finnies early in life. Early enough that Matt couldn't voluntarily cross his fingers but had to use one hand to move the fingers of the other into the crossed position. Recognizing a handicap, he started to keep the fingers on both hands in an almost constant cross. Every once in a while, he'd uncross them to let the game continue, tag and get tagged a few times, then laboriously recross his fingers. Each night after he fell asleep, I'd tiptoe into his room to uncross his fingers.

After a few days, though, I noticed Matt's malleable little finger bones developing a permanent curvature. Keeping his fingers uncrossed for the night didn't provide enough straightening time. I announced that the dinner table, for all meals, would be a last-tag-finnies-free zone. Everybody happily complied, especially Matt who had been having more than a little difficulty handling his eating utensils—new to him in any case—with crossed fingers.

After my edict, we always knew when Matt planned to depart from the table. He signaled his intentions by beginning the arduous process of crossing his fingers. He might overlook excusing himself, but he never forgot to cross his fingers.

Daddy and his mother continued to discuss which foods were good for one's disposition, with Grandma still insisting cheap, plain, cake-style, grocery-store donuts met her every dietary requirement. He argued the cause for more nutritional foods, but she grumpily refused change. So he tried to limit the doughnut supply, which, not surprisingly, didn't work.

If he didn't bring doughnuts home from grocery shopping forays, she'd make life miserable, whining—to use an unfortunate but accurate word—about the lack of love being shown to her. So, he'd buy some doughnuts and try to ration then, which only brought on the second verse of the same song. Grandma had Olympic gold medal whining skills, and nobody ever reached the limit of her stamina for the task.

You can take a stand on some points. On others, you realize it would be an exercise in futility. Daddy knew winning an argument about dietary failings with a mule-stubborn, cantankerous women in her middle eighties—especially your mother who thinks she's still in charge—landed squarely in the not-going-to-happen category. The doughnuts made a permanent return.

In the end, she ate all the doughnuts she wanted, along with as much meat and vegetables as Daddy could persuade her to accept. He jollied with her. He joked with her. He pleaded with her. Nothing doing. She wanted doughnuts—with perhaps chocolates, pie or cake for dessert to add a little variety.

Grandma's digestive system started to cause trouble, including much pain. Daddy made an appointment with the doctor and clued the doctor in about Grandma's donut fixation, suggesting a conversation about diet and nutrition. At the end of the visit, the doctor told Grandma, "Now, I don't want you to eat cookies, pies, cakes or candy. Promise me you won't." Acting like a stereotypical sweet, grey-haired grandmother the doctor apparently presumed her to be, she agreed. He asked again, adding a few more high-sugar treats to the list, and she agreed again.

As soon as they got back in the car, though, Grandma announced, a glowing self-satisfaction lighting her pugnacious expression, "He didn't say anything about doughnuts, so I can still eat all the doughnuts I want, and you can't stop me." Daddy tried to reason with her. He offered to take her back into the doctor's office so she could ask him about the doughnuts herself. She wouldn't budge. She had her answer, and she planned to stick with it.

Whether the doughnuts did it or not, Grandma developed colon cancer. During her last days, she continually called out for Josephine—Mother—the daughter-in-law she had always treated with disdain.

By now, Daddy did all the cooking and laundry. Mother helped with the dishes and did what housework she could manage. As long as she didn't overtire herself, she didn't appear sick. She participated in church activities, glad-hand-ing—her specialty—and making people feel welcome.

As time went on, Daddy found it harder and harder to do all he wanted to do, even though church members expressed their great satisfaction. While his work exceeded their expec-tations, his lack of energy bothered him. He never faced weakness before—and he would never welcome it into his life—so dealing with limitations vexed him.

Meanwhile, Mother had fallen in love with California during visits to Flo and Ed. She kept "hinting," with her usual lack of subtlety, about her desire to move there. The sledgeham-mer hints and his lack of energy finally got to Daddy, and he decided to retire. Since the Army had taken away his pension and he hadn't been with the Methodist Church long enough to build much of one, it would be financially difficult. He needed to produce some income.

He wrote to the Methodist Church's California Conference about part-time opportunities. They responded with a full-time opportunity in the middle of the desert—where the parson-age would be a mobile home. Neither the full-time aspect nor the mobile home housing enticed either of my parents. If he wanted full-time work, he'd happily stay in East Springfield. And Daddy didn't like to be in small spaces. Mother said the desert would turn her skin into leather without getting her close to Flo and the grandchildren. Daddy declined the job.

Then came an offer to be a part-time minister of visitation at First United Methodist Church of Huntington Beach, known as FUMCHUB to the members. Daddy met with the minister, Ed Erny, and found a good man he'd enjoy working with. Freeways would take them from Huntington Beach almost to Flo's door in a half-hour or so. He took the job.

Back in Ohio, Daddy told the Bishop of his retirement plans. Then, after four years as their pastor, he told his congregations.

They rented a no-pets-allowed Huntington Beach townhouse, so once again Mother sought a good home for the cat. It proved to be a cinch this time around. That cat's kind of entertainment doesn't come along every day.

When Daddy's retirement date arrived that June, we all gathered at the nearest Holiday Inn to celebrate. We had Daddy and Mother stay at the motel with us so they could share in our nonstop good times. Joe arrived in absolutely peak form and kept our ribs aching with laughter. Of course, we all joined in with our can-you-top-this attempts, but Joe outdid our best efforts without even breaking a sweat. Doing all of his around-the-world accents that could fool a native, he piled one joke on another in his rapid, stream-of-consciousness style. He went on for hours, taking us on a long, rambling journey into the bizarre and hilarious.

The rapid-fire repartee seemed to take the edge off of Daddy's need to walk away from something he loved. How can you wax nostalgic when you can't stop laughing? Or when you're trying to think of a topper?

On Saturday afternoon, we gathered by the pool. Some swam, and some sunned and talked. I kept an eagle-eye on two-year-old Matt, always as fast as a greased eel toward anything he found interesting—and he found everything interesting. As he got near the pool, I dropped into the water three or four steps away from him. Sure enough, he got too close to the edge and fell in. As I hauled him up into my arms, I congratulated him over and over on his wonderful dive. Terrified, he stared at me in wonder, but I wanted to keep him from the fear of water that had dogged me ever since I almost drowned in Trenton's canal.

As we climbed out of the pool and headed toward the family gathering, two people approached me at different points in my walk to congratulate me on the way I handled the situation. When I reached Daddy's chair, he wanted to know what they said to me. If they had been unkind, he intended to do something about it. Here we were, a grown daughter and her not-very-well father who still intended to protect his little girl from thoughtless people. I love you, too, Daddy.

On Sunday, we filled two pews at each of the churches. Good preacher's kids, we joined in enthusiastically. After the services we circulated among the people as Mother proudly guided us around so we didn't miss greeting a single soul.

As usual, I did the packing. By now I had a never-anything-broken record to defend. While Daddy finished up loose odds and ends at the churches, Mother sat and watched me pack, reminiscing about where she got each item and what it meant to her.

As we chatted, I noticed an almost imperceptible tremor in her left hand, a slight rolling motion. It surprised her when I mentioned it. She hadn't noticed the unintentional activity before.

HUNTINGTON BEACH, CALIFORNIA

Daddy's enthusiasm for his Minister of Visitation job moderated in fairly short order. For one thing, the gas to zing all over northern Orange County drank significant chunks of money. Maps hadn't kept up with the area's growth, making it a challenge to find the homes he planned to visit. Worst of all, he'd drive for miles to an appointment only to find nobody home. The California custom of making appointments without any intention of keeping them frustrated him no end.

While draining the gas tank getting lost trying to find an inexplicably vacant house sapped his energy, he did meet some wonderful people, many of whom became a regular part of the church—and of his life as well.

Meanwhile, a lady at the church approached Mother about teaching a Sunday School class of senior adults, "The Merry Methodists." The previous teacher moved away, and the dwindling class approached extinction. Without Mother, she implied, doom appeared certain.

Well, how could she say no? The lady's plea created a combination of a red flag taunting a bull with the sound of a fire bell rousing a fire horse—not to compare Mother with bulls or horses, but to explain the irresistible impetus to meet the challenge.

In short order, the class overflowed with members. Mother glad-handed them, helped them be part of a family away from home, honored everybody's birthday and taught a heck of a Bible lesson. Of course they came.

The tremor in Mother's hand grew more pronounced, and the doctor told her she had Parkinson's Disease, a specifically devastating diagnosis. Growing up, Mother knew a family friend, Mr. Appleby, who had had Parkinson's for twenty-five years. He spent most of those years bedridden and unable to speak. His ordeal terrified her young heart and made Parkinson's the one disease she feared. Cancer didn't frighten her. Heart disease caused no alarm. Name a malady, any malady, and she could deal with it—except for this one. The mountain might be steep and treacherous, but she would climb it, her faith overcoming any disquiet. But Parkinson's?

Struggling through her horror at the diagnosis took a while. For the first time in her life, doubt separated her from God. Could he really love her and yet require her to grapple with the monster she feared? Did the very precision of this hit have significance? Since God had to know Parkinson's loomed as her one and only fear, why didn't he protect her from it?

She and Daddy prayed. She prayed alone. She read her Bible. She wrestled for understanding and finally reached a place of certainty that God did care, he did love her and he would be with her, whatever happened.

But then a new snake slithered in to test her peace. Did her period of doubt mean she didn't have enough faith? Why had she let her crippling reaction control her? With enough faith, she wondered, shouldn't she experience equanimity, not doubt and fear? More darkness.

At that point, we arrived from Connecticut for a visit. Every first time visitor to Southern California seems compelled to visit Tijuana, and we invited her to join us. Warned against driving even an inch into Mexico, we parked on the U. S. side of the border and walked in, a significant hike.

Joanna and Matt walked with their father; I walked with Mother. As we walked, she confided her fears to me. She asked if her doubts meant she lacked faith. She reminded me the Bible says to always rejoice. She wanted to hear what I understood the Bible to say about it all. Sharing theology on a theoretical basis is child's play compared with reaching out to someone you love who is in spiritual pain. I poured out everything I had to offer.

I told her the Bible doesn't say to rejoice about any and all circumstances, but to rejoice in the fact we can depend on God regardless of life's ups and downs—which point she had already reached. I reminded her of Jesus's enormous pain when he realized his time—his test—had come and likened it to her original reaction. I talked about Jesus hanging on that dreadful cross, feeling God had abandoned him. I asked if she thought she had to be less human than Jesus. I said faith isn't something you measure. Never a matter of more or less—or of not enough—faith simply is or it isn't. You have faith or you don't have faith, and Mother always had faith, even in her darkest days.

It's a long walk into Tijuana, and we talked the entire way. By the time we reached town, we were able to laugh about whether, given the nature of Tijuana, that dusty stretch had ever heard a deeply theological discussion before. We concluded life held too many difficulties to assume any inch of the globe hadn't witnessed somebody reaching out to God.

Our talk seemed to help her spirit, but the walk obviously taxed her. We suggested that rather than hoof it back to the border, we pile into a cab. Mother too quickly agreed, saying she didn't think she could make it on foot. She had never waved the white flag of surrender before, and it surprised me by kicking me in the stomach. That was one tough day.

After two years of driving hither and yon tracking down church visitors, Daddy submitted his resignation. He spent almost full-time hours on it, most of the income went to gas stations and it wore him out, upping his nitro intake. Most significantly, Ed Erny retired. Daddy said the new minister, Al Jansen—Rev. Al—should be allowed to choose his own team.

About the same time, Mother realized the Parkinson's Disease was gaining ground, and she could no longer teach The Merry Methodists. Daddy took over the teaching—the part that exhausted Mother—while Mother greeted people and made them feel welcome. Teaching a Sunday School class can't hold a candle to pulpit preaching, but Daddy liked the thought process and study of preparing a lesson.

The team arrangement grew the class even more. But the loss of income made finances too tight, although nobody outside the family ever knew.

Charles stayed with Daddy and Mother during his business trips to California. His stays extended for two or three weeks at a time, with Daddy preparing Charles's favorite meals, so Charles gave them the per diem he received.

To provide a little extra income for them on a more regular basis than his sporadic trips, he suggested we each send them money each month. Of course we all agreed.

A stay-at-home-mom, I no longer had workplace income. Fortunately, I had participated in the employee stock purchase plan during my IBM days. My dividends exactly matched—to the penny—the amount Charles suggested. When the check arrived every three months, I sent it off to California with great pleasure. And every time IBM increased the dividend, they increased Daddy and Mother's income.

Daddy had mixed emotions about the agreement. He hated taking money from us, thinking the flow should go the other way. But the added income was critical, and he delighted that we wanted to give it. Mother appreciated the solution to a problem.

Many evenings found Daddy playing raucous games of Rook at Flo and Ed's kitchen table, always Ed and second son, Mark, against Daddy and eldest son, Fred. Daddy and Fred played conservatively; Ed and Mark took more risks. Ed and Mark erupted in great huzzahs when a risk paid off, only to listen to cheers from Daddy and Fred when their game-playing derring-do sent them down in flames. Daddy and Fred reacted with appropriate laughter, cheers or moans as their play worked or failed. Overall, wins and losses came out fairly even—one team's score steady-as-she-goes; the other's up and down like a yo-yo. But it was really never about the game.

Besides teaching The Merry Methodists, Daddy joined the church choir. He formed a men's chorus, The King's Men. He discovered two other trombone players in the congregation and formed a trio to occasionally play special music in worship services. He also taught the confirmation classes that prepared eighth-graders for church membership. He left a trail of encouraged people in his wake every time he crossed the church campus. And he gave nicknames to just about everybody, a point of pride for the recipients.

Some members considered him the father they never had, a role that pleased him. Others, since Daddy cared enough to listen, used him as a sounding board. People whose lives he touched learned, with astonishment, the lengths to which he would go. But nobody, not even Mother, knew how many lives he changed.

One FUMCHUB member, Bill Yunek, the son of an alcoholic father who still, somehow or another—although a tip of the hat to wife Benita, and certainly to God, wouldn't be out of order—turned out wonderfully well, said, "To be around your father was like having the hand of God guiding and keeping us on course. I always felt so safe around him." Like many others, he alternates between referring to Daddy as "Sir Charles" and "Saint Charles."

Mother decided she and Daddy would enjoy playing Yahtzee. For her, who never played games, it was about an evening's sociability. However, Daddy's natural bent and his years of playing Dominos with Grandma—with her card shark instincts—inevitably gravitated to strategy.

Since Mother focused amiss on camaraderie alone, Daddy often surprised her by suddenly claiming victory—before she even came close to filling all the slots.

Stunned, she'd blurt out, "How did you do that so fast?"

With his Cheshire cat smile, Daddy purred, "God smiles on me."

Well, that would never do. As she harrumphed that God could not possibly prefer him with her in the game, Daddy smiled benignly. Getting excited brought some of her old zip back.

And so it went. From time to time, Daddy gave her tips on strategy, which she ignored. She didn't care enough about winning to act on them. But she also preferred that he not win. How they could play without either one winning presents a puzzlement, but the oft-used "God smiles on me" line never failed to pump her up.

Upon occasion Mother triumphed and started a lengthy season of gloating. Whether Daddy found yet another way to say, "I love you" or she won fair and square, as she obviously took for granted, the world will never know. Either way she won.

When Daddy and Mother's fiftieth anniversary appeared on the horizon, a church-based celebration seemed appropriate. Besides family, the church offered all they wanted from life. I started planning a service of celebration, followed by a buffet, at the church.

It takes a certain amount of patience to plan a California celebration from Connecticut, especially with participants strewn across the country from coast to coast. But a day or so before the event, we all gathered in Huntington Beach to give it a go.

I asked Charles to select some music and make us all a choir. Flo invited Ivor Bosanko, a Salvation Army musician of extraordinary talent to accompany us on the piano, one of his many instruments. Better than even his talent, he offered the superlative attitude of being a sympathetic accompanist, that is to say, he covered when the singers get lost or broke down. We practiced, briefly, during a planned interlude in our usual storytelling sessions.

Joe and wife, Jo Anne, arrived prepared to sing "Because." Barney came ready to read the Scripture. We'd all be in the choir. Everybody would participate.

And so the appointed time arrived. The family came down the aisle as the congregation, a full house, sang the opening hymn. The service rolled along. When the "choir," about twenty or so strong, rose to sing, I'm not sure what our listeners expected, but we knocked them off their seats. Charles set us up with music that sounded complicated, but wasn't. Also, Joe, Jo Anne, Charles, Nancy, Ed and Flo all had choir-trained voices, while the rest of us added enthusiastic, even tuneful, bulk for a full sound.

Then I spoke about my parents and what they meant to us, and the service ended.

My uninspired plans for the celebration are my one regret in my life with Daddy. Without thinking about all that could be, I came up with a vanilla service to celebrate two very non-vanilla lives. At the very least, I could have finished with, "And now a word from the master," and turned the service over to Daddy. He would have loved that and so would everybody else there. And perhaps Joe should have had some time to do his thing. The service would have run long, but it would have been one memorable night. So many possibilities, all thought about too late.

Sheesh! Fifty years, and all they got was vanilla.

Daddy and Matt spent a lot of their time together lavishing compliments on each other. Matthew adored his Grandpa, an emotion fully returned, and one which apparently required constant verbalization to encompass the full extent of their devotion. Only their sincerity kept nausea at bay amongst the rest of us.

We went to a steak house where baked potatoes came with every meal. My kids, having never tasted a baked potato, hated them. Daddy asked Matt if he would take just a taste of his potato "for Grandpa." Would he try his potato for Grandpa? Would he fly to the moon for Grandpa? He could think of nothing in the world—indeed, the universe—he wouldn't do for Grandpa.

One taste did it. Finishing his potato with gusto, he asked Joanna for hers. She wanted nothing to do with the potato, but voluntarily giving something desirable to a little brother would break a major big sister rule. Like it or not, she'd have to eat the potato. One taste hooked her.

After that, both kids loved baked potatoes.

Daddy and Mother decided to go to Conference at Lakeside during one of their cross-country vacation swings. A few days into their stay, Daddy had another heart attack, twenty-two years almost to the day from his first—which also happened in Lakeside. He ended up in a Cleveland hospital.

Joe's son, Joey—now Joe, Jr—was deputized to get Daddy's car from Lakeside and drive it to Joe's Chicago area home. A daunting assignment, what with the ink on his license barely dry, but both he and the car arrived in good shape. He still remembers his death grip on the wheel for the whole distance.

Flo and Ed flew to Chicago to drive the car back to California. They were barely out of Chicago when a deer, doing what deers do, leapt onto the Interstate right into them. Now, Daddy's car wasn't the stuff of any car buff's dreams, but he loved it. Flo, already distraught about Daddy's heart attack, cried all the way from Illinois to California.

After the hospital released Daddy, he and Mother flew back to California, Flo and Ed met their plane and life resumed as if normal.

But life refused to become normal again, and Daddy's doctor decided—finally—to do an angiogram. It revealed badly blocked veins, but surgeons could do nothing because the first heart attack, all those years ago, destroyed the back of his heart.

What a man! A major part of his heart gone, and he put the Energizer Bunny to shame for years. No wonder fatigue set in from time to time.

Since Daddy rarely spoke about himself, the folks at the church didn't know he had had a previous heart attack. They also had no idea the doctor told him it was just a matter of time, maybe eighteen months at the most, before he died.

But what's the sense of being alive if you don't live? So, Daddy went back to The Merry Methodists, the choir, the trombone trio, The King's Men, teaching confirmation classes and playing rook. He just rested a little longer between events.

A year after the big 50th anniversary celebration, we moved to Arizona, which made visiting Daddy and Mother a lot easier. We bumped up our East Coast biannual visiting schedule to visiting every few months.

One Saturday, during my regular weekend call, Daddy said Rev. Al had asked him to preach a few weeks hence. Since teaching and preaching back-to-back took more energy than he had, he needed a substitute teacher for the Merry Methodists to accept Rev. Al's offer.

Close enough now, I offered to drive out to teach the class. Visit Daddy and Mother. Get up to be in the front of the room and do my thing. Take the kids to the beach. That would work.

The class started. I spoke with authority. I added a dash or two of humor. I threw in some little known facts. The class sat becalmed, solemnly taking it all in. No reaction, no response.

Unaccustomed to audience placidity, I cranked it up with more humor, more body English. No response from any of the obviously misnamed Merry Methodists, only tranquil repose.

So I stepped it up a little more, about to break out the straw hat and cane for a little tap routine—which, since I don't tap dance, probably wouldn't have been such a great idea. Smack dab in the middle of giving it everything I had, I saw Daddy standing in the door—aglow as always when I spoke, but obviously tickled.

My bag of tricks depleted, I soldiered on to the end of the hour, still at full tilt but wondering how I could bomb so completely. As in crater. In fact, a large, deep abyss.

But after the class mercifully ended, the members all gathered round to say how much they enjoyed my lesson. When they had gone, Daddy, still smiling at the mismatch of the audience's quiescence in the face of my escalating exertion, told me the class never showed any response. Never. You claimed success if they paid attention. According to him, I was a hit.

From then on, I showed up to teach the class any time he had a chance to preach. I don't know if anybody ever noticed this "coincidence."

One time, FUMCHUB had "Preacher's Kid Sunday," and Daddy, a preacher's kid, gave the sermon. Jay Cairns, a man the age of us kids and one of Daddy's trombone cronies, sang. After the service I asked, since participation in the service was limited to preachers' kids, how did Jay get to sing? Was his father a preacher, too? Daddy beamed, put his arm around Jay's shoulders and announced he had adopted Jay just for the occasion. After that I called Jay, "Bro."

As Matt approached the kitchen where Daddy and I were discussing something or the other, he could hear we had taken opposite sides of an issue to have a discussion. While he had no idea of the topic, Matt didn't approve of anybody disagreeing with Grandpa. Even in a friendly chat. Even his mother.

As he walked toward us he said, "Grandpa's right." Reaching us, he said, "Grandpa's always right." Passing by us, he said, "Grandpa's perfect." We sat agape, our eyes following his progress, our conversation on hold, as Matt strolled by declaiming his emphatic, tripartite announcement.

As he disappeared down the hall, Daddy grinned and blurted out a heartfelt, "I love that boy!" What a fabulous, feet-first-off-the-end-of-the-dock relationship!

One Sunday Daddy arrived at FUMCHUB early, as usual. He noticed a newcomer, a young lady dressed all in red. He went to greet her. She held a toddler and appeared very pregnant—and very troubled. She told him her story.

Her husband left her the night before. She had no job, no money and no family anywhere nearby. She didn't know what to do, so she came to this nearby church looking for peace and, she hoped, a word from God.

Daddy took her under his wing. Calling her Little Red Riding Hood in honor of her outfit on the day they met, he became her Daddy for more than two years—until his death.

He helped her get assistance to tide her over. He found an attorney to prevent her husband from taking all the assets while leaving behind all the responsibilities. He offered guidance in her job search. He encouraged her dreams and built her confidence. And he refused to let her bog down in the middle of any rough patch. Instead, he helped her through it.

Except for occasional mentions of somebody called Little Red Riding Hood, nobody knew about any of it.

We made good time as we drove out to California for Christmas, arriving about an hour ahead of schedule. Flo told me Daddy and Mother weren't doing well, but she had understated the case by about at least a mile.

We came in the door just as Daddy finished preparing dinner, a piece of toast for each of them. He hadn't been able to get to the store, and the refrigerator was bare. The pantry held plenty of canned goods, but they required recipes and preparation. Daddy wasn't able to spend an hour or so puttering in the kitchen. He was exhausted, his skin an ashy gray.

Appalled, I chirped around like Little Sally Homemaker pretending not to notice the sad state of affairs. Saying a piece of toast wouldn't satisfy their hunger for long, I announced my intention to poach some eggs, which both Daddy and Mother liked, and make a salad. I sent my husband to the supermarket to get groceries, lots of groceries.

During our week's stay, I cooked meals and stocked the freezer. Daddy regained some color and a little energy. He started introducing me as "my daughter who saved my life" while I wished I could.

Daddy and Mother joined us in our drive back to Tucson and stayed several days. Matt cheered Daddy with his usual good spirits and the ocean of blarney that flowed between them. Joanna spent time in enjoyable conversations with Mother.

During their stay, Matt attended a baseball camp, even on days when it snowed. Beyond amazement about snow in Tucson, the idea of playing baseball in snow captured Daddy's fancy. He and Matt talked and laughed about it. In all his baseball days, Daddy never played in snow.

Too soon we put them on a plane back to California. Even knowing his health problems, he seemed restored. It never occurred to me that I wouldn't see Daddy again.

About four in the afternoon the next Saturday, I made my usual weekend call. Mother said Daddy spent most of the day in bed, then called up the stairs for him to pick up the phone, "It's Bette."

Daddy sounded down. He saw nothing good about being sick, unable to go about his regular routine, allowing his body to trump his determination.

He'd prepared his Sunday School lesson during his day in bed, and we talked about the highlights. His Bible, lesson book and notes sat on the bedside table ready for Sunday morning.

He told me the priest at Joe's Episcopal Church had asked him to preach the next time he came to Chicago. He said he'd have to think about whether he wanted to preach or not. Laughing, I told him the only "if" came in the part about going to Chicago. Once there, the "if" would disappear into vapor, and he'd walk over hot coals to get to the pulpit.

We chatted and laughed for about an hour. The call lifted his spirits and by the end of the hour, he sounded good. I said, "I love you, Daddy," in closing and hung up.

With the first ring of the phone four hours later, I knew. I said, "It's about Daddy," and ran to answer. Flo was crying. Daddy had another heart attack, and doctors didn't think he'd make it. She'd call again when she knew more.

Mother had called to Daddy for help getting up the stairs to bed. He came down to the living, then half-carried, half-escorted her upstairs. As she went into the bathroom, he turned toward their bedroom, and she heard a thud. Daddy lay, unresponsive, on the floor, blood around a wound on his forehead where he hit the foot of the bed. First she dialed 911, then she called Flo.

The 911 emergency medical people arrived quickly and started CPR. That failing, they raced him off to the emergency room where doctors initiated heroic procedures.

Flo all but flew to the hospital, hurried in and asked to see Daddy. The hospital staff stiff-armed her and expected her to go away like a good little girl—proving beyond any doubt they had never before dealt with a Dowdell on a mission. Through her tears, she persisted, and at long last, probably in self-preservation, they let her in. Daddy had been dead quite some time. In fact, they believed he probably died as he fell. All the hospital heroics signified nothing.

In Tucson, while the rest of my family went to bed, I sat on the family room couch, shrouded in both the night's darkness and the gloom of my heart, thinking about Daddy and praying, too devastated to cry. I reflected on the fortuitous move from Connecticut to Arizona which put me close enough to visit frequently instead of every other year. I let my mind wander through our times together.

I prayed, of course, that he would be okay. But I also prayed that if this heart attack would make him an invalid, God should just take him. Dependency would simply be a slow death for Daddy, doubly painful since a wonderful place awaited him in heaven. Knowing I'd see him again—maybe sooner, maybe later—helped enormously.

Early Sunday morning, as the sun threaded tentative rose-colored shafts of light through the bleak sky, Flo called with the expected news. Daddy was gone.

Flo called Rev. Al with the news early Sunday morning. Al told The Merry Methodists, which left them sobbing. Then he told the choir, and they asked him to please not announce the news to the congregation until after they sang the anthem or they'd never get through it.

After the anthem, when he stunned the congregation with the news, Rev. Al said anybody who wanted to say something about what Reverend Dowdell meant to them should come to the microphone. Little Red Riding Hood came, along with ten or eleven others.

Little Red Riding Hood's story amazed everybody. Nobody knew all that Daddy had done, not even a hint. By the time all the others finished their similar—and similarly unknown—stories of incredible help, tears streamed down every face in the sanctuary.

Flo and I went to the funeral home, where Daddy had conducted so many funerals, to select a casket. As the funeral director started to show us the possibilities, I dismissed the first two caskets as too narrow. The funeral director, who knew and, of course, loved Daddy, took offense at my seemingly cavalier attitude and began to chide me ever so gently.

He didn't like my inference that Daddy needed a huge casket because he weighed too much. I hastened to explain that my comments had nothing to do with Daddy's waistline, but with his shoulders. "He has huge shoulders," I said, "that need a wide casket." The funeral director rewarded me with a skeptical look.

We finally settled on the widest casket in the place

The funeral director tried to dissuade Mother from the "viewing" she requested. "California people don't come out for viewings," he reported. "You'll sit here all evening, and nobody will come." Mother insisted people would come, so he acquiesced, but not without telling her she should know for sure everybody loved Daddy, whether or not anybody came. Despite the California setting, people came to the viewing, which gave Mother much comfort. And a bit of a triumph.

When I arrived at the funeral home just before visiting hours began, the director beckoned me to join him in his office. He wanted to thank me for insisting on a wide coffin. He exclaimed about the size of Daddy's shoulders and said they had a bit of a tussle even with the casket we chose. It may not have been what one could call a genteel remark, but he wanted me to know he now realized that my remarks about the casket's size weren't meant to demean Daddy. He assured me he knew I loved Daddy. I appreciated his effort to offer what solace he could. Remaining silent would have been easier.

Later the family gathered at Daddy's and Mother's townhouse to reminisce and tell our stories. It became a sort of variation on the theme of a raucous Irish wake. In the middle of it all, somebody remembered it was my birthday, and everybody joined in a rousing round of "Happy Birthday." The song's wish for my happiness sounded a little hollow, even though sincere.

We celebrated Daddy's life and said our good-byes on a bright, sunny Wednesday afternoon. Even on a workday, the church filled to overflowing, with people standing along the back and filling the entry area, to honor this once-in-a-lifetime man.

Daddy had never lost his love for the Salvation Army or its music. He'd asked Ed, the longtime bandmaster of the Tustin Ranch Salvation Army band, to have the band play at his funeral. He requested the "Red Shield" march, "Army Of The Brave" and "Peace Of Heart." Ed, always close to Daddy, readily agreed.

The Tustin Ranch band plays at a professional level, but it's a volunteer group. Members not only receive no compensation, but actually pay dues to belong. All the band members had full-time jobs. Ed told them he'd understand if they couldn't make it. But every bandsman showed up—on time and in spit-and-polish SA uniform.

Beyond the novelty of a thirty-some piece brass band playing at a Methodist funeral, it's rare to hear march music, full of flourishes and played with enthusiasm on such occasions anywhere. Even more unusual, "Army Of The Brave" is festival music, described by musicians as "bright," meaning it has lots of dazzle and high brass. Chances are you'd never hear that even at an Army funeral. Daddy's last choice, "Peace Of Heart," combines hymns into an upbeat medley. It starts with "Precious Name," has "There'll Be No Sorrow In God's Tomorrow," an old Army song that ends "He'll wipe away all tears," as its theme and ends with the tag "He Can Keep You From Falling."

Daddy's trombone stood on its stand in front of the casket. His liturgical stole, topped by his well-worn Bible, lay atop the bottom, closed portion of the casket. Flanking the bier stood the candles that symbolize Christ. Along with his family, these were the things he loved most.

As the organist Ray Rosson—another of Daddy's adoptees—played introductory music, Matt, as acolyte, came down the aisle to light the candles. Then the family took their places and the service began.

Rick Ertel, a young minister Daddy took under his wing—and called "Junior"—spoke of the guidance he received—and included all the humor it came packed in. Rev. Erny came out of retirement to talk about the first time he met Daddy and some of his minister-of-visitation adventures. Major Joe Noland, the Tustin Ranch Salvation Army Corps officer, offered warm memories of Daddy's frequent attendance at Corps events. Joe remembered our growing up days and told the story about the day Daddy carried the refrigerator.

Jay Cairns sang Daddy's favorite song, "I Walked Today Where Jesus Walked." The band formed a chorus and sang "Peace, Perfect Peace."

As the service went along with energy and humor, people started applauding each singer, speaker and number from the band. When the band played the "Red Shield" march, the applause rattled the rafters, while "Army of the Brave" brought the house down. Mother insisted the funeral be a celebration, and she got her wish—and then some. Everybody laughed, cried and applauded all at once, not knowing how to stop one and start another—or even which to choose.

Mother also wanted the funeral to end with the opportunity for people to make a commitment to Christ. Rev. Al rose to talk about the importance and power of Daddy's faith. He ended by asking the people to raise their hands if they wanted to make a commitment like Reverend Dowdell's, and hands went up all around the sanctuary.

Then the congregation filed past the casket to say their final good-bye. The family went last. I don't know what anybody else did, but as I passed, I leaned over and gave Daddy a quick good-by-for-now kiss on his forehead.

We sang a concluding hymn and thought the service had ended.

But Matt added a final exclamation point when he extinguished the candles. Usually the candles stand on either side of a cross, and the acolyte, in turning from one candle to the other, pauses in front of the cross. As expected, Matt extinguished the candle on the right, then turned to face the casket. Instead of simply pausing, he raised the long candle-lighter high and tipped it forward in a big salute, a good-bye to his Grandpa. Then he went on to snuff out the final candle, emotionally snuffing out a good part of the congregation as he did. Most of the audience knew about Daddy and Matt's very special relationship, and his salute finished them off.

If funerals can be wonderful, it was a wonderful funeral.

Immediately following the funeral, everybody gathered in Fellowship Hall for a buffet luncheon. Church members came to tell us Daddy's nickname for them. Woody, because he looked like Woody Hayes, the Ohio State football coach from days gone by. Buckeye, because she came from Ohio. And so it went.

During dessert, Rev. Al came to the table where our family sat and said people had been talking about an idea. Would we mind, he asked, if the church created a chapel in one end of the Education Building in honor of Daddy. The Dowdell Chapel. No, we most certainly wouldn't mind.

The idea would have surprised Daddy—and pleased him mightily. Later, the committee decided to add Mother's name, to honor her as well. He would have liked that, too.

Truth to tell, Daddy and Mother had already received enormous honor from the church members. From the day of their arrival, the people loved on them and appreciated them, and it washed over Daddy and Mother as pure joy.

They came to California in poor health, in the late twilight of their lives and did what they could push their health to allow, mostly loving and encouraging people. Now the church voted to build The Dowdell Chapel in return. Amazing.

AFTERWORD

The Dowdell Chapel arose from gutting and rebuilding one end of the FUMCHUB Education Building. What had been classrooms became a mini-sanctuary comfortably seating about seventy people. It had new carpeting, new pews, new lighting, new sound system, new pulpit, new communion rail, new piano, new organ—new everything. Four gothic-style stained glass windows—a dove of peace, a descending dove, a rainbow and a fisherman—designed and created by a young couple who loved Daddy and who happened to be in the stained glass business—topped it off.

As completion neared, I asked Rev. Al what the chapel committee wanted but couldn't afford. That would be my gift. As it turned out, the chapel wanted for nothing; people gave well beyond the chapel's needs.

Rev. Al couldn't remember a time when a church project took in so much more money than requested. Just meeting minimum goals brought jubilation; exceeding the targeted amount took everybody into unknown territory, a splendiferous (to quote Mother) place to be.

Mother, the Dowdell kids and a selection of grandchildren returned to Huntington Beach for the dedication of the Dowdell Chapel. We started it off with a celebration service, along with our best wishes and appreciation.

Today, the Merry Methodists, the Sunday School class Mother brought back to life and Daddy taught for years, meets in the Dowdell Chapel each week. The preschool uses it for their little chapel program twice a week. It also provides a perfect fit for small weddings and services. And its very presence continues the memory of two extraordinary people.

Mother lived seven difficult years before she went to be with Daddy. Now free of Parkinson's Disease, her energy returned, she lives a life of joy that will never end.

I never heard my father curse, tell a dirty joke, make a *risqué* remark or speak unkindly. He walked always in peace and showered love and encouragement freely on everybody he met. He accepted people with all their foibles, growing frustrated only when they let fears and habits control their lives and keep them from moving onto success. He tried to instill the confidence it took to reach for the heights, to go for the gold. Perhaps most of all, he loved to share his knowledge of how life with God could take people higher and farther than they ever dreamed—as nothing and nobody else could.

Daddy lived a congruent life. Whatever swirled around him, he walked his talk. I'd like to say I knew him inside and out, but who can fully know a genius, let alone a saint? Especially one so comfortable in his own skin he never felt the need to explain himself?

What great good fortune, then, that I realized when Daddy sat at the kitchen table nursing his cup of coffee, it was an invitation to talk. He wouldn't presume on anybody, but would wait for a response to his silent offer. We had many long, long conversations over gallons of coffee.

When I taught The Merry Methodists, they'd tell me they thought I took after Mother until I started speaking—at which point I became Daddy. Their comments flatter me far too much, delighting my Daddy's girl heart. I can't imagine anybody not wanting to be like Daddy.

The Bible says when death comes, our final destination, whether heaven or hell, is fixed by our lifetime choice. Beyond that, though, there's a judgment where we receive our reward for what we do with our lives—whether that moves us to the deepest depths of hell or the highest reaches of heaven—or anywhere along the way in either direction.

That being the case, the first thing I plan to do when I get to heaven is go find Daddy. That way, I can get at least a little peek at what the best part of heaven looks like.

And a chance to apologize for my fiftieth anniversary brain freeze.

I found the following hymn in Mother's papers. She wrote it for a contest and won an honorable mention—which both pleased and miffed her.

The Hymn Of Praise

Sung to the tune: Hark! The Herald Angels

1. *Ever onward, Thou hast led us,*
   By Thy great and powerful hand
   Thou has ever brought us forward
   In this great and glorious land
   By Thy Word our strength has been;
   In Thy Son the world has seen
   Man redeemed and raised to bless
   All mankind with righteousness;
   So may we Thy servants be
   Dedicated, Lord, to Thee.

2. *Through the fire and through the tempest*
   Finding courage by Thy side
   Thou didst give a vision glorious
   To Thy servants far and wide,
   God the Father, God the Son,
   God the Spirit, Three in One;
   Thou didst show Thy power and might
   Through Thy children in the fight;
   So may we Thy servants be
   Dedicated, Lord, to thee.

3. *God of triumph hear us sing*
   Hallelujah! To our King.
   Great Creator of mankind
   And the universe combined,
   Thou are worthy of our praise;

Lead us on in heavenly ways;
Christ Thy Son has been our theme
And Thy blessing rich has been
So may we Thy servants be
Dedicated, Lord, to Thee.

—Josephine Dowdell

I tend to be a little skeptical when people start talking about visions they've had. Maybe yes. Maybe no.

So when the church secretary, who had known Daddy only the last two years of his life, said she'd had a vision of Daddy, I didn't exactly click my heels and plan to get excited about the details. But she clearly wanted to tell me about it, felt she had to in fact, so I listened.

She said Daddy was running a relay race, about to transfer the baton. He had a wide, jubilant grin that animated his face more than she'd ever seen before.

She said he was younger, maybe in his thirties. She described his big barrel-chest, which, although she didn't know it, was perhaps the most noticeable feature about Daddy in his thirties. Maybe Mother said something, though it didn't sound like her.

She said he was already bald, but with the same fringe of hair, now a medium brown, not the snow white she had known. Daddy's hair had, in fact, been a medium brown. Maybe that was a lucky guess.

305

Then she talked about a little curl of hair on the top of his head, in the center of what would have been his hairline. It was the curl I played with as a little girl. She had no way of knowing about that little curl. She had, in fact, had a vision of Daddy.

She said he told her to tell everybody that he was passing the baton on to them, and they should run their race with enthusiasm.

So I pass those words on to you: Run your race with enthusiasm. Grab God's hand and truck on with joy. The path is sometimes steep and rocky, but persevere. A wonderful prize awaits at this life's finish line for those who run after God.

And if you get there before I do, go find Daddy and tell him I said "Hi."

And that I miss him.

INDEX

Hire Bette Dowdell to speak at your next seminar, conference, etc.

- She's knowledgeable
- She's funny
- She's motivational
- She's a hit with both secular and Christian audiences.

You can contact Bette via:

E-mail:	Bette@ConfidentFaith.com
Phone:	800-235-4235
Mail:	Confident Faith Institute LLC
	PO Box 11744
	Glendale AZ 85318
Fax:	623-572-5082

And be sure to go to www.ConfidentFaith.com to:

- Read about Bette's books
- Check out her blog
- Hear her speak
- Sign up for a FREE e-mail subscription to her original, take-the-hill quotes.

LaVergne, TN USA
26 November 2010
206349LV00008B/16/P